Children's Encyclopedia of

The Arts
of the World

Compiled and edited by Kenneth Bailey

Collins

Glasgow and London

Contents

Written by Desmond O. Ward, David Roberts, George Beal

Designed by David Nash

Illustrated by Max Ansell, M. J. Atkinson, Thelma Bissex,
Ronald Embleton, Gwen Green, Harry Green,
Richard Hook, Angus McBride, John Marshall,
David Nash, Christine Robins, Gwen Simpson,
John Smith, Charlotte Snook, Bill Stallion,
George Thompson

First published 1976
Second impression 1977
Published by William Collins Sons and Company Limited, Glasgow and London
© 1976 William Collins Sons and Company Limited

Printed in Great Britain

ISBN 0 00 106164 X

Art and Architecture

The word 'art' can mean many different things. Music is an art, and so are poetry and ballet. Cookery, too, may be considered an art, and so may needlework or even fishing. But if we speak of Art—with a capital A—we usually mean some object deliberately and skilfully created for public exhibition. To make something is art, if the aim of the maker is to create an object worth placing before his fellow man for appraisal and understanding. In olden days when a skilled craftsman made a new coach for the squire to travel in, he set out to fashion a vehicle that would serve its owner well, one that would be strong, light, comfortable and steady. In doing all these things he was being a good craftsman. But when in addition he came to make the coach elegant and well-proportioned, then he became an artist.

Art and Design

Today there are artists designing detergent packets, newspaper pages, street lamps, radio cabinets, and thousands of other objects. Like the old coachbuilder they must consider such things as use and weight and cost, and this is a matter of design. But when they begin to think about the appearance of the object they are designing, in order to make it beautiful and satisfying to the eye, then they become artists. Architects are subject to the same rules. A building may be just a serviceable building, but if its designer succeeds in making it a delight to the eye, then it becomes an architectural work of art. Even a pigsty can be a work of architecture if its proportions are pleasing and satisfying to the eye.

We are all artists to an extent – some of us more than others. When we change our hair-style or select what clothes to wear we are creating an image to be seen. It is the same basic activity as Michelangelo exercised when he painted his famous frescoes for the pope in the Sistine Chapel in Rome. Of course Michelangelo was an all-time genius who had been trained since boyhood for his work, so it is pitched at a far greater intensity than that of the 'everyday' artist. It also contains deeper meaning. In his great ceiling paintings he tried to sum up all the philosophy of his time; to link Christian beliefs with the ideas of the ancient Greek thinkers. There was much more involved than merely choosing a tie to wear or deciding on a hair-style; but in a sense it can all be considered as art.

The Purpose of Art

In the pages that follow we shall attempt to understand something of the world's art over the whole period of man's activity as an artist. We shall see that in those thousands of years, practically all artists' work has been produced for some definite purpose. The purpose has changed from place to place and from time to time, and with it the character of the art has changed. Everywhere the artist has been asked to perform a useful service, which he has done as a good craftsman should, but at the same time he has tried to make the object of his art worthwhile as a thing in itself. It is this that makes him an artist. Art is often required of him from the outset but frequently he is asked only to provide good craftsmanship. The art he then brings to his work is thrown in as a gift.

At times artists have been specialists —gifted people selected and trained to become expert in the choice of excellent forms, colours and lines. They seek to portray truthfully the visible world or to make images that express truths about the invisible world of the spirit. For several centuries in Europe the aim has been to create a tradition of realism, while in other parts of the world artists have

been concerned with different versions of reality expressed by symbols or by the conscious distortion of the real facts.

The Architect

Architecture is a form of art in which the designer is asked, first and foremost, to construct a building for use. If he is asked to design a cathedral, he must then provide a building that will keep a multitude of people dry and warm, and give as many as possible a clear view of the priest at the altar or in the pulpit. There will be other requirements, but these are the main ones. In addition to these practical considerations the building should impart a feeling of reverence and inspire the worshipper. It should create a sense of wonder and a desire to praise, and in every way be suitable as the Christians' house of God. The designer of a Hindu temple or a Mohammedan mosque will have equal but different responsibilities. Thus, in some measure all architecture demands a craftsman's solutions to practical problems and an artist's solutions to whatever spiritual problems are involved.

When a cathedral, or a temple or a mosque, has been erected, other artists may be called in to add to its beauty. These may be sculptors or painters, or workers in mosaic, tapestry or stained glass. Some may be chosen for their excellence in decoration, but all will be able to convey meanings beyond the scope of architecture alone, however noble and inspiring the building may be. Their images will be able who may have died centuries ago— to us; messages that cannot be conveyed in words, but only in visual images.

In cathedrals and temples, and many other kinds of building, the paintings and carvings and other adornments have usually been made to fit into a special place and so blend with the architectural design. Much of the world's greatest art has been of this kind. But there have always been portable works of art as well. Many of these have been objects for use, such as hand mirrors or fans or weapons of some kind, that have been made good to look at as well as being serviceable. Nowadays, however, pictures and small sculptures are often made by artists who have no idea where they will be seen or even who will eventually own them. They are conceived and executed by individual artists,

Laocoön and his sons assailed by serpents, a marble group (2nd-1st century B.C.) by the Rhodian sculptors Agesander, Polydorus and Athenodorus (left). *Fluorescence* by the Swiss artist Paul Klee (above). The Château de Chenonceaux at Touraine in France (right).

to join with all human experience and human vision, bridging past and present and offering a link with the future. By the choice of his images as well as the way in which he treats them, the artist can convey meanings to our minds—meanings that are limited only by his ability to conceive and express them and our ability to understand them. Complex messages will pass from the artist— each working alone in his own style, and are purchased and owned simply for the sake of their artistic value. Today we are used to this, but it is really a very recent idea. Most of the world's art has been required for a definite purpose and produced to serve that purpose. To appreciate it fully we must understand why it was required and something about the culture that required it.

Prehistoric and Ancient Art

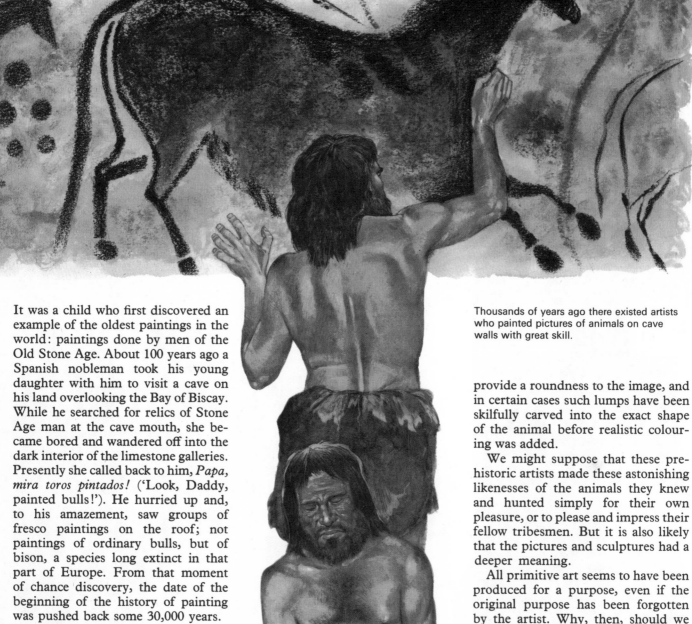

It was a child who first discovered an example of the oldest paintings in the world: paintings done by men of the Old Stone Age. About 100 years ago a Spanish nobleman took his young daughter with him to visit a cave on his land overlooking the Bay of Biscay. While he searched for relics of Stone Age man at the cave mouth, she became bored and wandered off into the dark interior of the limestone galleries. Presently she called back to him, *Papa, mira toros pintados!* ('Look, Daddy, painted bulls!'). He hurried up and, to his amazement, saw groups of fresco paintings on the roof; not paintings of ordinary bulls, but of bison, a species long extinct in that part of Europe. From that moment of chance discovery, the date of the beginning of the history of painting was pushed back some 30,000 years.

Cave Paintings

As the years passed, other caves were explored in northern Spain and south-western France, and many more cave paintings were discovered. It became clear that thousands of years ago there existed artists who painted pictures of animals with great skill. They observed and depicted the beasts they hunted with extraordinary truth and vividness. At first they used a simple engraved outline but later their paintings were in full colour. Each one is an isolated, perfect representation of an individual animal, sometimes shown in a well-observed moment of its normal life, sometimes as wounded or dying. Occasionally a suitable lump on the surface of the rock was used to

Thousands of years ago there existed artists who painted pictures of animals on cave walls with great skill.

provide a roundness to the image, and in certain cases such lumps have been skilfully carved into the exact shape of the animal before realistic colouring was added.

We might suppose that these prehistoric artists made these astonishing likenesses of the animals they knew and hunted simply for their own pleasure, or to please and impress their fellow tribesmen. But it is also likely that the pictures and sculptures had a deeper meaning.

All primitive art seems to have been produced for a purpose, even if the original purpose has been forgotten by the artist. Why, then, should we suppose that this one kind of painting should be art for art's sake? Why, too, are the subjects almost always just those animals needed for food? One would expect the artist to choose the more dramatic giant bears and cave lions or even human beings, which hardly ever appear without animals. Then again, why do we so often find one painting executed over another and partly hiding it, and why, with all their skill, did these artists rarely group their animals or set them in a landscape? And, most important of all, why did they so often take the trouble to journey back into the most remote and inaccessible galleries of the caves, when plenty of good rock surfaces were ready to hand near the cave entrances where the people lived.

These cave systems are extremely large and complex, and the passages extend back and back into the heart of the mountains. Many paintings have been found in remote places that Stone Age people would never have seen in their normal lives. Clearly this suggests that the cave paintings were more than just a pastime.

The actions and beliefs of other primitive hunters may give a clue to the purpose of Stone Age art. The Bushmen of the Kalahari Desert, for instance, often make a picture of the animal they intend to hunt and then shoot arrows at the picture. Having performed this ritual slaying they believe success will be more certain when they hunt an animal in the flesh.

Images and Magic

It is a widespread belief among primitive peoples that the image of a thing is identical with the thing itself and that the possession of an image gives one power over whatever is represented. In Europe, in days gone by, a tiresome neighbour would be dealt with by making a little wax image of him. A spit or skewer would then be stuck through the figure and it would be slowly melted over a fire. As the last drips of melting wax dropped on to the embers the unpopular neighbour was supposed to die, so close was the supposed connection between the thing and its image.

It seems more than likely that the artists among Stone Age hunters were, in fact, sorcerers. By creating paintings so very true to life they were seeking to guarantee success in hunting the animal depicted.

There may also have been another and more important motive. In the Old Stone Age many little carvings sorcerers may have believed they were securing for their tribe a continuing abundance and increase of those animals. If this were so it would answer many of our questions about this fascinating kind of art.

Animal Artists

We can never share the thinking of early men, who are so remote in time and whose life was so very different from our own, but we can certainly enjoy the artists' eager interest in the animals they depicted, and share a delight in their skill in making those animals live on rock walls deep within the mountains.

A quite separate and much later tradition of rock painting has been discovered in Africa in the centre of the Sahara Desert. By about 4000 B.C. the artists there had become herdsmen, living in the New Stone Age

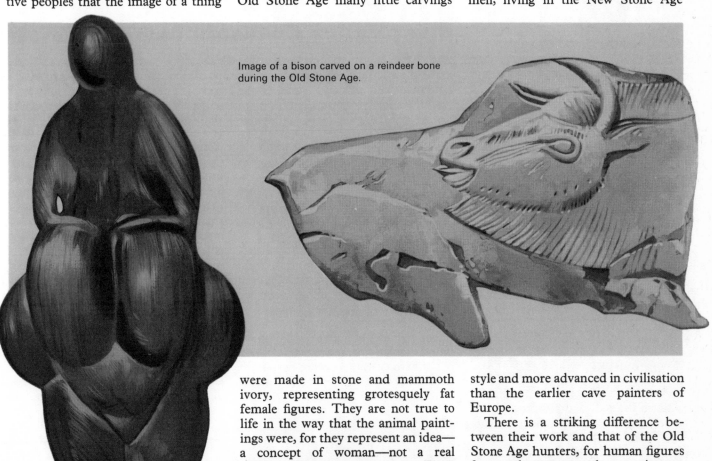

Image of a bison carved on a reindeer bone during the Old Stone Age.

were made in stone and mammoth ivory, representing grotesquely fat female figures. They are not true to life in the way that the animal paintings were, for they represent an idea— a concept of woman—not a real woman. They represent the Earth Mother, the fertility goddess of early times. The Earth Mother, or Mother Earth, was a concept widely held for many thousands of years. She was the chief deity of the fertility cult that was perhaps the earliest of all religions.

By creating exact images of their food animals in the very centre of a mountain—as if in the womb of Mother Earth herself—these artist-

style and more advanced in civilisation than the earlier cave painters of Europe.

There is a striking difference between their work and that of the Old Stone Age hunters, for human figures frequently appear and are as important as the animals. Men and animals are grouped to describe situations and narrate stories. As exact representations of nature these paintings are less accomplished, but the aim was to tell a story and for that they are perfect. In time this region of the Sahara became increasingly dry and as desert conditions encroached on the lands of the people who lived there, so their art tradition came to an end.

Typical 'Venus' figure, representing the fertility goddess of early times.

The Pharaoh Mentuhotep (XI Dynasty, about 2000 B.C.), a statue of painted grey sandstone found at the funerary temple of Deir el Bahari at Thebes in Egypt.

Wall painting from a Theban tomb.

River Valley Civilisations

The slow drying-up of climate that made the central Sahara almost uninhabitable had, in other parts of the world, already compelled certain groups of hunters to make the change in their way of life that was perhaps the most important that man has ever made—the change from hunting to agriculture.

At first groups of cultivators were small and their methods so primitive that the crops they grew barely sustained them. They needed constantly to abandon their fields as the soil became exhausted, to move on to new ground and break it up. In time people found that by combining together they could move into the valleys of great rivers and take advantage of the richer soil and abundant water to be found there.

Numerous workers were needed to raise banks to control the surging water in times of flood and dig ditches to eke out the feeble trickles in times of drought—for these great rivers were wayward. By means of such irrigation works the valley cultivators acquired for their crops the richest of soil under a hot sun, with river water close at hand. The river also provided a highway for moving produce. The people no longer had to move every few years and could settle in one place. As life became easier and wealth increased, their settlements became towns, and eventually cities. There was more food and clothing than the labourers in the field needed and this was available to support specialist workers, among them the artist-craftsman. In this way a number of civilised, art-producing communities came into being.

By about 2000 B.C. four such centres of valley cultivation existed, one in the Euphrates valley (now Iraq), another in Egypt, and two more, one in the

Temple at Deir el Bahari, partly carved into the surrounding mountainside.

10

Indus Valley and another farther east, in China. Of these four, the civilisation of Egypt is closest to Europe and has influenced European art most strongly. Also its art tradition continued unbroken for more than 3,000 years.

Egyptian Culture

Ancient Egyptian culture was dominated by the need for continuity: for continuing prosperity in this life and for the life which would continue after death. In very early times it was their ruler, the Pharaoh, whose life beyond the grave the people strove to secure. Pharaoh was deemed to be a god in his lifetime, and after death it was necessary that he should take his place among the other gods as their equal. The whole population demanded this.

When Pharaoh died his body was embalmed to continue as a dwelling-place for his soul, but in case some accident should occur, another man-made body was provided. Craftsmen had to fashion an exact replica of the

practically the whole of their output was devoted to this purpose. Much of the art of Egypt was laid away with the dead kings, never to be seen again. In later times other important people, besides Pharaoh, were given elaborate burial equipment.

The need to provide their god-kings with dwellings and equipment for eternity required the use of the most perfect and permanent materials available and the highest degree of craftsmanship. All carvings or paintings were designed to be as true to life as possible. They had to serve as real people and objects for ever. This need led to an approach to art that is unique and peculiar to ancient Egypt.

These ancient Egyptian artists were not attempting to create for the on-looker the effect of a scene or an experience, which is what many painters in modern times have tried to do.

Blue ceramic figure of a hippopotamus, an animal both hated and worshipped by the Egyptians.

The Tombs of the Pharaohs

Concern for permanence also influenced the Egyptian architectural tradition. Sun-dried mud-bricks, which were used for most of their buildings, were a very impermanent material. Even the divine Pharaoh might live in a mud-brick palace in this life, but after death his dwelling had to be eternal and for this purpose the hardest stone was used.

It was a widespread custom in early times for kings and chieftains to be buried in stone chambers covered with great artificial mounds of earth. Even in far away parts of northern Europe this was the case. The early Pharaohs were also given similar artificial mounds. At first these mounds were of mud-brick, and were called mastabas. But before long the Egyptian builders invented building in stone, and stone mounds—almost stone mountains—

Royal tombs in Egypt have yielded jewellery of great beauty such as this pendant ear-ring (left). Scarab beetles (below) were seals usually mounted in a ring and used to stamp clay sealings on letters and also carried as protective amulets.

were constructed. The great pyramids at Giza are examples. Each pyramid had, deep inside it, the body and belongings of a dead king.

Egyptian temples were built of the hardest and most durable stone. Colonnaded courtyards and halls full of columns led to a small central chamber housing the statue of the god, or of a dead Pharaoh—himself a god. Because Egypt produced no timber for roof joists, doorways were made narrow and columns wide and massive and placed close together. They could then be spanned by stone lintels in place of timber joists, for the Egyptians never discovered a way of constructing arches. Walls and columns alike were covered with relief carvings tinted with flat, clear colours that glowed with a superb richness in the dimly lit interiors. The whole effect was awe-inspiring and mysterious, perfectly suited to the needs of that strange religion in which the gods and goddesses were part human and part animal.

king to be ready for his death. They also had to equip him with everything he would need to meet the other gods as their equal. Every necessity or luxury he had owned in real life was buried with him for the life after death. In earliest times Pharaoh's attendants were killed and buried with him so that he might have fitting company on his journey after death, but later carvings and paintings were substituted for real people.

These ceremonies placed a great demand on the work of the artist-craftsmen of Egypt, and at one period

They were creating a replica of something as it existed to their eyes. That is what they were required to do, and they did it perfectly. We must not be tempted to think their art childish or incompetent, for it is, in fact, perfect for its purpose. The dominating need to create, in paint, replicas of reality for the after-life so influenced Egyptian art that this approach persisted in all work, for whatever purpose it was produced. The attempt to reproduce the truth exactly was linked with a superb sense of decoration and design.

Nomads and Barbarians

While the people in Egypt and the other valley civilisations were perfecting the art of irrigation and building their rich and splendid civilisations, other less fortunate groups were developing their own special methods and traditions. The people of the steppes of Central Asia and eastern Europe led a very different kind of life. On bare grasslands lived various groups of herdsmen—cattle and horse breeders—who were not concerned with agriculture. They were nomads and had no permanent dwelling-places, but moved with their herds from one pasturage to another in regular annual journeys, taking all their possessions with them.

Over a period of roughly a thousand years various groups of these nomads moved away from their homelands on the steppes and began long, slow journeys outwards in various directtions. On their way they met new conditions and differing customs. Most of them ceased to be merely herdsmen and took to agriculture as well, learning many new skills from the tribes they came across on their travels. In many cases they mingled with people of other cultures. Even when enormously outnumbered, they tended to form a ruling aristocracy,

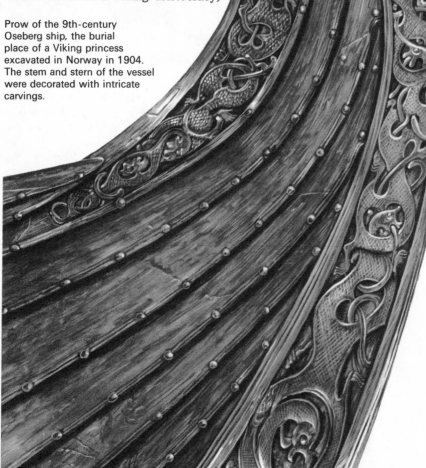

Prow of the 9th-century Oseberg ship, the burial place of a Viking princess excavated in Norway in 1904. The stem and stern of the vessel were decorated with intricate carvings.

Celtic bronze mirror (1st century A.D.) decorated with a design typical of the period.

for they were masters in the art of dictatorship. Yet many remained faithful to certain of their own traditions—their Aryan form of language, for instance, and their religion, also their habit of indulging in strong liquor and their love of hearing long epic poems chanted by a professional musician while they feasted at night. They kept their admiration for physical courage and their ideal of the indomitable hero figure. Most of them made war in chariots, drawn by fiery little horses, a new method of warfare as decisive then as the tank was in the First World War. In the field of art, too, they carried with them their own peculiar excellence and even certain favourite subjects which continued to be popular as the centuries passed.

The Scythians

Typical of these nomadic herdsmen in their original state were the Scythians. They were fierce and ruthless horse breeders who did not, in fact, migrate but remained on the steppes. Being nomads they could not amass bulky possessions or erect magnificent buildings. Instead they developed a tradition of the goldsmith's art, making for themselves exquisite little pieces of relief sculpture in gold, to serve as cloak brooches, belt buckles or ornaments for horses' harnesses. Their subjects were mostly animals, rendered simply to suit the methods of making them, but full of vigour and writhing, struggling movement. A favourite subject or motif of theirs is called 'animal conflict', in which two wolves, perhaps, or a bear and a wolf, are locked in perpetual battle. Each holds the other in the inescapable grip of its powerful jaws, neither can win the battle and neither dares to let go. This state of savage stalemate seemed to hold a fascination for the Scythian goldsmiths and it was to have the same appeal for craftsmen in other materials and in distant places, as we shall presently see.

At about the same time that the Scythians were perfecting the art of working in gold, away in the east another Aryan-speaking people, the Celts, were drifting slowly westwards across Europe. Eventually some of them found their way into Britain and even reached Ireland and the islands of the Outer Hebrides in the Atlantic. Working chiefly in bronze, the Celtic craftsmen were not so much concerned with representing animals or anything else in nature. Their special genius was in decoration, and they could endow slender, winding forms and engraved lines with a weaving movement that makes these shapes live for us as though they represented truly living things.

Teutonic Art

We shall meet the Celts again but first we must turn to another group, the people of Teutonic stock who followed the Celts outwards, but on a slightly more northerly route, which took them to the shores of the Baltic Sea. These included the Norsemen of Norway, north of that sea, and the Danes to the south, and related peoples such as the Angles and Saxons who followed the Celts into Britain. These Teutonic peoples possessed a tradition of art rather like that of the Celts, but they were more concerned with representation. Their delight was to depict imaginary monsters, not real, natural animals, and to convey in them a sense of supernatural power. They were skilled craftsmen in timber, and much of their finest work was carved in wood —a dragon's head for the prow of a Viking ship, or interlocking monsters round the doorway of a timber building—an art reminding us of the work of the Scythians.

Unlike the art of the Egyptians, which was based on thought and

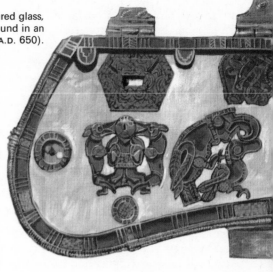

Lid of a purse set with garnets and coloured glass, part of the Sutton Hoo treasure found in an Anglo-Saxon burial ship (c. A.D. 650).

understanding, this northern work is an art of feeling and fantasy. It springs from the regions of the mind from which come our dreams and our moments of sudden understanding: we call this the unconscious mind, or intuition. The other part of the mind that we use consciously we call the intellect. So we see here a striking contrast between two forms of art, the Egyptians creating mainly from the intellect, and the northerners from the intuition. All art is two-fold. Sometimes the intellect will dominate, sometimes the intuition; often they are in balance. We see this throughout the long story of the world's art.

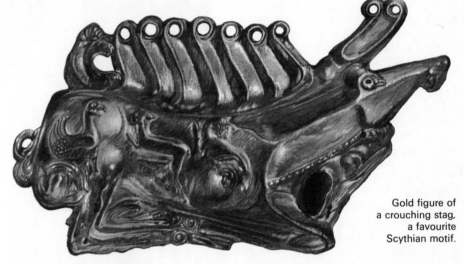

Gold figure of a crouching stag, a favourite Scythian motif.

Bronze figure of a tribal chieftain from Sardinia (10th–5th century B.C.).

When the Celts of Ireland became Christians, this stimulated them to produce an art in carved stone, and in book decoration that has never been equalled in its particular excellence. This was Ireland's great moment in the realm of visual art. Isolated in the remote west and cut off from the rest of civilisation by heathen Saxons, Franks and other unlettered nations, the Celtic Christians kept alive the arts and ancient learning.

Carved on stone crosses erected in the open air or painted on the parchment pages of books in monastery libraries, Celtic art reached its perfection about A.D. 700. Here, too, one often discovers, hidden in a maze of winding, plaited bands of intricate ornament, eight legs, two tails and two heads, together forming two complete monsters, each grabbing the other in a deadly grip. It is the old 'animal conflict' of the Scythian goldsmiths reappearing 2,000 miles to the west of the steppes and over 1,000 years later in time.

The Classical Tradition

Turning back in time to about 2000 B.C. and looking eastwards to the eastern end of the Mediterranean Sea, we see two rich civilisations—that of Egypt on the southern shore and the other on the island of Crete to the south of the Aegean Sea. The Cretans were an island people, a seafaring nation. They voyaged far and wide carrying both merchandise and new ideas wherever they went.

As one might imagine, Cretan art echoed the free-roving, enterprising character of the people. Their wall paintings and painted pottery were gay and vigorous—full of movement and energy. Their sculpture was carried out in bronze, ivory and coloured, glazed earthenware (faience). The fortress-palaces of their kings and chieftains were skilfully planned, with colonnades, majestic stairways, and halls gay with mural paintings.

This early Cretan culture is called Minoan after the legendary King Minos, who once ruled in Crete from his stronghold at Knossos. Minoan influence was supreme in the Mediterranean region for more than 1,000 years. One country where it was felt particularly strongly was the mainland of Greece to the north. Here there developed an art style, inheriting much from Minoan art, which excelled in gold, silver, bronze and copper metal work, also in vase painting and gem engraving. This culture is called Mycenaean, from the ruined stronghold of Mycenae in Greece, where relics of this period were first found.

The Fall of Knossos

About 1400 B.C. disaster struck the island of Crete. The fortress-palace at Knossos was destroyed and the Minoan civilisation came to a violent end. The blow may have been struck by raiding invaders from the mainland of Greece, but it may also have resulted from natural causes such as an earthquake. In Greece, for about two centuries, Mycenae and the rest of the country had been under the control of newcomers, a migrating, warrior nation who called themselves Achaeans. They spoke an early form of Greek, a language of the Aryan group, and dominated Greece without destroying the Mycenaean style of art which they found there.

It was of these Achaean chieftains that Homer wrote in his great epic poem the *Iliad*. Odysseus, hero of the other Homer epic, the *Odyssey*, was one of the Achaean princes who dominated Greece. They were a typical Aryan-speaking ruling aristocracy, and each lord with his Achaean supporters was served by a submissive native population. Their fortified palaces were nobly planned. The central feature was a great hall, or megaron, with a colonnaded portico. When they died the Achaean princes were laid in beehive-shaped tombs (tholos tombs), large and skilfully built and covered with a dome of soil. They were really very majestic versions of the burial-mounds or barrows in which chieftains were then buried all over Europe.

The Achaean lords had ruled undisturbed for about 500 years when their security was shattered by the arrival of invading Dorians. These newcomers also spoke a form of Greek, but they were a harsh, uncultured people, expert in war and manly sports, but caring nothing for beauty or gracious living. Then the light of learning and art was put out all over Greece and a 'dark age' set in which lasted several centuries.

When the turmoil and destruction of the invasions had subsided, designs in metal work and painted pottery were produced once more. At first the designs and figures were stiff and formal. Angular, geometric patterns

Partial reconstruction of the Palace of Knossos at Crete.

Examples of Greek black figure painting (left) by the vase-painter and potter Exekias and (above) an Attic red-figured drawing.

were employed, and when animals and human figures were depicted these, too, were made angular and geometric. Funeral processions, armies with chariots, and lions, birds, ibexes and the like were converted into powerful, conventional patterns, and the Greek genius for design already showed itself in the perfect placing of bands of ornament or pictures on the pottery vessels.

After about 300 years this severe, geometric form gave place to a style strongly influenced by work then being produced in nearby Asia. Bold curves and bulging forms appeared in strong contrast to the rigid angles of the earlier style. This phase lasted about 100 years, and then, about 600 B.C., the true genius of the Greeks reasserted itself.

Athenian Style

At this time the city of Athens was becoming more and more powerful and Athenian artists came to set a standard for the whole of Greece. Unlike the artists of Egypt and the other river valley civilisations, those of Greece were not slaves working in teams. They were free men. They were not bound by rules and age-old customs enforced by a rigid and binding kind of religion. The Greek religion provided inspiration and opportunities, not restricting formulas.

Under these favourable conditions the Greek art tradition quickly came into being. Style and skill developed side by side. Never before had such a development occurred in so short a space of time. Not only in art and architecture, but in science, mathematics, literature, philosophy and drama the Greeks found a new approach and a new perfection. They set the world a standard that has been an inspiration ever since and, of its kind, has never been surpassed. This style of the Greeks and of the Romans after them, we call the classical tradition.

The Greek Gods

Much Greek art was concerned with religion and with those deities which formed the Greek family of gods and goddesses called the pantheon (a Greek word meaning 'all the gods'). To the people these Greek deities were not remote and aloof but very real. Some expressed a particular aspect of human character, but in its essence and perfection. Ares, the war god, expressed the ideal of male courage and energy; Athene, the ideal of wisdom and the working of intellect; Ceres was the life-force seen in the plant world, especially in the renewal of the farmers' crops; Pan, half man and half goat, expressed the forces filling the whole of nature and the power of man's unconscious mind. Everything experienced was expressed in human

Greek sculptures: (below) *Man with Calf* (c. 560 B.C.) and (right) *Marsyas*, sometimes called *The Dancing Faun*, a copy after the celebrated Greek sculptor Myron.

or semi-human form, and Greek artists were mainly concerned with perfecting their powers of depicting and making expressive that human form.

A combination of truth and realistic perfection was their aim, but not just truth observed, as in the art of the prehistoric cave painters. For the Greeks truth had to be analysed and understood, and then used to express the artist's meaning and intention. In their quest for understanding these early artists achieved an unsurpassed mastery in representing the human figure, and the greatest of them used

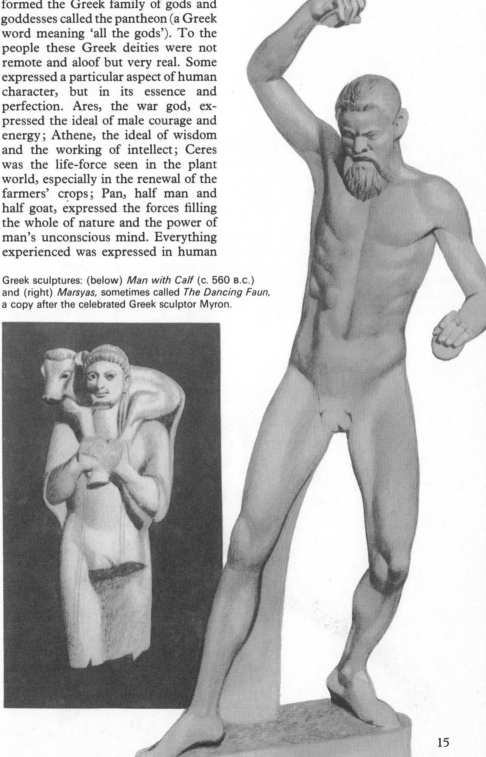

this mastery to produce the noblest art of its kind.

We know from various writings that wall paintings by the best Greek painters were greatly admired in their own day. They understood perspective and foreshortening, but to what extent they used this knowledge we shall never know, for no paintings of this kind have survived. In the early days of Christianity the newly converted Christians believed it their duty to destroy all images of heathen times, and the paintings were an easy target.

On the other hand many vase paintings have survived. Sometimes the subject may be taken from Homer's poems or from stories of the gods and heroes, at other times from scenes of real life. To begin with the figures are black on the natural red colour of the bases (black-figure style), later the figures were red on a black ground (red-figure style). They were painted with swift certainty on the hard, curved surfaces of the vases, and no changes or corrections were possible. As is fitting and right for paintings done in this way, the lines and areas of colours are simple and clear. The figures are placed against a plain background as though they were actors in a tableau on a shallow stage, and their actions and emotions are expressed with superb assurance. This assurance was only possible because these painters had achieved a knowledge of the human figure and a skill in depicting it through generations of experience and eager endeavour.

Greek Sculpture

Greek sculpture has survived in greater quantity than the paintings, though much of it is broken, but even the small fragments are often art treasures. It is in sculpture and architecture that the Greeks left us their greatest works of genius.

At first the Greek sculptors were much influenced by those of Egypt. Their figures were rigid and formal, but they steadily gained skill and confidence, and their own natural temperament soon began to assert itself. Poses became more natural and varied, and the modelling more subtle and lifelike. In the space of 250 years Greek sculptors gained complete mastery in their rendering of the human figure. But they were not satisfied with mere skill, they put that skill to such good use that their finest works of sculpture have been recognised as supreme masterpieces ever since. In imagining their gods and heroes they visualised whatever is finest in every aspect of human character, and in their art they achieved superb expression of those visions.

In later years pride in technical skill outpaced sincerity of expression, and the newer generations began to lose sight of the true aim of art. In their eagerness to make their work intricate and smooth, and sweetly pleasing or forcefully impressive, their art became comparatively trivial and commonplace, a sad story often repeated since then in the long history of art.

When the Romans overpowered the Greek city-states and brought Greece into their growing empire in the second century B.C., in a sense it was the Greeks who gained the greater victory. The Greek ideals in art were spread far and wide within the Roman Empire, and it was largely the artists and craftsmen of Greece who were employed in adorning the great buildings and monuments in Rome itself. The Greeks created the classical tradition, and then the Romans made it world-wide.

Greek Architecture

In architecture, too, the ancient Greeks reached a level of perfection that has set a standard for all time and established a classic tradition. Their own homes appear to have been simple and unassuming but when they designed and built dwellings for their gods they made certain that no thought or care was lacking. The Greeks knew how to build arches but only used them where they would not be seen, as for instance in their drainage systems. In their temples they preferred the dignity and restfulness of the monolithic type of structure of vertical columns and straight horizontal lintels, as in the great monument at Stonehenge in Britain.

The Greeks built without mortar, laying their blocks of perfect marble in place and leaving the force of gravity to hold them there. When we look at their noble temples we see at a glance that their structure is sound and logical, and this sense of sound structure satisfies and pleases us more than any lavish ornament could. A Greek temple stands on a platform (stylobate) with steps leading up to it from every direction. In the centre stands a hall (naos) in which the statue of the god was erected. This is usually surrounded on all sides by covered colonnades. The smallest shrines have columns at the end only, but the largest temples have columns, sometimes two deep, round all four sides.

There are three distinct styles in Greek architecture. They are known as the three orders, and are easily distinguished by the kind of capital used at the top of the columns. The earliest was the Doric order, with capitals shaped like simple saucers, then came the Ionic, with capitals showing twin ram's-horn spirals, and last the Corinthian with acanthus leaves carved on an inverted bell-shape. Their use and popularity overlapped in time, and a Greek architect

Young jockey astride his horse, a bronze sculpture of the Hellenistic Age (c. 110 B.C)

often had a choice. But when he had chosen to use one of these orders he did not try to make any bold changes. He merely sought to achieve greater perfection within the limits of the style of his choice. This quest for even greater perfection is typical of Greek art.

Each order consisted of the vertical column with its base and capital, and the horizontal bands of masonry resting on it. The lowest of these was the architrave, above this the frieze, and topmost the projecting cornice. These three together form the entablature. This arrangement was kept constant by the Greeks as well as by the Romans who came after them, and by architects of later times who have chosen to work within this classical tradition.

The Perfect Building

As each new generation of Greek architects strove to make their buildings ever more perfect they became

Reconstruction of a part of the Parthenon, the Greek temple to Athene on the hill of the Acropolis in Athens. It is considered the most perfect example of Doric architecture. The architect Phidias (5th century B.C.) is shown conducting a party of visitors over the building as it neared completion.

aware of certain optical illusions that distorted very slightly their true aspect. Certain edges, for instance, if made perfectly straight appeared to be slightly curved. From the normal viewpoint of a person standing on the ground, the steps of a temple platform (stylobate) appeared to sag slightly in the middle. Any architect, after checking and finding them perfectly straight, might well have been satisfied, but not the Greeks. In future buildings the steps would be made very slightly curved, the centre being raised a few inches. Columns too were given an imperceptible bulge (called entasis) in their outline, to counteract an illusion of being narrower half way up. Those columns on the corners, which were normally seen dark against a light background, were made slightly thicker and set slightly closer together than

Floor mosaic from Pompeii. Such pictures were common in ancient Rome and many of them bore the words *Cave Canem,* or 'Beware of the Dog'.

their turn demanded richness and grandeur. The Romans themselves originated little in the field of art. They took their ideas from others, mainly from the Greeks, and adjusted them to their more wordly outlook. But they did provide a rich market for works of art and much employment for artists. They also maintained law and order over a vast area for a long time, so that art was able to prosper, though with lessened sincerity.

Roman architects made bold use of the round arch, and also the barrel vault. In their temples they modified the Greek tradition, but they extended their range of sumptuous buildings to include palaces and large private houses, public baths, triumphal arches, courts of justice and sports arenas. They took over the three Greek orders, altering them to serve their own tastes, and added two more, one which combined Ionic and Corinthian, and another called the Tuscan order, which resembled Doric. They liked to contrast the right angles of the orders with the bold curves of round arches, producing an effect of great richness and vigour.

The homes of rich Romans were often decorated with mural paintings. Many buildings at Pompeii were buried in volcanic ash when Vesuvius erupted in A.D. 79 and some mural paintings were preserved. These revealed that painters then had attained a high degree of realism. Roman sculptors were expert in casting bronze and carving marble. Some of their best work is in portraiture. In their pictures of the emperors and other dignitaries, they often managed to combine a convincing likeness with the appearance of authority required in such official portraits. Relief sculptures of complicated subjects such as triumphal processions show great skill in the arrangement of figures.

In more recent times it has often been this worldly Roman work that has revealed the classical tradition to nations further west, rather than the more spiritual art of the Greeks who originated it.

Bronze sculpture by Apollonius of a Roman boxer (mid-1st century B.C.).

those usually seen against the shadowed wall of the naos. This corrected the impression that the end columns were more slender and spread out than the others, an impression which would have been given had they all been the same size. By means of such tiny adjustments, a feeling of perfect stability and strength was achieved.

The Art of Rome
Where the Greeks sought a quality of serene perfection, the Romans in

Reconstruction of a street in Pompeii which lay buried for hundreds of years after the eruption of Vesuvius in A.D. 79. The city's ruins were so well preserved that when they were excavated much was learned about everyday Roman life.

The Middle Ages

At the height of its power the Roman Empire extended from the desert east of the Jordan in Palestine to Hadrian's Wall on the border between England and Scotland, and from the River Danube in central Europe to the Sahara Desert in north Africa. Over this great area the classical tradition in art and architecture became firmly established. At the same time a new religion, Christianity, was quietly gaining converts throughout the same area, a situation destined to have a great influence on both art and architecture in the years to come.

At that time the war-like movements of peoples on the borders of the Empire were intensified, and there was a grave danger that its defences might be overrun. No one was more aware of this than the great emperor, Constantine, who became sole governor of the Roman world in A.D. 323. Constantine realised that the most serious threat was from the east and so moved his headquarters from Rome to the city of Byzantium near the eastern border of the Empire, making it his capital and renaming it Constantinople after himself.

The future of European art was determined by this decision. Rome and the western half of the Empire eventually broke away and were overrun by hordes of nomadic barbarians eager for plunder. Constantinople and the eastern half of the Empire stood firm. There the light of learning and art continued to burn brightly for over 1,000 years. We call this culture Byzantine from the early name of the city, Byzantium.

Constantine adopted the Christian religion, probably more for political purposes than from conviction, and decreed that Christianity should become the official state religion of his Empire. From then on its priests and soldiers were united in their struggle against the enemies of Christianity. We need to understand this situation in order to appreciate Byzantine art. The Christian church, previously oppressed and persecuted, had suddenly become triumphant, and was recognised as the state religion of the Empire, whereas the Empire itself was threatened on all sides by enemies upholding other religions. It was natural that the art of the eastern Empire was dedicated to proclaiming the power and majesty of the Christian God and his Church.

This was an entirely religious art and totally Christian. It was not the gentler aspects of the Christian story that were emphasised, but the aspect of authority and power. Not the Christ who walked among men, preaching and healing, but the Christ who was to come to glory on Judgement Day, the stern king and law-giver.

Church Building

It was only natural that most of the important new buildings in Constantinople and the surrounding lands should have been churches. These were mostly quite unlike the western type of church with its long, high nave flanked by lower side-aisles. The typical Byzantine church had a tall, square central area and extended out from this equally in all directions.

The Byzantine builders frequently had to rely on brick and concrete, for Constantinople had no good building stone. They did not spurn the use of the arch as the builders of ancient Greece had done 1,000 years earlier. In fact they rejoiced in it, making great use of domes which, in a sense, are just arches extended to become continuous surfaces. They went far beyond the Romans in this, for they used an ingenious method of fitting a circular dome onto a square building,

This 4th-century medallion is a fine example of Byzantine portrait painting.

a thing the Romans never achieved. Their development of the dome was made possible because Constantinople stands on the boundary between Europe and Asia, and in nearby districts of Asia experiments had been made for some time in the building and positioning of domes.

Religious Images

Byzantine art possessed very little sculpture. The reason is that the eastern Church took very seriously the commandment, 'Thou shalt not make to thyself any graven image or the likeness of anything'. We must remember that Christianity had only just emerged triumphant from a long conflict with the religions of ancient Greece and Rome and their multitudes of gods and heroes. The ancient religions had always been personified by works of sculpture, such as statues of the gods found in and on the temples. The early Christians made sure, whenever they could, that these heathen statues were destroyed. They also took the commandment literally when it came to Christian images. There were periods when even paintings of Christian themes were forbidden and those that existed were destroyed as idolatrous. At such times many Byzantine artists would journey westwards, greatly enriching the art of the west. This destroying of paintings and sculptures is called iconoclasm (image breaking).

However, most of the time, images were permitted, and even encouraged, provided they were purely two-dimensional. In fact many Byzantine buildings were adorned with some of the most impressive and beautiful images ever produced.

The bare brickwork of Byzantine churches cried out for some form of rich decoration. Inlay of marble slabs in various colours looked superb, but new brickwork takes time to settle, and a long period of waiting was required before the unyielding marble could safely be fixed over the settling bricks. A perfect solution was found in mosaic, a method so far used mainly to cover floors. In mosaic work small cubes (tesserae) of marble and tile of various colours were pressed onto a surface of wet plaster which held them firmly when it dried.

The Beauty of Mosaic

The Byzantine designers discovered that cubes of glass could be used in this way to provide a surface that gleamed and glittered softly in the dim

Byzantine mosaic figure of Christ (c. 1000).

15th-century Flemish painted wooden shield.

interiors of the churches. Each cube was coloured or gilded on one of its six surfaces. This coloured surface was set in place on the inner side, so that the colour was perfectly protected, while the outer surfaces of the cubes were of shiny glass. They all lie at slightly different angles and as one moves past, each little square shines out and fades in turn, producing a magical effect impossible to describe.

This mosaic technique does not lend itself to the achievement of realistic effects, and it would be wrong to expect them. The designers were required to enrich the walls with designs that inspired reverence and awe—designs rich with spiritual meaning—and this they did perfectly. Colours and patterns are strong, with lavish use of gold. Figures are arranged on a single plane without depth or movement. Everything is stylised and conventional, but the effect is magnificent in its glowing stillness.

The style demanded by mosaic influenced other forms of Byzantine art. Illustrations and decorations on the parchment pages of books, or single framed paintings on wooden panels (ikons, from the Greek word for images) share the same limitations and some of the same splendours that

20

we find in the mosaic designs. Ikons executed in this style have been produced in Russia right down to the present day, but Constantinople itself was taken by the Mohammedan Turks in 1453 and its churches destroyed or turned into mosques. So the true Byzantine tradition ended in disaster.

The Dark Age

While Christian art flourished in the Byzantine Empire, what of the western half of the old Roman Empire? Rome itself was sacked by barbarian strangers in A.D. 410 and again in 546, and prosperity and culture dwindled until the classical tradition was only a memory, a memory kept alive mainly by the debris of Roman greatness. The marble temples, theatres and baths were in ruins, and in the comfortable houses the rich mosaic pavements and mural paintings were open to the sky. Only here and there, mainly in small Christian monasteries, did anything of the old culture survive, and there the light of learning burned only dimly.

For some 400 years the Dark Age continued. The art of western Europe during that time was basically that of the barbarians—the Lombards, Goths, Teutons and Celts – who were jostling for territory over the whole area. Sometimes they tried to capture the style of the Roman craftsmen, but they could not become Roman, so their attempts did not succeed. In the end no direct link survived in most

Examples of Celtic and Byzantine jewellery.

places with the craftsmen who had understood the style and techniques of Rome, no tradition was directly handed down – no skills were passed on from master to pupil.

Yet one slow change was taking place during this period that was destined to nourish the growth of a great new movement in art and architecture in the years to come: the barbarians everywhere were forsaking their old gods and becoming Christians. In fact it was among the small bands of monks that the seeds of art were kept safe, ready to germinate when conditions were right. In the monasteries patient hands faithfully copied and re-copied the old books. Sometimes they were adorned with gold and colours, in designs and pictures that dedicated to the new faith all the decorative genius of the barbaric nations. Only the monks possessed any education, and education and art were preserved during these days in the Christian communities.

Charlemagne

As the various peoples settled down and conditions in Europe became stabilised, the time came when the arts could begin to live again. One might have expected this to happen first in Italy and the south, where the country was littered with relics of the finest Roman work and where the Byzantine tradition was a living force and influence close at hand. But this was not so. Perhaps the very presence of so much that was old prevented the birth of something new in art. In actual fact it was in the kingdom of the Franks, where the northern frontier of France now runs, that the great change was centred. Here in the far north-west there was little of the old to influence the new, and the Byzantine Empire was far away, so the techniques of art and architecture had to be discovered afresh.

The history of this period is dominated by one very great man, Charlemagne (in Latin, *Carolus Magnus* or Charles the Great) (742–814). He was a soldier and ruler, and soldiers did not then much concern themselves with books. Charlemagne, however, gave full honour to learning and the arts. He encouraged the founding and growth of monasteries, where this learning and the practice of the arts were mainly fostered, and by his success he provided, for a time, a unity and stability over most of western Europe in which a new artistic tradition could come to life.

Virgin and child by the Italian painter Duccio (*c.* 1255–1319), a fine example of the Byzantine style.

The new art style which resulted is called the Carolingian School (sometimes Carlovingian) from the Latin form of his name *Carolus*. The word 'school' used in this sense means a situation where a number of artists, working at the same time and within a given area, create a distinct style belonging particularly to that place and time.

Romanesque Architecture

The new style of architecture that grew out of the early work of the Charlemagne period is called Romanesque, suggesting that it is an imitation of Roman work. This it was, for the first attempts to build in stone often amounted to collecting columns and other items from the ruins of ancient Roman buildings and re-using them to meet the needs of a new, rising civilisation. In this re-using of old materials the new builders, who were skilled craftsmen in timber, but not in stone, learned some of the skills of the Roman tradition.

They learned also from the craftsmen of the Byzantine Empire. This was particularly so along the shores of the Mediterranean Sea, for there was much coming and going in the course of trade to and from Constantinople. The Romanesque style in architecture continued until about A.D. 1200. In England this period is divided into Saxon and Norman; but both together form English Romanesque. Romanesque architecture is marked by a bold simplicity in the forms of columns and arches, roofs and towers, and in their arrangement—and absence—of trivial detail. The same can also be said of the work of the Romanesque period in the other arts.

Most of the skilled artistry of those times was devoted to serving the Christian religion. This is not surprising, because here Christianity had recently triumphed over the pagan religions of the barbarians just as it had when the Byzantine tradition was formed a few centuries earlier. Here, in western Europe also, the Romanesque painting, carving and the other forms of art were almost entirely dedicated to the advancement and glory of the Christian Church.

Romanesque art, like Byzantine, is very unlike most of the art of our own times, and to understand it we must also gain an understanding of the needs and ideals that shaped it. In the bold, swinging lines of the paintings, and the deep cutting of plaited curves of much of the carvings, this art

The Piazza del Duomo in Pisa is sometimes called the Piazza dei Miracoli (Square of Miracles), for it contains breathtaking examples of Romanesque architecture unmatched in beauty. Standing in a green meadow are the three principal structures, the Cathedral, the Leaning Tower and the Baptistery. The drawing below shows the original design for the Baptistery (right) as well as the Gothic additions which were made in the 13th century.

The Leaning Tower, Pisa's best known building, now overhangs its base by about 4 metres (nearly 14 feet). The tilt is caused by subsidence in the ground which began almost as soon as the tower was built in the 12th century. It is estimated that in modern times the tilt increases by almost one millimetre each year.

is not far removed from that of the immigrant Celts and Teutons, the forefathers of the population of Western Europe. We see, too, frequent cases of influence by Byzantine work from lands away to the east, and here and there a small pinch of the classical tradition added to make up the mixture.

The House of God

So much for the basic ideals, but what of the needs? One of these was to adorn the new churches and cathedrals fittingly to be the houses of God. Wherever it was possible to find a place for a painting or a carving, these adornments were provided. In time the glowing richness of stained glass was added, so that every surface might be splendid with colour and meaning.

Another need was the need to instruct. Few people except monks and priests could read in those days, not even kings and noblemen, so the sacred stories had to be written in pictures. For this purpose a style of painting was developed that needed no words. This need, perhaps more than any other, determined the Romanesque style in art. Each incident in the holy stories had to be explained so clearly and simply that there could be no doubt or confusion in the telling, and the art style was perfect for this purpose. This work may seem childish to us at first glance, but we must not make the mistake of thinking so, for it is extremely skilled and suited to the needs of the times.

Was there also, perhaps, some survival here of the old belief in the

The Cathedral of Pisa, which is seen in longitudinal section below was built between 1063 and 1118 by the architect Buschetto, and the Leaning Tower, originally a bell tower, was begun in 1173 to the design of Bonanno Pisano. The Baptistery, one of the world's most magnificent buildings, was begun in 1152 and completed about 1280. The Cathedral contains a celebrated bronze lamp known as Galileo's Lamp, since it is said that by watching its swing to and fro the great scientist was able to formulate his theories about the pendulum.

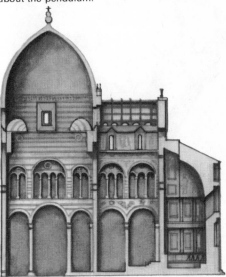

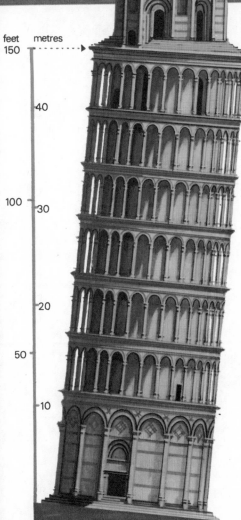

magical power of pictures? Only a little earlier the people of northern Europe had believed in and worshipped the crude gods of the barbarians. Perhaps they felt that by depicting God and his saints and angels they were in some mysterious way filling their new churches with the presence and power of God and his heavenly companions.

Almost all the work of the Romanesque artist-craftsmen was produced for the Christian religion, and many, if not most, of those artists were monks. All books were then manuscripts, written by hand by the monks and owned by the monasteries. Many were enriched with designs and pictures in gold and gay colours. There was also a need for rich caskets (reliquaries) to hold relics of the saints and other more perishable possessions, such as robes and vestments for those performing the rituals in the churches.

A mark of Romanesque workmanship is the straightforward simplicity of its forms and ornaments. Lines are bold and colours simple and strong. Carving was deeply cut, a treatment needed inside buildings where windows were small and closely shuttered in cold weather, for glass was for the richest only. Of course styles varied from district to district. One remarkable exception was in England where,

for a time, the Winchester School provided a charming and delicate style of line illustration in their books, quite unlike most work of those times. After the Norman Conquest in 1066 this style was lost—perhaps one of the greatest losses suffered by the English at Hastings in the final count—for this could have become a rich chapter in the history of the book.

Medieval Illumination

During the 300 years when Gothic was the universal style in architecture over the greater part of Europe, the other arts shared its character and virtues. Very few of the wall paintings of the period have survived for us to see, as image-breakers have done their work in those countries where Protestants broke away from the Church of Rome. Many paintings and statues were then destroyed or damaged, for they were considered Popish. Churches, which had previously been filled with painted and carved images, became bare and austere. The richly illuminated manuscripts were easier to hide away, so numbers of them have been preserved. They were written on parchment pages by skilled scribes, and painted and gilded decorations and illustrations were added. The scripts in which they were written are splendidly decorative

23

The Devil's head depicted in stained glass that is contemporary with the building in which it is contained, the 15th-century church of St Mary the Virgin in the Gloucestershire town of Fairford in England.

small and an exceptional feature.

In the making of stained glass the colour is added to the glass when it is in a molten state. When it has hardened it is cut into small, irregular pieces which, when fitted together, will make up the picture or design already determined. Certain pieces are then painted with different features, such as eyes, ears, hair or fingers, and these are heated in a kiln to fuse the surface paint with the glass. The small pieces are then fitted together. Bars of lead hold them in place and separate one from another, forming a kind of stiff net of lead bars which keeps the whole area of coloured glass firm and flat. Every change of colour is defined by a bar of lead.

This process imposes strict limitations on the artist, but in the early years the artists in every medium were limiting themselves. Their aim was to tell stories clearly without words, and for this purpose stained glass was admirably suited. But the artists' aims gradually changed. A more complete rendering of scenes as they actually appeared to the eye was attempted, and for this the stained glass technique could not serve so well and some of the early splendour was lost.

Towards the end of the Middle Ages heraldic designs took on great importance. Noble families vied with each other in displaying in their homes the coats of arms of other great families with which they were connected. For this purpose stained glass served excellently and there was a great demand for it to fill the windows of manor houses as well as churches.

Tapestries

Another art form that became important towards the end of the Middle Ages, especially in the north of Europe, was that of tapestry. When defence ceased to be the main concern in domestic buildings, comfort could be considered, and heavy tapestry hangings provided some degree of protection in the draughty houses of those times. In Shakespeare's play *Hamlet*, poor old Polonius found an easy but fatal hiding place 'behind the arras'.

in their changing styles, while the illustrations developed in the course of time from a flat and conventional style which tells its story clearly without words and at the same time skilfully decorates the page, to a more three-dimensional treatment which introduces distance and perspective.

At first the columns of lettering and the pictures in these manuscripts were carefully restricted to limited areas on the page, but in time the confining lines began to sprout tendrils and branched out into the empty margins. Then human figures and birds and animals began to creep among the foliage, which grew more extensive until it formed solid borders occupying the greater part of the margins. In early times the scribes and illuminators were nearly always monks, but as the Middle Ages drew towards their close more and more laymen were involved in this kind of work.

Stained Glass

The stained glass that came to play such an important part in adorning churches provides some of the finest examples of medieval art. Many people feel that it was not in the later years of the Middle Ages, when glass was plentiful and windows large, that the finest stained glass designs were produced, but in earlier times, when glass was still very scarce and windows

The Syon Cope, one of the most famous of all church vestments, is a fine example of canvas embroidery in the 13th-century style known as *Opus Anglicanum*.

The 13th-century cloister of the Benedictine monastery of Mont-St-Michel, on a small rocky island near the coast of France.

Miniature illumination of a knight of Prato on horseback from an Italian manuscript of the 14th century.

The city of Arras, in northern France, became so famous for its rich tapestries that every tapestry was known as an arras. Because tapestries were mostly intended to be hung in houses and not in churches, their designs often included scenes or pictures of courtly life.

When the Middle Ages began there were only two important classes in society – the nobility and the peasantry, but as life became more complex a third, middle class grew to be important. This consisted of the merchants and master craftsmen who lived in the quickly growing towns. They were concerned with the prices and qualities of merchandise of all kinds, and attention to these material values was their business. This attitude became more apparent in medieval art as time went on, for the payment of artist-craftsmen came more and more from members of this class. A worldliness was affecting the Church also, for many abbeys were becoming large business enterprises, and the same materialism which governed the lives of merchants was creeping into the outlook of priests and monks as well. We see these changes reflected in medieval art, as it changed from the serene, devotional spirit of the early Middle Ages to the richness and intricacy of the final period at the end of the fifteenth century.

15th-century pendent vault of Henry VII's chapel in Westminster Abbey, London, seen from above.

Medieval Architecture

Large Romanesque buildings were nearly all either churches or castles. Time has not been kind to the castles. If they were not damaged in war, many were wilfully destroyed to make them useless in the event of war, and neglect has continued the destruction. However, sufficient have survived to show us that many ranked high as noble works of architecture. Romanesque churches, on the other hand, have been more often lost through being modernised in later times, yet many remain to impress us with the grandeur of their tradition.

The larger Romanesque churches follow the plan of the earliest of all Christian churches in and around Rome. A tall nave is flanked by lean-to side aisles. The main windows are high up above the side aisle roofs. A chancel extends the nave eastwards, and where nave and chancel meet, two transepts, to north and south, form the arms of a cross in plan. A tower often stands over the crossing, between the two transepts. This has remained the traditional plan of all western churches ever since, very different from the Byzantine churches in the east.

The round arch was always used, and columns are based on those of the Corinthian and composite orders of ancient Rome, though many strange and remarkable changes were made in them. The arcades of arches that separate nave and aisles are frequently carried on piers of enormous thickness.

In fact everything about Romanesque buildings, especially those in the north-west, tended to be massive and solid. This was often an attempt to use sheer weight in place of skill to provide strength, for the builders' knowledge of erecting large buildings in stone was only recently acquired.

The round barrel-vaults of the Romans were known, and these were often intersected to form the cross-vault. In time solid ribs were introduced in those parts of the vault where the greatest strength was needed. This allowed the intervening panels of masonry to be of lighter construction. At first, vaulting was used in the main only over the narrow side aisles. The wider roof of the nave was usually of timber, but this was a constant fire hazard. The great aim of the builders was to be able to span these wider spaces with stone vaults in place of timber.

To do this two difficulties had to be overcome. One was concerned with the distribution of weight. In vaulting of this kind the great weight of stone exerts pressure downwards and also outwards. The outward thrusts tended to push the walls outwards at the top. Wherever the greatest thrust was exerted, the Romanesque builders strengthened their walls with shallow buttresses.

The second main difficulty lay in the construction of the vaults themselves. In rib vaulting there are arched ribs forming a square, called a bay. In these the strong, round arch was used. But there are also diagonal ribs forming a St Andrew's cross in every bay. These diagonal ribs have a wider space to span, and if the whole roof is to maintain an even level, they naturally have to be of a shallower, weaker curve. Here was a great point of weakness in these early vaults, especially when a very wide span was involved. Many experiments were made to overcome this, and the Romanesque style came to an end largely through the final success in mastering these problems.

The Gothic Style

This occurred about A.D. 1200, when the round-arch Romanesque gave place to the pointed-arch Gothic style which continued until the end of the Middle Ages. It was as a means to a structural change that the greatest value of the pointed arch was found. If pointed arches enclosed each bay on the four sides of its vault, then the diagonal arches of that bay could become strong round arches instead of the weak, shallow arches previously used. When this change was made in Gothic structures, it was a real breakthrough in vault construction and provided the strength needed to span the widest spaces.

The wider span then increased the force of the outward thrust, but this problem too was overcome. Buttresses were made heavier and given greater depth, and the thrust of the nave vault was carried clear above the side aisle roof by flying buttresses. These arched downward on to the main outer buttresses, which were extended and enlarged until they radiated outwards from the wall. The walls themselves then became mere screens, for they did not carry the weight or withstand the thrust of the roof. They could be of stone or glass, for the structure of piers, vault-ribs, flying buttresses and main buttresses made a perfect frame which would have stood, perfectly stable, even if there had been no walls. In the end the spaces between the great main buttresses were often filled with stained glass held in a slender tracery of stone, and the buildings had very little in the way of wall.

A New Christian Spirit

With the coming of the Gothic style and its technical improvements great new opportunities were available, and just about the same time a new spirit was inspiring the Christian church. During the Romanesque period the

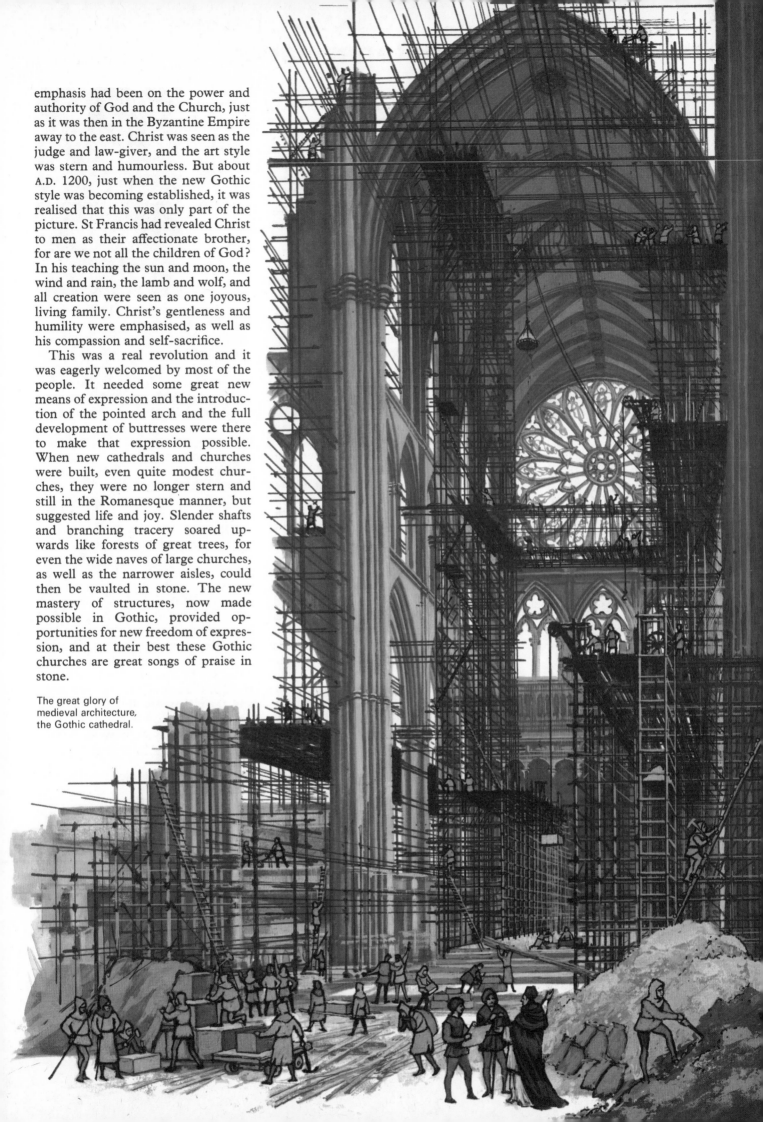

emphasis had been on the power and authority of God and the Church, just as it was then in the Byzantine Empire away to the east. Christ was seen as the judge and law-giver, and the art style was stern and humourless. But about A.D. 1200, just when the new Gothic style was becoming established, it was realised that this was only part of the picture. St Francis had revealed Christ to men as their affectionate brother, for are we not all the children of God? In his teaching the sun and moon, the wind and rain, the lamb and wolf, and all creation were seen as one joyous, living family. Christ's gentleness and humility were emphasised, as well as his compassion and self-sacrifice.

This was a real revolution and it was eagerly welcomed by most of the people. It needed some great new means of expression and the introduction of the pointed arch and the full development of buttresses were there to make that expression possible. When new cathedrals and churches were built, even quite modest churches, they were no longer stern and still in the Romanesque manner, but suggested life and joy. Slender shafts and branching tracery soared upwards like forests of great trees, for even the wide naves of large churches, as well as the narrower aisles, could then be vaulted in stone. The new mastery of structures, now made possible in Gothic, provided opportunities for new freedom of expression, and at their best these Gothic churches are great songs of praise in stone.

The great glory of medieval architecture, the Gothic cathedral.

Giotto's campanile in Florence

The Renaissance

Renaissance means rebirth, and we think of this period in the history of art as the sudden rebirth of the classical tradition, and this to some extent is true. But the Renaissance is really the striking climax of a period of change that had been gathering strength for a long time.

During the Middle Ages Europe had been slowly changing from a purely agricultural society to one in which tradesmen took a leading part, and the simple, unquestioning faith of the peasantry gave place to the shrewd independence of the middle class. People began to think for themselves and to question old beliefs and old knowledge. Spiritual truth was no longer all-important and scientific truth was sought for its own sake.

Painters and illuminators were caught up in this movement and began an intensive research into the appearance of things around them: the shape and structure of objects, and the nature of the light that revealed them, the laws governing shadows and reflections, and perspective, which expressed recession into the distance. Little by little painting began to create the impression that the viewer was actually present and viewing the scene as though through a window.

The invention of printing, which brought less expensive books to middle class readers, helped this movement forward. The books being printed were not all by recent writers. Some were by ancient Greek and Roman authors. These came as a revelation to the readers of the fifteenth century, for the quality of their scholarship and the ideas expressed in them. Soon many educated people were fired with enthusiasm to discover all they could about the classical world of ancient Greece and Rome.

Humanism

The study of classical writings and art gave great encouragement to the growing independence of thought seen everywhere. The ordinary man found that he could make decisions on his own and form his own opinions without referring to the Church for guidance. Man's full honour and dignity were restored to him. This movement is called humanism, and in this movement the artists of the Renaissance were deeply involved. They were full of enthusiasm and optimism. There seemed to be no limits to their ability and everything seemed possible. They spoke of their creations, thus claiming even god-like faculties.

Detail from *La Primavera* (Spring) by Botticelli, the head of Flora.

In Italy the artists of Florence took the lead. That city was a great centre of trade, and its art and architecture were closely bound up with a certain powerful family – father, son and grandson – who were not artists at all, nor aristocrats, but bankers. This was the family of the Medici.

Florence was then a republic, and power was in the hands of the businessmen. Through their ability and increasing wealth, the Medici gained a strong hold on the affairs of Florence. But they were not merely businessmen. They were deeply involved in the growth of humanism and developments in art, and gave great encouragement to scholars, writers and artists. Their intelligence and enthusiasm, combined with their great wealth made them ideal patrons of the arts. Lorenzo de Medici (1449–92), called Lorenzo the Magnificent, founded an academy in imitation of the academy of the philosopher Plato in ancient Athens. There, all the leaders of thought and art in Florence could meet, and their shared enthusiasm, backed up by the enthusiasm of Lorenzo himself, brought astonishing results.

A stone copy of Donatello's heraldic lion stands before the Palazzo Vecchio in Florence.

Della Francesca's portrait of the Duke of Urbino (detail).

lived not as a painter, but as a prince'. Within the space of one century the whole concept of the artist had been completely changed, and from this time on we know the names of even the less important artists. In earlier times their names were seldom recorded.

The real breakthrough from the medieval period to the Renaissance came early in the fifteenth century, and was led by the sculptor, Donatello (*c.* 1386–1466) and the painter, Masaccio (1401–28). Donatello was one of the greatest artists of all time. His

over 1,000 years. In portraiture he excelled in the rendering of strong, rugged character, and his sculptures of babies have all the smooth softness of youth. In his reliefs he equalled the painters in the delicate suggestion of depth.

Perspective in Painting

Masaccio did for painting what Donatello did for sculpture. He died aged 27, but in his short life he achieved the true Renaissance style, using light and shadow and scientific perspective in his quest for a fully three-dimensional rendering of his figures and their settings. He convinces us of the weight and volume of his figures, but we are also convinced of the shape of the spaces between them. Above all, he expressed the ideals of the humanists superbly in giving his characters a sense of immense nobility and self-confidence.

Not until the end of the fifteenth century do we find artists to equal these two great men of genius. It was then that the artists of central Italy

Raphael was commissioned by Pope Leo X to design ten tapestries to be hung on the walls of the Sistine Chapel in Rome. Raphael's designs, or cartoons, were enormous paintings, 5.2 metres (17 feet) high and up to 6.1 metres (20 feet) wide. Their subjects were inspired by the Acts of the Apostles, and a detail of one is shown here.

All this led to a great change in the status of artists in society. At the beginning of the fifteenth century they were regarded merely as craftsmen, like plumbers or blacksmiths – members of a craftsmen's guild. By the beginning of the next century things were very different. An artist received honour according to his merit and was valued for his individual qualities. The man of genius had come into his own and supreme honour was given to supreme genius. It was recorded of the painter Raphael that 'indeed he

work was so many-sided, and his vigour and enthusiasm so great, that he broke new ground in every aspect of his work. In his bronze David he was the first since classical times to choose the nude figure to express a deep intellectual meaning. His equestrian portrait, the Gattamelata, was a triumph of bronze casting. Nothing of such difficulty had been attempted for

achieved the full aims of the Renaissance. This short period which happened around the year 1500 is called the High Renaissance.

A painter who must certainly be mentioned is Botticelli (1444–1510), that master of dancing line and pale, silvery colour. When his subjects were not from the Bible he sought his inspiration from Roman mythology.

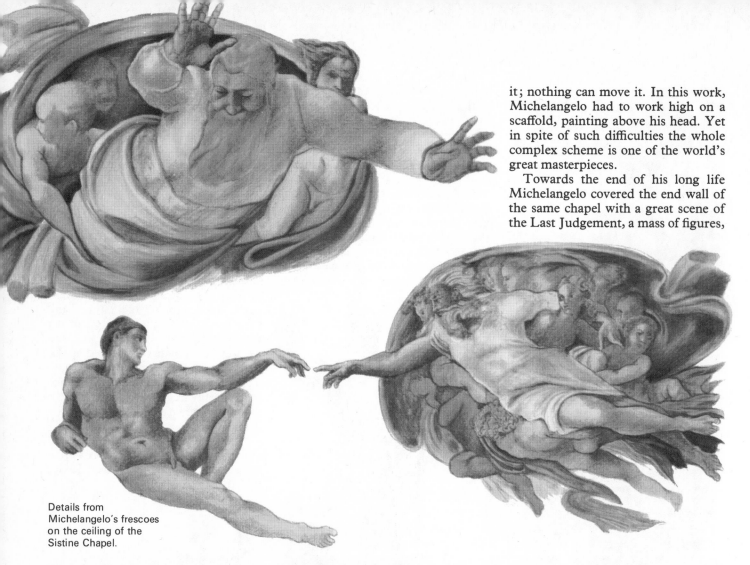

Details from
Michelangelo's frescoes
on the ceiling of the
Sistine Chapel.

it; nothing can move it. In this work, Michelangelo had to work high on a scaffold, painting above his head. Yet in spite of such difficulties the whole complex scheme is one of the world's great masterpieces.

Towards the end of his long life Michelangelo covered the end wall of the same chapel with a great scene of the Last Judgement, a mass of figures,

We can enjoy his paintings simply as exquisite illustrations of their subject, or for the more profound meanings they contain – meanings often concerned with the affairs of Florence and the Medici family or with eternal, unchanging truths as revealed by the humanist philosophers, for Botticelli was closely concerned with the beliefs of Lorenzo's academy.

Michelangelo
One of the supreme artists of all time was Michelangelo (1475–1564)—sculptor, painter, architect and poet. Above everything he was a sculptor, for in his paintings and even his architecture, we can see the mind of a sculptor at work. In his art he found expression almost entirely through the human figure, searching all the time to make the figure, especially the nude figure, express and convey the most profound truths and the deepest feelings.

His marble David expresses not only the courage and confidence of Florence when confronted by her more powerful enemies, but far more. It is a supreme tribute to all human courage and confidence in the face of overwhelming difficulties. Michelangelo covered a vast range of human feelings

and situations, from the brooding tenderness and sadness of his *Pieta* (Mary mourning the dead Jesus) in St Peter's Rome, the stern energy of Moses, his figures of bound captives struggling to be free, to his last religious carvings full of a tragic sense of grief and compassion.

Michelangelo's greatest paintings are in the Sistine Chapel of the Vatican Palace of the Popes in Rome. Early in his life he covered its ceiling with scenes from the book of Genesis, and with many other figures taken from Christian and heathen writings. Together they set forth the beliefs of Christians as revealed in humanist philosophy. In his youth Michelangelo had been befriended by Lorenzo de Medici and taken into his household where he met all the most advanced thinkers of the day.

These great paintings are frescoes, as were those of Masaccio. In this method, sufficient plaster for the day's work is laid on the wall or ceiling. The outline is transferred onto it from a prepared drawing, and the painting is done in water-colour onto the drying plaster. While it is drying, plaster is extremely absorbent and the paint is sucked right into it. So long as the plaster survives, the paint survives with

superb in their expressiveness of many varying emotions.

Another great fresco painter of the High Renaissance was Raphael (1483–1520). He lacked the fire and intensity of Michelangelo, but achieved such a perfect mingling of design and expression that he brought the Renaissance style in art to its final perfection. He probably had a greater influence on the art of the periods that followed than any other Renaissance artist.

Leonardo da Vinci
One other great figure of this period must also be mentioned, Leonardo da Vinci (1452–1519). He left us very few finished works, but in his own lifetime and ever since he has been judged one of the greatest artists and greatest men of all time. His interests took him in many directions. The anatomy of men and animals fascinated him, and so did many engineering and scientific problems, such as the designing of aeroplanes and submarines, schemes of fortification and the improvement of firearms. His enquiring mind and fertile imagination were tirelessly at work, and he recorded facts and inventions in his famous notebooks.

Leonardo's surviving paintings include the well-known *Mona Lisa*, a portrait that has gripped and fascinated generations by its mysterious half-revealed meaning. In his *The Virgin of the Rocks*, Leonardo stirs our wonder and imagination by revealing certain selected details in strong light, while concealing other parts in the gloom of the shadowed passages. In this he provided a prototype for styles of painting yet to come, for up to that time no one had perceived the moving power of this kind of painting.

Northern Renaissance

While the great changes of the Renaissance had been taking place in Florence and Rome, the north-west of Europe had not been at a standstill. The focal point of change there was Flanders (now Belgium). Like Florence in the south, the cities of Ghent and Bruges were great centres of trade.

At the time when Masaccio was developing the southern Renaissance style of painting, the Van Eyck brothers, Hubert (*c.* 1370–1426) and Jan (*c.* 1389–1441), were doing the same for Flanders. Their most important work was a great altar-piece of which the central subject was the 'Adoration of the Lamb', the lamb being a symbol for

hand in their home. Every detail of the figures, clothing, furniture and the floor and window are lovingly portrayed. The brass chandelier, Jan's outdoor clogs, the rug on the floor are described for us with diligent truthfulness, and above all the convex mirror in which the whole scene is repeated in reverse. This is one of the first paintings of an everyday scene and so marks the beginning of what is called genre painting, later to become so important in the art of this region. It is also probably the very first group portrait and marks the beginning of another type of painting known as the conversation piece. Shortly before this, the only acceptable way for a patron to have his portrait painted was to commission some religious subject and to have his own likeness introduced kneeling in adoration in one corner of the picture. In the nature of its subject as well as the skill of its execution this picture is another breakthrough in the liberation of painting.

It is often stated that Jan van Eyck discovered the technique of oil painting, but this is almost certainly untrue. What he probably did was to see the great possibilities of oil paint and

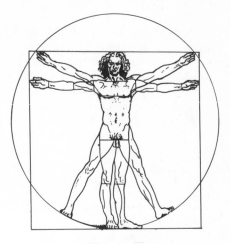

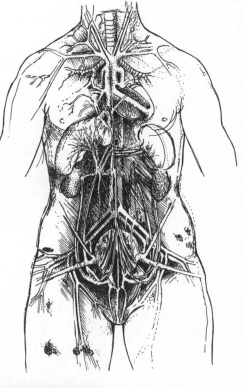

Jesus. It was recorded that Hubert, the elder brother, began the painting and after his death Jan finished it.

These two painters and their followers had no classical tradition to inspire them and they had very little chance to see Greek and Roman work at first hand. They had thus no urge to attempt the noble grandeur of southern art, nor to express their meaning through the medium of the nude figure. Their art was a splendid climax to the movement which for many years had led northern painters especially those engaged in painting miniatures in manuscript books— to observe and record the appearance of the world around them.

Genre Painting

Jan van Eyck's genius is well seen in his double portrait of the Italian merchant, Jan Arnolfini and his wife and their pet dog. They stand, hand in

At the top of the page is Leonardo's drawing which illustrates the statement of the Roman architect Vitruvius that the span of a man's outstretched arms is equal to his height. Below it is one of the artist's many detailed anatomical drawings. Above left are the heads of Christ and four apostles from Leonardo's painting of the Last Supper. On the left a detail from the painting known as *Lady with an Ermine*.

to demonstrate its effective use to others. The tempera technique with egg as its binding substance, was an excellent and very permanent method, but with oil as their medium the van Eycks and their followers produced a richness and gem-like brilliance which gave them a far greater capability to paint what they saw with complete truth.

Jan van Eyck, in his lifetime, brought the art of this early Flemish school to its full perfection. Others who followed used his technique to add those special qualities which belonged to their own personalities, but there was little left that could be added to the general merit of Flemish painting of this period.

There are several artists, who were not necessarily better as painters than

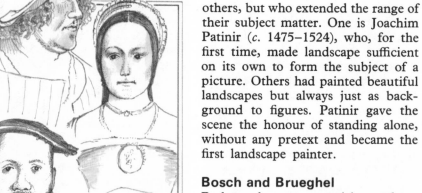
Sketches of heads by Holbein.

others, but who extended the range of their subject matter. One is Joachim Patinir (c. 1475–1524), who, for the first time, made landscape sufficient on its own to form the subject of a picture. Others had painted beautiful landscapes but always just as background to figures. Patinir gave the scene the honour of standing alone, without any pretext and became the first landscape painter.

Bosch and Brueghel

Perhaps the most surprising and remarkable of these early northern painters was Hieronymus Bosch (c. 1460–1516) whose fantasies, filled with the most grotesque and improbable images, gave the foretaste of the Surrealist paintings of our own times. No dream image was too absurd for Bosch: a hedgehog in religious vestments conducts a strange ritual, fish stamp about on dry land in enormous boots, and young girls are threatened by monsters, part-fish, part-insect—his inventions are endless. Everything is most skilfully and beautifully painted.

Pieter Brueghel (c. 1520–69) was another Flemish painter who could invent the most outlandish and often terrifying fantasies, but his best known pictures show the ordinary, simple people of his own times at work or enjoying their brief moments of jollity. He recorded their rough crudeness with a mixture of satire and sympathy, and so powerfully that the most everyday scene becomes strangely memorable.

Brueghel was born at the time of the High Renaissance in Italy. He was a Fleming, but by his time the main centre of change in the north had moved into Germany. Wood-carving was an important art form there, and so also was the engraving of woodcuts to be printed as small black and white pictures. The wood-carvers made much of the ample draperies of the sacred figures they represented, exaggerating every fold and kink of the cloth to produce a very complicated, rich effect. This exaggeration was echoed by the engravers of woodcuts. They emphasised every change and detail of drapery, plant, figure or building, and achieved a splendidly rich effect.

The greatest German painter of that time was also the greatest wood-engraver. His name was Albrecht Dürer (1471–1528). He has been called the 'Leonardo of the North' for, like Leonardo, he was a tireless student in

Detail from one of Bosch's realistic paintings of life among the very poor.

every aspect of representation. The laws of perspective and the quest for ideal proportion, the structure of human anatomy, and of plants and animals, everything in nature was his concern, and he approached every task with supreme confidence.

Like many other northern artists Dürer visited Italy. The lesser men often seemed to lose something of their own individuality after viewing the splendours of Italian art, but not Dürer. His personality and his self-confidence were so strong that the visit did him nothing but good.

One other great German painter must be mentioned—Hans Holbein (1497–1543). All across northern Europe the Reformation, when the northern churches became Protestant and broke their allegiance to the pope in Rome, almost completely destroyed the tradition for religious pictures. The main demand then was for portraits, and fortunately Holbein was one of the most gifted portrait painters of all time. During the latter part of his life he lived in England painting superb and extremely honest portraits for Henry VIII and members of his court circle. The drawings which Holbein made as preparation for his portraits are perhaps even better than the finished portraits themselves.

Venetian Painters

With some understanding of the Renaissance art of Florence and Rome in central Italy, and of Flanders and Germany in the north, we are better able to understand the superb paintings of the Venetians. Separated from

Dürer's painting of St Eustace, one of the wings of the Paumgartner altarpiece.

central Italy by the Apennine Mountains and from Flanders and Germany by the Alps, the area of the valley of the Po, with its great seaport of Venice, developed very much in its own way.

Venice was an international port with close links with the continents of Asia and Africa. It was a distributing centre for merchandise from all over the known world. The men of Venice were mostly merchants, accustomed to

judging the value of all manner of merchandise. Material values were their business, and this was naturally reflected in the quality of Venetian art. The smooth softness of flesh and the silky sheen of a woman's hair, the deep, rich pile of velvet and the subtle patterning of brocade, such things were relished by the painters and their merchant patrons. But this worldly approach was strangely blended with a strong poetic tendency which fortunately saved Venetian art from becoming vulgar.

It may have seemed a quite unimportant event when a painter from Sicily in the far south arrived to work in Venice, but strangely enough he brought with him the knowledge of the oil techniques of Flanders in the far north-west. His name was Antonello da Messina (c. 1430–79). Tradition tells that he had been as far as Flanders on his wanderings and had become a pupil of Jan van Eyck. But this is unlikely. How and where Antonello had picked up his skill we shall probably never know, but it was a great gain for the painters of Venice.

Like the Flemish painters, the Venetians were keenly interested in landscape with its changing moods controlled by shifting light and the differing pattern of weather. They were fascinated by the effect of vapour in the air as it reduced the sharpness of form and colour in distant objects, fusing all into a unity and mystery. Now, having the advantage of oil paint, with its thin, luminous glazes over solid underpaint, the Venetians could pursue this interest with exquisite results, and they produced one of the most splendid traditions of painting in the whole history of art.

Detail from Brueghel's painting *Children's Games*.

They were equally successful with figures and landscape.

In Florence light and shade had for the most part been used to separate and define objects. Colours too had been thought of as the colours of different objects and substances, useful for defining and separating them. Colour and light were used separately as unrelated elements. But now, in Venice, a painter named Giovanni Bellini (c. 1430–1516) led the way in bringing colour and light so closely together that they united the different objects and substances into a harmony never before imagined, never before observed or expressed so superbly.

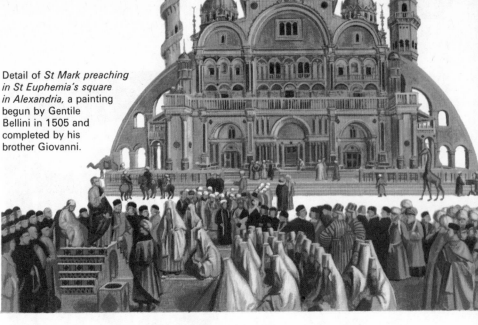

Detail of *St Mark preaching in St Euphemia's square in Alexandria,* a painting begun by Gentile Bellini in 1505 and completed by his brother Giovanni.

The Venetian painter Titian at work.

Titian

In Giorgione's lifetime he was assisted by Titian (c. 1490–1576), and after his death Titian went on to bring Venetian painting to its highest point. He was one of the world's greatest colourists, supreme among the Venetian painters who in this period were famed as colourists. When we say this of these painters, we are not speaking of colours combined for their own sake as they might be in a modern abstract painting or a fabric design. Titian and his fellow Venetians linked the light that flooded their canvasses with the arrangement of objects and figures. The composition and the light were felt as one, and the colour arrangement was closely linked with the light. In fact all the different elements were fused in one superb plan.

This fusing of the various aspects of painting is often spoken of as 'orchestration', for subject, action, movement, light, form, colour and distance are like the instruments in an orchestra, and the painter is both composer and conductor, controlling his 'instruments' to produce a single great harmony. Titian's skilled and beautiful use of the paint itself contributed greatly to the excellence of each complex masterpiece.

Titian's pupil Tintoretto (1518–94) excelled in very dramatic subjects, using not only colour but strong light and shadow to intensify the sense of drama. Paolo Veronese (1525–88), who followed, loved to depict marble palaces and great, ceremonial occasions. He would convert simple, homely scenes from the life of Christ into great tableaux crowded with many richly-clad figures and lavish decoration, and all bathed in beautiful, pearly sunlight and painted with the utmost skill. His enormous paintings are executed in oils on canvas.

The next link in the chain was Giorgione (c. 1478–1511). It is one of the great tragedies of art history that his brilliant career was so short, for he died when he was only 32. But in the few years of his working life he took Venetian painting another step forward. In painting portraits, or the nude figure, or religious subjects, he showed himself a real poet with paint. But it was in his landscapes that Giorgione was unique. There he achieved a splendid unity of soft, glowing colour which joined figures and landscape in a still, dream-like reality—not quite the reality of everyday life, but of some lovely fairyland of his imagination.

Renaissance Architecture

Renaissance architecture sprang from the same movement which sent scholars, especially those of Florence in Italy, searching everywhere for the writings of ancient Greek and Roman authors.

The Gothic style of building had never been accepted with enthusiasm in Italy. True, the pointed arch and Gothic structural methods were adopted, but in their hearts the Italian builders were still loyal to the old classical ideals. So it was that Italy readily took the lead in the breakaway from Gothic, and brought about the reintroduction of classical ideals and forms in the art of architecture. The

apprenticeship, he was capable of taking on the most difficult tasks of construction and achieving the noblest designs.

Brunelleschi took the old classical forms and with them expressed the new spirit of the Renaissance. There was nothing of slavish imitation here. The old forms of Roman architecture were given new life and a character of serene simplicity. From that time the architects of Florence, and soon of the whole of Italy, thought no

was by no means uncommon. As the new style in architecture became the fashion, so these powerful families began to vie with each other to possess the most modern palace.

The early Renaissance palaces remained stern and fortress-like on the outside, but inside they possessed colonnaded courtyards where all was grace and elegance. Slender columns supported round Roman arches, and these in turn often supported balconies with more columns and arches. After a time the outside of the palaces were enriched with pilasters and other features of Roman origin. Both inside and outside the building everything was arranged in perfect balance and carefully considered proportion.

The dome of the Cathedral of Santa Maria del Fiore in Florence was designed by by Brunelleschi.

Although it contains the work of many artists, St Peter's in Rome owes most to the genius of Michelangelo.

Italians were aided in this by the presence of the remains of ancient Roman buildings still surviving in almost every Italian city.

Brunelleschi
One of the first and greatest of Renaissance architects was Filippo Brunelleschi (1377–1446). He was a friend of the sculptor Donatello and the painter Masaccio in Florence. In those days any lad who wanted to become an architect would seek to become apprenticed to some well-known architect in his neighbourhood —not so Brunelleschi. He took himself off to Rome and there began to explore and study the many abandoned ruins of ancient Roman buildings. He dug away the debris of centuries that half-buried many of them, taking measurements and making drawings, trying to find out the principles on which the Romans worked. He then returned to his native Florence and set about proving to his fellow citizens that, although he had never served an

longer of using the foreign, Gothic forms. Their art became entirely Italian.

At that time the great families in cities such as Florence lived in magnificent palaces. Each palace was a fortress, for feuds between the various families and factions were the rule of the day. The situation of Shakespeare's Romeo and Juliet with the Montagues at war with the Capulets,

Among the ancient writings which were discovered and published about this time were those of a Roman architect who lived during the first century A.D. His name was Vitruvius and he was a great student of ideal proportion in everything. He believed that perfection could be attained and taught, and he made rules to guide architects and artists in this quest. His writings were eagerly followed by

Renaissance architects and artists, and from that time ideal proportion became their main concern. Vitruvius taught that the circle and the square were the two perfect shapes, and should form the basis for all good design. He also set down rules governing correct perspective which enabled painters like Masaccio to work confidently and precisely in creating the illusion of depth in their paintings.

Naturally the architectural orders, with their vertical columns and horizontal entablatures, took on great importance in this revival of the Roman style. Sometimes they were true, free-standing columns, but often they took the form of shallow pilasters or half columns, used merely to break up an otherwise bare wall surface. On some large buildings, the orders were used, as in the ancient Colosseum in Rome, one tier of columns above another, each row standing upon the horizontal cornice that crowned the tier below. At other times the columns would be carried up the whole height of a building, their tall vertical lines binding its height together just as the entablature with its bold horizontal shape bound its width together. This was known as a giant order.

The Palladian Style

At first the Renaissance style was slow to extend outside Italy, but in the sixteenth century a very great architect named Andrea Palladio (1518–80) appeared in Venice. He too would probably have had little influence on the rest of Europe except that he wrote a book on architecture which was translated and published in most countries in Europe. This introduced architects everywhere to the Renaissance style.

Until that time buildings outside Italy had often possessed a strange mixture of styles. Classical features were inserted into designs which were still mainly Gothic in their character and construction. In England, for instance, Renaissance details, such as round arches and classical columns, began to appear here and there early in the sixteenth century. But it was almost another hundred years before any British architect had sufficient knowledge and confidence to plan and design a whole building fully in the Renaissance way. The most important British architect was Christopher Wren (1632–1723). By that time the architects of Italy were already developing a changed style called Baroque.

Andrea Palladio built the Palazzo Chiericati in Vicenza in 1550. In many of his designs for domestic buildings he introduced the Roman idea of a colonnaded loggia in front of the house.

Baroque and Rococo

The ideals of Italian artists during the fifteenth century were fully realised in the High Renaissance by Leonardo, Raphael and Michelangelo in central Italy. Leonardo died in 1519 and Raphael the following year. Michelangelo lived another 40 years but by 1520 he had reached the summit of his success and Titian had by that time reached a pitch of brilliance in Venice where no living painter could vie with him. With every ambition accomplished by these giants of art, what could the new generation of artists strive for?

Supreme skill in technique was theirs, but what is the value of skill when everything seems already to have been accomplished? They could repeat the achievements of their elders, but the thrill of discovery had gone and their works were comparatively lifeless. Yet art must always change, must always go forward to attempt new excellence, to accept a new challenge. The younger painters were competent and skilful, but no challenge presented itself.

Some, in order to be different, adopted strange exaggerations of style and drawing. Because of these strange mannerisms they are called mannerists. But the changes they made tended to be artificial and contrived. Others saw that they could never surpass the drawing of Michelangelo, the composition and style of Raphael or the colour of Titian. But they thought that if they could combine all these qualities in their work they might surpass any one of those giants through multiplying their virtues. They are called ecclectics, meaning that they collected up and combined numerous qualities in their work. Again, we can admire their skill, but the fire had gone. All they achieved was a kind of stale medly of second-hand success.

El Greco and Caravaggio

Yet there are two artists of this time who did manage to find new paths to tread. Very different in their outlook and work, both were ardently sincere and individual.

The first, El Greco (the Greek) had an extraordinary career. His real name was Domenico Theotocopulos (1541–1614). He was a native of the Greek island of Crete where the ancient Byzantine tradition of art lived on. While still a young man he left Crete for Venice where he acquired the Venetian method and technique of painting and the ability to orchestrate

Miniature of Mary, Queen of Scots by the Elizabethan artist Nicholas Hilliard.

colour in the Venetian way. Then he journeyed, by way of Rome, to Spain, where he lived and worked for the rest of his life. There, in an intensely religious environment, his own nature and Christian beliefs could expand, and there El Greco developed his true genius. Byzantine, Venetian and Roman influences merged, welded together in the fire of his ardent temperament. In a sense El Greco was one of the mannerists, for his work is full of strange exaggerations. In his case, however, the mannerisms grew directly from his feelings and were not assumed artificially. The strangely tall, thin figures and the fitful gleams of unnatural light in his pictures are a necessary expression of the spiritual aims of his work.

Unlike El Greco who left scarcely any mark on the work that followed, the Italian painter Caravaggio (1569–1609) passed on to future periods a powerful means of dramatic expression. Leonardo had seen the dramatic possibilities of strongly contrasted light and shadow and of keeping parts of a painting concealed from the spectator in the gloom of shadowed areas. Tintoretto had also seen this. Now Caravaggio made it the main feature of his work. This strong contrast between light and shadow came to be called chiaroscuro (clear-obscure). Caravaggio aimed to make the subjects he depicted vivid and powerful and completely convincing as part of the real, everyday world. The people he painted were those he saw around him every day. Nothing must be idealised or even improbable. Yet he wanted the effect on the onlooker to be supernaturally powerful, and that is where the use of strong chiaroscuro served him well.

Baroque Architecture

For 100 years after the High Renaissance the architects of central Italy had been happy to work within the limits of the classical tradition, following the advice of Vitruvius. They admired the simplicity of the ancient work of the Greeks and Romans and they asked no more.

Detail of Caravaggio's *The Fortune Teller*.

But in time younger artists began to grow tired of the rigid limitations of these ideals, and they found their enjoyment in making the classical elements perform strange and unorthodox antics. They were weary of the still dignity of repeated rectangles, especially in the ground plans of their buildings, and longed to bring a sense of movement into their designs. Boldly curved surfaces began to appear and sweeping flights of steps zig-zagged up to great columned porticos, their balustraded hand-rails criss-crossing each other when viewed from above or below. Statues on Roman-style pedestals and many new forms of decoration adorned these rebel buildings. Fountains and balustraded terraces surrounded them, domes and cupolas surmounted them and the ancient Roman forms were combined in an entirely new and florid style called Baroque.

During this period a strong missionary movement surged through the Roman Catholic Church. The disaster of the Reformation, when most of northern Europe had abandoned its loyalty to the pope in Rome, had been a shattering blow to the Catholic cause. Now great efforts were being made to stage a come-back and recapture the north for the older faith. This movement is known as the Counter Reformation. Also the task of converting the natives of the new Spanish and Portuguese colonies in the Americas was a stimulating challenge, and the Catholic Church was stirred to great activity.

This movement required many new churches both in Europe and Latin America—churches which expressed the ardent religious fervour of the moment—and the Baroque style, with its freedom from rules and restraints, was well suited to accept the challenge.

We must not suppose that all Baroque architecture showed the same flexibility and ornamentation that is seen in the most extreme examples. In Protestant countries, where sober respectability was the prevailing ideal, the style was modified and restrained, although still distinctly Baroque in essence. In France too, though the country was mainly Catholic, it was the policy of Louis XIV to create an image of authority and power, and the riotous extravagances of full-blooded Baroque did not serve this aim. So his great palace at Versailles is square and stern outside, although inside the inventiveness of Baroque designers was given free play.

Ornament and Design

Baroque spirit is present in all the arts—literature, music and drama—and the character of Baroque architecture influenced all the visual arts. Some of the most fantastic and exaggerated Baroque designs were the elaborate settings constructed for the masques, the dramatic performances of the time. On the inside of churches and palaces the sculpture and painted decorations linked up with the architectural structure until often one could not tell where structure ended and painting began. The designing of furniture, coaches, and even ships was made a pretext for lavish and often overloaded ornament, and clothing and hairdressing followed the trend to produce rich and exuberant effects. Europe followed the Baroque style for 100 years or more.

Baroque was the art style of the seventeenth and the first part of the eighteenth century. Then a new variation took its place, called Rococo. There was no abrupt change from Baroque to Rococo, but a change of taste leading to a new way of using the same materials and motifs. There was little difference in the outward appearance of buildings, but a new spirit was seen in the decoration of their interiors. Rococo ornament was on the whole daintier and smaller. The earlier Baroque interiors had nearly always given the reassuring impression of being sound and stable. Then painted structures were added to reinforce this impression, even when the work was already grossly overloaded. The arrival of Rococo was a reaction against this ponderous use of excessive ornament.

Fashionable taste began to demand a lighter touch. This affected not only architecture and interior design, but the design of furniture, coaches, ships, clothing and hair styles. Men gave up the great curling periwigs for neat tie-wigs fastened at the back with a black bow. Horses, even, had their hair styles changed. The long, flowing crimped manes and tails were seen no more. Instead, manes were hogged and tails docked. During the eighteenth century everything tended to become dainty and neat.

Baroque Sculpture

Sculpture was an art form highly prized during the Baroque period. From the most famous sculptor to the humblest craftsman, whether working in plaster or timber, all were in great demand, for architects and their patrons required lavish enrichment, both outside and inside their buildings.

Portrait busts were fashionable and single statues, which were much used to crown the skyline of churches and great houses. Fountains were popular and were often furnished with marble tritons, nereids, dolphins and seahorses. Tombs and monuments were regarded as symbols of great importance from modest stones in graveyards to pretentious mausoleums inside churches. The altar

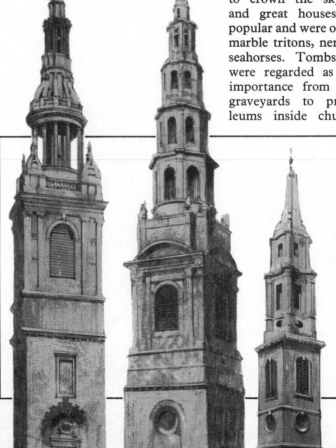

The great British architect Christopher Wren is best remembered for his masterpiece St Paul's Cathedral in London. He also built many churches in the city, each with its distinctive spire. Those on the left are (left to right) St Mary-le-Bow, St Bride, Fleet Street and St Vedast, Foster Lane.

pieces in some of the new Catholic revival churches were enormous. They seemed to be intended to overwhelm and stupefy the worshippers with their vast size and the colossal energy of their treatment. They were often enriched with sculptured figures of saints and angels. Sometimes they contained carved architectural features, rocky cliffs and floating clouds. Flesh, hair, feathers and draperies with their varying textures were brilliantly reproduced in marble and bronze.

In most periods sculptors have kept their figures still to give the viewer a feeling of security, for otherwise the weight of stone or bronze would seem unbalanced. Baroque sculptors, on the other hand, frequently disregarded this. Their figures often appear to be hurtling through the air precariously supported by sculptured clouds or their own flying drapery. Many of the figures are clearly inspired by pagan Roman examples which were enlisted in the cause of furthering Christian aims. Nymphs serve to represent such abstract ideas as Hope or Peace, and sometimes the angels can barely be distinguished from Roman deities of ancient times, for everything Roman was in fashion. Rich men sent their sons to visit Rome, and educated people were expected to lace their conversation with Latin phrases and quotations and allusions to classical mythology.

The technical skill displayed in much of this sculpture is truly amazing. The craftsmen who worked on plaster ceilings or carved fruit and foliage on timber stair-rails, or on coaches or state barges, or on the poops of ships, often showed astonishing ability and brilliance.

Some of the finest work of the English artist Grinling Gibbons (1648–1721) is found in his wood carvings on the choir stalls in St Paul's Cathedral in London.

Bernini

At the summit of this accomplishment we must certainly place the Italian Lorenzo Bernini (1598–1680), who was really responsible for establishing the Baroque style of sculpture. In his lifetime Bernini himself invented and accomplished almost every feat of skill and ingenuity used by sculptors in this period. Extreme naturalism of surface and hurtling movement are seen in his *Apollo and Daphne*; intense emotion is expressed in the *Ecstasy of St Teresa*; and when he designed an enormous shrine for St Peter's Chair in St Peter's, Rome, he introduced columns, clouds, saints, angels, sculptured rays of light and other motifs. All the figures appear in dramatic attitudes or violent motion. It is a work that displays all the supreme technical skill of Baroque art.

Baroque Painting

It was the Baroque fashion to enrich such apartments as the throne room of a palace with paintings which cover walls and ceiling alike. If the architect had already broken up the wall and ceiling surfaces with structural features, the painter would often add his own architecture in paint so that one cannot tell where solid structures end and painted ones begin. Sometimes a ceiling would be painted with tier upon tier of architecture, the columns and arches extending upwards so that they give the illusion of a real extension of the room into the infinity of the sky above. The painted architecture and the floating figures would all be correctly painted as

Velazquez's portrait of Pablo
de Valladolid, a court jester.

though seen from below when viewed from the correct point on the floor. In these grandiose schemes of decoration many figures from classical mythology would be depicted hurling themselves through the air or perilously supported on small floating clouds.

Of course such elaborate mural decorations were rare. The usual kind of painting was the framed picture, and the most common of all, the portrait. Many artists painted nothing but portraits, but the most famous were known for their subject pictures. In this class, classical subjects were then popular—scenes from stories of the gods and heroes of ancient Rome. Religious subjects too were in demand, principally as altarpieces in churches. In Catholic lands we see painters of exceptional genius earning great favour and often great riches, living like lords and winning the friendship of monarchs. Their work was mostly large paintings for churches and palaces.

Among the great Baroque artists of Catholic lands the Fleming, Peter Paul Rubens (1577–1640) was the earliest and perhaps the most typical. He was sixteen years older than Bernini. Everything about Rubens's paintings suggests that he really enjoyed life to the full. He liked the soft sheen of satin, the strength and courage of a good horse, the company of happy, plump women, in fact, all the good things of life. This he expressed with riotous energy and supreme skill in the use of paint in the Venetian manner. He had learned this when he stayed in Italy as a young man. Towards the end of his life Rubens turned away from the invention of great subject paintings to landscape. In this he had a great influence on the future of landscape painting. Today some people find him too robust and sensuous in his figure subjects, but few can find fault with his landscape.

Rubens's pupil Anthony van Dyck (1599–1642) had all his master's skill, but with it an elegance and refinement that made him the perfect court portrait painter. At that time great painters were sought by monarchs who liked to have them attached to their courts as official artists and so add lustre to the royal image. Charles I of England was fortunate in persuading van Dyck to come from his native Flanders and become his court painter. In time artist and king became close friends. For some years Van Dyck portrayed the king and his family and many members of the court circle, creating a world of truly regal elegance in which his noble sitters were represented. Van Dyck always achieved a likeness at once true and flattering. He died just before the outbreak of the Civil War in England.

French Painters

The two greatest French painters of this period worked mainly in Italy. Nicolas Poussin (1594–1665) based his style on the work of Raphael, using precise drawing and clear colours to separate and define the figures and other forms in his carefully arranged paintings. He chose subjects mainly from classical stories. His fellow-countryman Claude Lorraine (1600–82) found his inspiration more in the work of the Venetians, sharing with them a delight in linking light and colour, fusing everything into a mysterious unity. His still, carefully composed landscapes contain Roman temples and harbours where idle ships lie at anchor. Their centre and focal point is usually a hazy distance, empty of life or movement, where soft sunlight and silent mist blur all definition in a golden glow of magic light. Claude established a style of classical landscape which remained a standard for such pictures for many years.

The Spaniard, Velasquez (1599–1660), was the same age as Van Dyck. He too was a great court painter and the friend of a king, but with a very different temperament. Velasquez was dogged, diligent and very conscientious. He tried to record his world with the utmost faithfulness and the keenest observation. His style progressed from painstaking and detailed description to an amazingly free, almost impressionistic shorthand in paint. In this he was a strong inspiration to the French artists of two centuries later. Yet, although his aim was never to change or modify the image that his eye received, his paintings possess a dignity and tastefulness that distinguish Velasquez as a nobleman among artists.

Rococo Painting

During the eighteenth century painting made the same change from a bold vigour to a dainty sweetness that we see in decoration. France was the focal point of this phase.

First to feel the need for such a change was Antoine Watteau (1684–1721). In his pictures, movement is slow and staid, manners are gentle and courtly, and we sense that soft music is quietly throbbing in the still air. Elegant ladies and gentlemen while away their leisure in green forest glades where everything is pleasant and peaceful. Yet we sense a pervading sadness, as though each charming picture was a lament for the gentleness and courtesy that Watteau found lacking in real life. His pictures, with their feathery brush-work and beautiful but subdued colours, present a gracious fairyland that is haunting and unforgettable.

The most typically Rococo of all painters was probably François Boucher (1703–70). He gladly adorned the French court with brilliantly executed paintings of shepherds and shepherdesses, nymphs and satyrs, gods and goddesses, all depicted in a style that is utterly pleasurable and delightful. Boucher was an expert in design and skilful composition, and in figure drawing and painting technique. He was lucky in being perfectly in his element in fulfilling the demands of the pleasure-loving French court. Jean Fragonard (1732–1806) too was a delightful painter of all manner of courtly frivolity, with a superb gift for subtle and lovely colouring.

Another French painter of this time was Jean Baptiste Chardin (1699–1779). He was completely different. He depicted scenes from everyday life, and simple still-life subjects. He could find in the sight of a maid servant going about her work or a loaf of bread and a pewter tankard, such beauty and meaning that the humble subjects seem to be given an importance quite beyond the everyday world in which they existed.

In Italy, Giovanni Tiepolo (1696–1770) continued the tradition of mural painting, but with a light touch and freshness that were completely in keeping with the Rococo taste. He could open up a ceiling with his brushes to suggest an expanse of sky above, peopled with charmingly painted figures disporting themselves among fleecy clouds. Tiepolo moved from one country to another delighting his wealthy clients with his charming inventions.

His fellow countryman, Canaletto (1697–1768) was known far and wide for his views of Venice, which were taken home as souvenirs by visitors from abroad. Like many other popular painters from Raphael onwards, Canaletto employed many assistants. His was really a picture factory. Some of the pictures may have received finishing touches from the master himself; others he probably never saw. But when he did execute a picture entirely with his own hand, Canaletto was one of the greatest of landscape painters.

The Dutch Masters
When we move from Catholic to Protestant countries we see a striking

Pottery figure from the German porcelain factory at Meissen established in 1710.

change. A country like Holland was free from the frivolity and luxury of a royal court. Its purely middle-class citizens were exulting in their newly won freedom from Spanish rule and their growing success in prosperous seaborne trade. There were no nymphs and tritons here. Instead the Dutch artists painted scenes of everyday life (genre) and we see farmers and housewives, merchants and sportsmen as they are, eating and drinking, receiving or writing letters, cooking or entertaining visitors.

The Dutch burghers of the seventeenth century loved to have their portraits painted, but they were small, sober portraits. Exceptions are the large group portraits in which the members of some society or homeguard unit are depicted together. A painter who was specially successful in these pictures was Franz Hals (c. 1580–1666). He could group eight or a dozen sitters, all with equal prominence, yet give the whole painting an interesting variety, free from the even monotony that it might easily have possessed. Above all, Hals could paint with such brilliance and directness that he could convey the impression of a face, or a hand, or a lace cuff with a few, slashing brush-strokes, using an

impressionist style of his own inventing. In this way he could capture a fleeting expression in a way that made him unique among painters.

Fifty years later, Jan Vermeer (1632–75) developed a rather different impressionist approach, altogether more deliberate and thoughtful. He noted the exact colour and degree of darkness of each area as revealed by the light, and placed the correct tints side by side. He then broke up the large areas into smaller ones until he brought his painting to quite a high finish. Vermeer was supremely aware of the poetry of light and also of the harmonies and contrasts obtainable

Detail from one of Canaletto's many paintings of Venice, *View From the Grand Canal.*

with varying shapes and proportions. In his paintings of people going about their ordinary business in their homes, he links these two factors—the mellow appeal of soft daylight and the beauty and interest created by contrasting shapes.

In their landscapes, too, the Dutch artists were quite happy to portray their own surroundings. There were no ruined Roman temples or made-up scenes of Arcadia—their own land was interesting enough. Among a number of other excellent landscape painters one might single out Jacob van Ruisdael (*c*. 1628–82). He understood and loved the dramatic changes by which cloud shadows and sunlight could bring magic to the most humdrum scene. The scenes of Albert Cuyp (1620–91) are just the reverse. In these all is stillness and the air full of golden haze. There is a sense of eternal waiting.

Rembrandt

At this time in the seventeenth century Holland produced one supreme genius, Rembrandt (1606–69) whose paintings, drawings and etchings outclassed those of all his contemporaries. In the early part of his career he was a highly successful portrait painter, but the time came when he began to paint, not to please wealthy clients, but just for himself. He broke with Protestant convention by taking many of his subjects from the Bible. Others came from classical stories. Always he expressed understanding for the character and feelings of his figures and the tensions and intensity of the situations they were in. When he painted portraits he often chose the toilers and unfortunates of the slums of Amsterdam.

Rembrandt was the first to exploit fully the possibilities of etching for artistic expression. In this technique, the drawing is scratched in the wax which covers a copper plate. This is then placed in acid which eats into the copper where the wax surface is scraped away, forming engraving lines. The wax is then removed from the plate which is next coated with ink, and wiped clean once more, leaving the ink only in the sunken lines. When it is passed through a printing press under great pressure, the ink is dragged out of these grooves onto a sheet of paper which has been placed to face it. Many prints can be made from one plate. If lines are forcibly scratched in the copper it is called dry-point. Rembrandt often combined

dry-point and true etching with acid in a single plate.

In his etchings, paintings and his many brilliant, quick drawings, Rembrandt was years ahead of his time. It was another 200 years before his true greatness was realised.

As Dutch painting declined, art in England was poised for a period of new vigour. The sober English, with their German royal family, never accepted Rococo as a popular style, though the qualities of daintiness and neatness belonging to Rococo were in fashion in England as everywhere else.

One remarkable English artist of this period was William Hogarth (1697–1764), a painter and engraver of prints. He was a Londoner and was intensely aware of all the folly and vice of that great international seaport. He was a very fine craftsman with paint and as an engraver, but his fame comes mainly from his persistent determination to expose in his paintings and engravings the evils of his time. His best known works are his series paintings, each on a given theme. For instance, *The Rake's Progress* shows in several stages the sordid career and final downfall of an unscrupulous young villain of London society. No other artist has so diligently and powerfully set out to reform the world as William Hogarth.

Rembrandt's portraits are among his greatest works.

43

Romantics to Impressionists

The Rococo style had been popular with the French court, but was discarded along with the royal family when France became a republic in 1792 after the Revolution. Because the revolutionaries looked for inspiration to Rome as the ideal republic, artists also sought their inspiration in ancient Roman art, and a movement known as Neo-Classicism arose. It had converts in other European countries, but a rival movement was then coming into being spontaneously throughout Europe. This was known as the Romantic Movement and found support in literature and music as well as art.

The word 'romantic' is often used to mean simply romantic love, but this is really only part of its meaning. In talking of art, romantic means the qualities involved in feeling, but feeling of every kind. It is the opposite of classical which implies the use of reason. So we have the arts of reason and of emotion—classical and romantic— the two extremes in art.

Neo-Classicism
The leader of French Neo-Classicism was Jacques Louis David (1748–1825). The clear-cut, orderly, classical style appealed to his temperament

as well as his politics, for he was a staunch republican. His was an art of thought, more than feeling; classical, more than romantic. When Napoleon came to power, David became a supporter of his régime and was employed to enhance the image of Napoleon by painting large canvasses filled with notable personalities set in the glamour of the Imperial court. He also painted many subjects

David's portrait of Napoleon, painted in 1810 when the French general was 40 years old, shows him in his favourite uniform of a colonel of the guard.

from ancient classical history, all with great precision.

On David's death it was his pupil Jean Ingres (1780–1867) who assumed the leadership of the Neo-Classicists. By that time, however, they were being challenged by the rival Romantic Movement, led by Eugène Delacroix (1789–1863) who preferred to express his ardent temperament with scenes of tragedy and disaster. If his subjects were tranquil ones, he

Detail from Goya's *The Parasol,* a cartoon for a tapestry painted in 1777.

required them to be set in some remote and exotic country. These became the favourite subjects for his followers in the Romantic Movement, for mystery, tragedy and violence were their choice, in contrast to the clarity, stillness and tranquillity of their opponents, the Neo-Classicists.

Constable and Turner
During most of this time France and Britain had been at war and British painting developed independently. Where the Romantics in France emphasised the human figure, the corresponding Romanticism in Britain

was based on landscape. The two great leaders of change in Britain were John Constable (1776–1837) and Joseph Turner (1775–1851), very unlike each other in temperament, but sharing the same interest in effects of light and atmosphere.

Constable rejected the fashionable idea of inventing timeless landscapes in the classical manner of Claude Lorraine. He took his paints and brushes out of doors, making small, quick sketches direct from nature, seeking to capture effects of quickly changing light and weather during the brief moment that they remained. From these quick colour notes and his drawings he painted large, rapidly executed versions of his subjects, aiming to retain and recapture the effect he had observed on the spot. The third stage was the carefully finished picture, ready for exhibiting. Constable, like the English romantic poet Wordsworth in literature, spent his life becoming more sensitively aware of the reality of nature. This was another and gentler aspect of the Romantic Movement, very different from the tension and violence of French romantic painting, and altogether English.

Turner's work covered a vast range

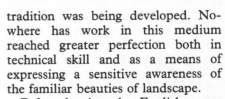

Turner retouches a painting during varnishing day at the Royal Academy in London.

John Constable.

of subject and treatment. He understood well how to construct a made-up, classical landscape, and his mastery and invention were superb. In some of his paintings violence and tension were the themes, but the wind and waves were his heroes, not men, and he could equally well create a serene and sunny scene.

In time Turner became less concerned with solid forms and facts, and more and more involved with the whole effect and spirit of a scene. The unifying influence of light and vapour

in the air was his constant interest. At times he seems to be painting the light and mist alone, with almost no suggestion of anything solid. Unlike the simple, conscientious Constable, Turner manipulated nature to suit himself. With enormous self-confidence he rejected, altered, subdued and emphasised as his dramatic aim of the moment demanded.

In addition to oil paintings Turner worked a great deal in water-colours, a medium recently become popular. In England an excellent water-colour

tradition was being developed. Nowhere has work in this medium reached greater perfection both in technical skill and as a means of expressing a sensitive awareness of the familiar beauties of landscape.

Before leaving the English scene we must consider one other great name, that of William Blake (1757–1827), the poet and painter. He was unique in his own time and, indeed, in all time. His subjects were not taken from the real world of nature, but from his own inner visions. His art was more akin to that of the Byzantine or early medieval periods than to anything of his own day. His images were a means of making real his daydreams. By many he was considered mad, but this was because he was so utterly original. To understand Blake's work one must begin where dreams begin, in the deepest layers of the imagination.

Goya

There was one very great Spanish painter in the eighteenth century, Francisco Goya (1746–1828). At the half-way point of his long life he was a very gifted and popular painter, and most artists would have been content; but not Goya. After a very serious illness that left him almost completely deaf he seemed to begin a new career. His portraits became so sensitive and revealing that only Rembrandt's perhaps surpassed them. When Goya felt sympathy for his sitter no likeness could be more tender and respectful, but if he saw the signs of stupidity or evil, he was merciless. Even the Spanish royal family were revealed by him in all their corruption and foolishness. In this, as in everything else, Goya was fearlessly honest.

His subject pictures and etchings are also largely concerned with the same stupidity and evil in human nature and the brutality with which men treat each other. His series of etchings, *The Disasters of War*, record the horrors of the conflict between Napoleon's invading troops and the Spanish patriots. With his usual complete honesty Goya did not express

45

loyalty to one side or the other. He was not concerned with politics or propaganda, but with human nature in all its weakness and savagery, its courage and loyalty.

Late in his life Goya painted a number of works known as the 'Black Pictures'. Some are simply haunting and mysterious, others are truly horrifying. It seems as though Goya felt compelled to ransack all the secret corners of his mind for those doubts and terrors which we all possess, and he made them real by creating these strange dream images. In this he forestalled the Surrealist movement of modern times.

The Realists

In France a new revolt occurred in art at the height of the conflict between Romanticists and Classicists, a revolt against exotic or historical subjects. Its leader, Gustave Courbet (1819–77), held that the ordinary world around us should provide the subjects for art. His first important work, *Burial at Ornans*, is a large canvas depicting the people of an ordinary French village at the graveside of one of their neighbours. This strong, forthright record of a simple, contemporary scene was a great shout of defiance which enraged established painters and critics alike.

Courbet was a superb painter and also an exhibitionist who sought opportunities to flout public opinion. He became involved in revolutionary intrigues and ended his life as an exile in a foreign land. But he was the hero of a small number of painters calling themselves Realists who were tired of the artificiality of established art. A group of these worked in the village of Barbizon in Fontainebleau Forest. Most were landscape painters but one, Jean François Millet (1814–75) a peasant boy turned painter, recorded the toil and struggle of the French peasants which he had shared in his childhood. He depicted their everyday occupations with a simple strength that made his paintings masterpieces. Millet's city counterpart was Honoré Daumier (1808–79). Besides being one of the first and best of political cartoonists, he depicted the washerwoman and other toilers of Paris with a simple boldness that was lacking in most established contemporary art.

One of the greatest of the Realists was Edouard Manet (1823–83) who, like Courbet, flouted the fashion of his day and suffered for his courage. At that time the nude figure was considered perfectly respectable in art if it appeared in scenes from ancient times or distant places. Manet depicted naked people in settings of his own time and that, of course, was considered a crime. Not only that, he painted these scenes in true, clear daylight in a way that he had learnt

Manet's painting *Olympia* (1863), now considered a masterpiece, caused a great scandal when it first appeared.

from the works of Velasquez in Spain. Such truthfulness in rendering the effect of cool daylight was itself a shock in a society used to the older traditions of painting. For these crimes Manet was derided by most of his contemporaries, but he, in turn, was regarded as a hero by the art rebels of the younger generation.

The Impressionists

These young rebels were the Impressionists, who took the search for realism to its final conclusion. In the public exhibitions of that time a slick, descriptive skill and a subject that appealed to the average person were all important. The Impressionists discarded both. They formed a close-knit group in Paris, each gaining support and encouragement from the other members. Some were concerned with subject matter up to a point. Pierre Renoir (1841–1919) chose the

Detail from Rossetti's *The Bower Meadow*.

nude figure and scenes of lively enjoyment at cafés, while Edgar Degas (1834–1917) preferred the background of the racecourse or the circus or the ballet. Others discarded all interest in subject matter. Their concern was the light reflecting from objects in front of them. So long as those objects provided an opportunity for a lovely harmony of shapes and colours, they were acceptable. Claude Monet (1840–1926), the most single-minded of the group, took an old haystack as the basis for a whole series of pictures, painting it at every time of day, from dawn to dusk.

The Impressionists had a hard struggle to win recognition, for few people could understand and appreciate their aims. But in time the public and critics were won over and the style was accepted all over Europe, though too late to benefit the original members of the group.

An American painter, James McNeill Whistler (1834–1903), like the Impressionists, turned from subject matter in quest of creating harmonies of colour and proportion in his pictures. Working in England, he carried on a one-man campaign in this cause. To emphasise this belief

Detail from Millet's *The Gleaners*.

he gave his paintings titles taken from the language of music, such as *Nocturne in Blue and Silver* or *Symphony in White*.

The Pre-Raphaelites

In England, at that time, a group of young artists were carrying on a parallel revolt against the slick skill with paint which passed for art in

most of the popular work at that time. They called their group the Pre-Raphaelite Brotherhood, meaning that they were trying to emulate the work of Italian artists who lived and worked before Raphael. They wanted to be as humbly painstaking in their search for visual truth as those neglected early painters, and to set aside the clever accomplishments of the much admired followers of Raphael.

In spite of a common aim in their

The young lovers from Renoir's painting *La Bal à Bougival*.

search for the appearance of nature the Pre-Raphaelites varied a great deal, one from another. For instance, Ford Madox Brown (1821–93) devoted himself to pointing out social evils, and Holman Hunt (1827–1910) to portraying incidents in the Bible,

while Dante Gabriel Rossetti (1828–1882) and Edward Burne-Jones (1833–1898) looked back with yearning to the Middle Ages for their inspiration. In this they found support from William Morris (1834–96) who campaigned for good and honest design at a time of ruthless industrial growth, when ignorance and bad taste were seen everywhere.

During the century following the French Revolution sculpture had been pursuing a course parallel to that of painting. The classical fashion was expressed in the still, smooth marble statues of the Italian Antonio Canova (1757–1822) and his many followers, while the romantic approach is seen in the great energy and violence of Antoine Barye's bronze animals. Realism, and even Impressionism, also found supporters among the sculptors. But the one really outstanding sculptor of this century fits neatly into no single group. This is Auguste Rodin (1840–1917), without doubt a great genius.

Rodin could work in the fashion of the day when he chose, but he usually rejected the soft smoothness of the imitation Roman statues that were so popular just then, preferring a rough, clay-modelled surface. He used this to emphasise the tension and energy that were his main interests. He was a Realist and often chose momentary poses for his figures in contrast to the posed stillness favoured in the classical style. But his figures were not all just Realist sketches. They expressed universal human emotions and endeavours. Rodin, too, was rejected by the fashionable art world, just as the Impressionists were, but

buildings in styles from the past. Some chose Baroque, others Gothic. In Britain the 'War of the Styles' raged bitterly: on the one side the classical faction, on the other the architects of the Gothic Revival. Some very fine buildings were designed in Victorian Gothic, perhaps the best of all being the Houses of Parliament in London, planned by Sir Charles Barry (1795–1860) in the Tudor style.

When nineteenth-century architecture at last found a style of its own, it came directly and logically from new basic materials and structures. The Industrial Revolution was in full growth and one of its products was

cast iron—a new material at that time. When a huge building was required quickly for the Great Exhibition in London in 1851 it was designed by the architect and gardener, Joseph Paxton. He based his structure on the rib-pattern of the leaf of a giant water-lily, and the iron ribs of the building were prefabricated and assembled quickly on the prepared site. The spaces were then filled in with glass. This was the famous Crystal Palace. Many other similar structures followed. The Eiffel Tower in Paris, the rear part of St Pancras Station in London and the Clifton Suspension Bridge near Bristol are examples.

This construction in iron was a real revolution in building. At first many people refused to call it architecture, but it had come to stay, and soon the fancy dress buildings of the classical and Gothic revivals gave place to other styles belonging more honestly to their own times.

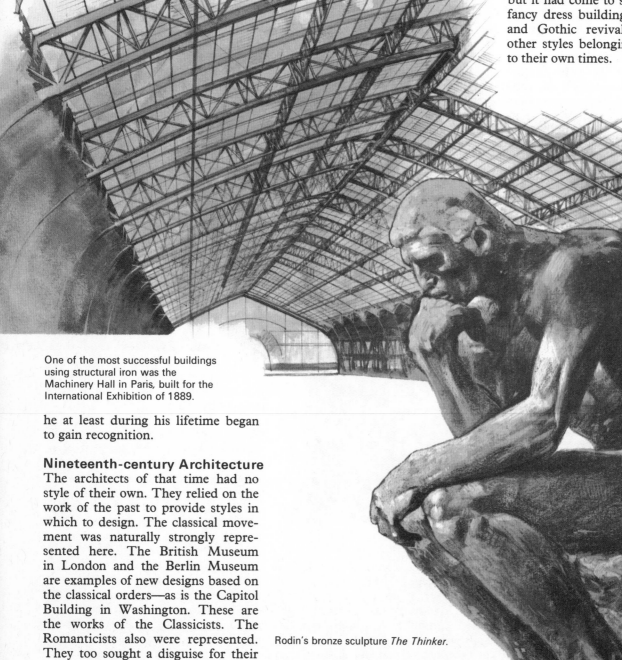

One of the most successful buildings using structural iron was the Machinery Hall in Paris, built for the International Exhibition of 1889.

he at least during his lifetime began to gain recognition.

Nineteenth-century Architecture

The architects of that time had no style of their own. They relied on the work of the past to provide styles in which to design. The classical movement was naturally strongly represented here. The British Museum in London and the Berlin Museum are examples of new designs based on the classical orders—as is the Capitol Building in Washington. These are the works of the Classicists. The Romanticists also were represented. They too sought a disguise for their

Rodin's bronze sculpture *The Thinker*.

Modern Art

The Impressionists really formed the final link in a long chain of experimenters reaching back to Jan van Eyck and beyond; a chain of painters intent on creating the illusion that a person viewing the flat surface of a picture was actually looking at a three-dimensional scene. The Impressionists seemed to have taken this quest to its final conclusion, and there was little chance of a new generation of painters finding fresh discoveries along this path. They had to establish a new direction, and some found the achievements of the Impressionists a jumping-off point for their experiments, while others turned back to old styles from which to seek inspiration. Unlike the Impressionists these innovators each worked in isolation, searching out his own way forward. We call them the Post-Impressionists.

Cezanne and Seurat

Paul Cézanne (1839–1906) found the Impressionist approach lacking. The effects of light, which were their main interest, were too transient and superficial for him. He was impelled to probe beneath the light reflected from objects and to search into the forms and structures of those objects themselves. Whether they were mountains, or men, or apples, it mattered little to Cézanne. He spent his life finding out more and more about the basic nature of the shapes of the objects in his paintings and how to render and relate those shapes in a concise and orderly way.

Since the time of the Renaissance, European artists had been expressing the solidity of objects by increasing and reducing the darkness of their surfaces as they turned—we call it shading. The most heavily shaded areas always tend to become dingy, and the Impressionists had striven to keep them fresh and clean. But this was a compromise. Cézanne discovered that he could express solidity of form by giving every new angle of his surface a slightly different colour, modelling by colour alone. He was wealthy enough to have lived all his life in idleness. He toiled ceaselessly to make himself perfect in his self-imposed task of representing nature in all its solidity in the simplest possible terms, and at the same time make every work perfect in itself.

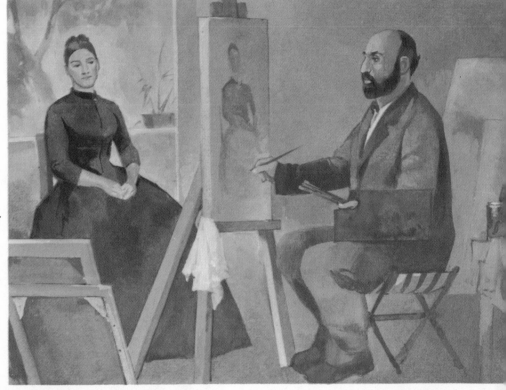

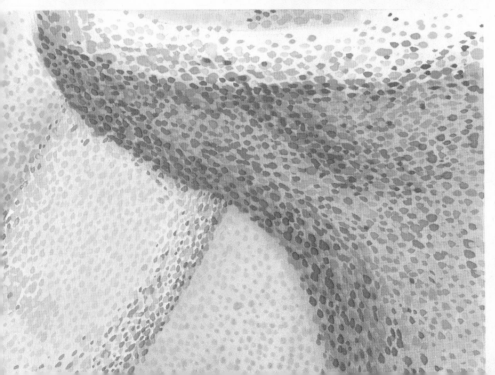

(Right) Cézanne at work on a portrait. (Left) Detail of Seurat's painting *Young Woman with a Powder Puff* with (below) a close-up showing the method by which the artist applied tiny dots of colour.

During this time another painter, Georges Seurat (1859–91), was carefully developing a different method. The scientific study of colour had shown that white light is made up of all the bright colours of the spectrum. Seurat realised that if he placed tiny dots of the spectrum colours next to each other in the correct proportions they would be blended by the eye of the spectator and, when viewed from a distance would produce all the soft tones that he might need. This avoided the dulling effect produced every time several colours are mixed on the palette. When mixed by the eye they give a greater sensation of brilliance. This method is called pointillism or divisionism. Monet and others of the Impressionists had been

49

doing this kind of thing, but only instinctively, never systematically.

Seurat's intellectual approach is also seen in the careful way in which he planned his compositions, almost as an architect will design the facade of a building. He looked for shapes and angles which he could repeat again and again in different, carefully chosen positions on his canvas, emphasising some and subduing others—again like the instruments in an orchestra— and so produce a balance and harmony that is both stimulating and satisfying. Many colour sketches and tone drawings were done in preparation for the final picture.

Van Gogh and Gauguin

When we turn from the two Frenchmen, Cézanne and Seurat, to the Dutchman, Vincent van Gogh (1853–1890), what a difference we see, for Van Gogh's art was of ardent feeling

and white-hot enthusiasm. He worked from the heart, not from the head. At first he painted subjects of poverty and toil in sombre colours. Later he went to Paris where he turned to the clear, luminous colours of the Impressionists. Later, at Arles, in the sun-drenched south of France, he painted everything around him, using brilliant colours applied in thick, bold brush strokes. His method was so direct and spontaneous, his vision so keen and his feelings so powerful that the effect is amazingly vivid. In two years at Arles his output of pictures was prodigious, but his end was a sad one. After a period under treatment in mental hospitals, he shot himself. He was only 37 years old.

The other great Post-Impressionist painter, Paul Gauguin (1848–1903) was also an artist of the heart. When he was 35 he gave up his promising business career, left his wife and

children and accepted a life of extreme poverty in order to become a full-time painter. He found he could not afford to live in Paris, so he moved to Brittany where he developed his style, using areas of brilliant, glowing colours in his pictures, rather like stained glass and reminiscent of the work of young children. He believed that an artist must select and exaggerate those qualities in a scene that are important to him personally, neglecting everything else. Removing himself even further from city life he sailed to the Pacific Islands, to look for the simple, primitive life that he craved and for subjects of primitive life to stimulate him. There he produced rich, glowing paintings of the islands and their native inhabitants, developing and perfecting the simplified richness of his very personal style. He died alone on one of the most remote Pacific islands.

One other very great artist of this generation must be mentioned. This was Henri de Toulouse-Lautrec (1864–1901). He was the son of a wealthy family, but an accident when he was a child left him deformed. Later he shunned fashionable society and sought the company of artists and the poor people of Paris. He was not a real Post-Impressionist for he found the style that suited him in the work of such painters as Degas, merely pitching his work to a new intensity.

Like Goya, a century earlier, Lautrec was very cynical, though like Goya he could be respectful and tender when his sympathy was aroused. But he often treated his subjects of city life with a strong tinge of caricature. His sarcastic wit may have been an unconscious way of hitting back at fortune for inflicting on him his absurd appearance and awkwardness, but his paintings, prints and drawings are brilliant, forceful and often very beautiful.

Les Fauves

The story of the Post-Impressionists brings us into the twentieth century and the beginnings of modern art. Of course many artists still chose to represent nature faithfully, and still do—and probably always will. But the Post-Impressionists, each in his own way, had succeeded in freeing the artist from the necessity of being true to actual appearances. Photography was already taking over much of the descriptive work previously done by artists, who no longer needed to try to compete with the camera.

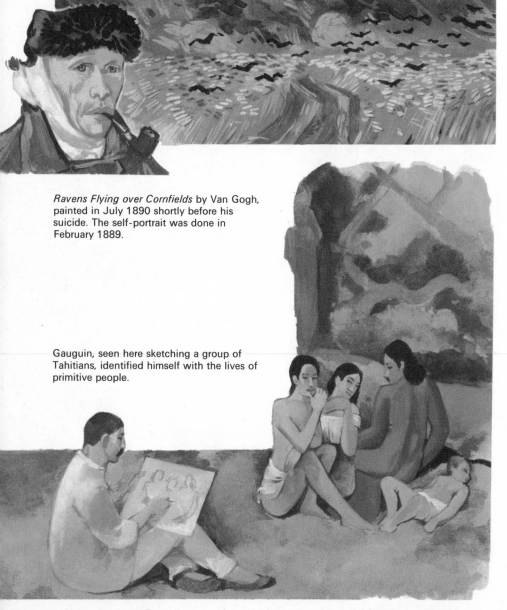

Ravens Flying over Cornfields by Van Gogh, painted in July 1890 shortly before his suicide. The self-portrait was done in February 1889.

Gauguin, seen here sketching a group of Tahitians, identified himself with the lives of primitive people.

50

They were free to take liberties with the realities of appearance and many eagerly seized the opportunity.

One of the first of the new generation to do so was Henri Matisse (1869–1954) who led a group of painters dedicated to winning freedom from the need to keep to the actual colours of objects. Why should one not paint green nudes on pink grass? Inspired by Japanese prints and the art of Mohammedan lands, in which shading is not used, Matisse explored all kinds of methods of using colour independently and creatively, simplifying his drawing to provide a pattern of forms and abandoning the exact perspective that artists in past times had taken such pains to achieve. A shocked and disgusted critic called Matisse and his followers *fauves* (wild beasts). They adopted the name defiantly and are called *Les Fauves* to this day.

Toulouse-Lautrec chose his subjects from the world of cafés, bars and dance halls of Montmartre in Paris. On the right is his poster of Jane Avril, who befriended the crippled artist.

Braque and Picasso

Another liberation movement in art was begun by Georges Braque (1882–1963) and his Spanish friend Pablo Picasso (1881–1973). They were inspired by Cézanne's belief that 'everything in Nature is based on the sphere, the cone and the cylinder', and by their discovery of the strange beauty of African carvings. In these the figures are reduced to geometric forms in bold, clear-cut planes, thus seeming to put Cézanne's belief into practice. For some time Braque and Picasso worked together, experimenting in reducing objects to their basic shapes. Others joined them and the movement came to be called Cubism. Their experiments led them to represent objects as though taken apart, each part or facet on its own. Then they began to assemble compositions of various objects reduced to their most basic flat shapes. Finally they tried pasting together all kinds of items such as bus tickets and playing cards, and making pictures by adding lines, colours and textures—an art that we call Collage.

Picasso's *Family of Saltimbanques,* a painting of circus folk belonging to his Rose Period (1905).

Detail from a lithograph of
The Scream by Edvard Munch.

Artists were now completely free, if they so wished, to depart from depicting objects accurately. Many new experiments were made, and new 'isms' came thick and fast, some to disappear as quickly as they came. We have considered Classicism and Romanticism, Realism, Impressionism, Fauvism and Cubism. Italy provided Futurism, in which the emphasis was on breaking with tradition and expressing the spirit of the new mechanised age, with great emphasis on rendering movement. In representing an aeroplane it was the sweeping lines of its flight that were stressed, not the shape of the aeroplane itself. The movement was led by the poet Filippo Marinetti (1876–1944), and the most influential artist was Umberto Boccione (1882–1916).

In Russia, Casimir Malevich (1878–1935) led a movement called Suprematism, aiming to detach art from representation completely. Art was to become the direct expression of the artist's feelings to be conveyed to the spectator by lines, shapes and colours without representing anything in nature. In poetry we are moved by the poet's meaning, and also by the ring of the words on our ear, but if we hear a poem in a foreign language we hear only the ring of the words and are moved by that alone. The aim of Malevich and Vasily Kandinsky (1866–1944) was to achieve this in art—expression without descriptive meaning.

Two Russian brothers Antoine Pevsner (1886–1962) and Naum Gabo launched another movement, called Constructivism, in which structures of wire, metal and plastic materials were put together to challenge traditional sculpture as an art form. In Russia their outburst of rebellious change following the Revolution soon won the disapproval of the Bolshevik authorities, who insisted that old-fashioned figurative methods must be used for propaganda. Russia was the loser here, and the western world benefited as the most gifted Russian artists moved west, disillusioned exiles from Communism.

The Bauhaus

Some of these exiles were welcomed in Germany by Walter Gropius, the architect and founder of the famous, new-style art college called the Bauhaus. There the latest ideas in fine art and design were developed, and the school provided a strong influence in the years ahead, not least when Hitler and his Nazis came to dominate Germany. But they, in turn, found the new art movements intolerable and the Bauhaus was closed. Once more its brilliant staff members scattered as exiles, carrying their ideas and ideals far and wide, some to settle in America.

In modern times the contemplative artist who has sought to find a new discipline in art has followed one of two main paths. One of these is to represent real objects, but to strip them of everything superficial, retaining only what is essential to his purpose. Each makes his own selection of what to emphasise and what to discard, according to temperament and intention. The other method is to abandon all subject matter and make a selection of shapes, colours and tones without reference to anything observed. Those who follow this course are the purely abstract artists.

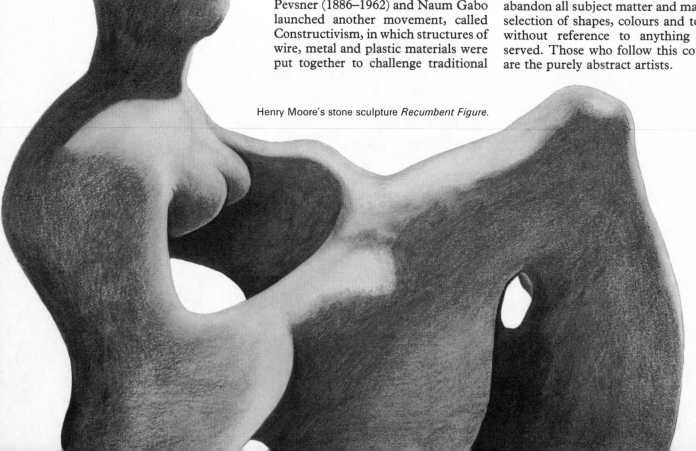

Henry Moore's stone sculpture *Recumbent Figure*.

Decorative fan and sculpture from the Art Deco period of the 1920s.

The great English sculptor Henry Moore has based his work mainly on the human figure, but selecting only those qualities that serve his aim of expressing massive importance and power. Barbara Hepworth, on the other hand, has attained a serene refinement of forms which bear no distinct resemblance to anything in nature. Abstract sculpture includes Naum Gabo's breath-taking structures of perspex and nylon thread, and Jean Arp's arrangements of solid shapes suggesting, but never representing, human flesh.

Abstract painters of the more classical kind have usually kept to purely geometric forms. A typical example is a long series of pictures by Josef Albers entitled *Homage to the Square*, each of which contains a series of perfect squares of various colours, one inside another.

Expressionism

If we look at the work of modern artists of the more emotional kind, we find abstract work there also, for in contrast to the still perfection of the geometric school, a strong, emotional excitement can be expressed by swirling shapes and lines and by colours. Such ardent emotion in art has become known as Expressionism. A striking example of this in abstract art is seen in the Abstract Expressionism of Jackson Pollock (1912–56) in America. His method of laying his large canvasses on the floor, and dripping and dribbling blobs and streams of paint very deftly onto them has been called Action Painting.

Not all Expressionism is abstract, in fact most has been figurative, for when artists are driven to express strong feelings they usually want to express them about somebody or some situation. Long before Pollock developed his abstract style in America, Van Gogh had been painting strongly expressionist pictures in southern France. This was natural enough, for he was a Dutchman, and the Teutonic race has for thousands of years shown a strong tendency towards Expressionism. Georges Rouault (1871–1958), a Frenchman, depicted Christian subjects and scenes from the Paris underworld in a strongly expressionist way, using harsh, bold outlines that remind us of stained glass. They are often deeply tragic and sometimes pitilessly cynical. Picasso, too, a Spaniard, has a strong expressionist strain in much of his work. But this extreme in modern art is most often found in Germany and other Teutonic lands.

A Norwegian painter and printmaker, Edvard Munch (1863–1944), depicted human situations and emotions stripped of the social disguises with which they are usually concealed. In *The Scream* he shows emotion in its most uncontrolled violence. His work from the years between the wars, is often marked by the bitterness and cynicism which comes from despair and frustration.

We must remember that most people, and most artists, are neither entirely intellectual nor entirely emotional, so most art lies somewhere between these two extremes. This applies also to modern art. Much good work is still produced in a thoroughly traditional way, for even today art does not have to be extreme to be acceptable.

Surrealism

Expressionism is an art of feeling, often of unrestrained feeling, and our feelings spring from the deepest and least understood layers of the mind. We have seen that Goya and others were impelled to express in their work

Jackson Pollock.

the content of these deep, unconscious regions. It was only a step from Expressionism, in which emotion is to some extent criticised and curbed by the conscious mind, to Surrealism, in which the unconscious urges have free play.

Modern psychology has made known the existence and importance of the unconscious mind and the role of our dreams which arise from it. The idea is very simple. Our minds have a conscious part which is obedient to our intentions year in and year out. We are conscious of what is happening there. But there is also an unconscious part over which we have little or no control. We are not aware of what is taking place there except through our dreams, which emerge from it along with certain strange impulses which sometimes we do not understand. Our dreams appear as images which can be very disquieting, for in them the laws of everyday life do not apply. They present themselves as dreams in our sleep, or in very abnormal circumstances in our waking hours, but with practice an artist can record them as easily as he can represent a remembered scene. This is just what the Surrealists aim to do.

The Surrealists differ a great deal from one another. Giorgio de Chirico's dream cities lie unpopulated, lit as though by some unfamiliar moon. Paul Klee (1879–1940), part serious,

part humorous, created new creatures to inhabit new worlds of his own imagining. Max Ernst, perhaps the greatest of Surrealists, painted strange scenes which haunt us with their reality, though it is not the reality of everyday life. They are so factual and convincing that we could almost believe that it is the real world that is unreal. René Magritte (1898–1967) paints what are virtually visual puns, in which objects which resemble each other become identical, with the strangest results. The most popular and sensational of the Surrealists is Salvador Dali who presents his world of strange, dreamlike images with the actuality of a coloured photograph.

A very recent form of art, related to Surrealism, is called Pop Art (Popular Art). It is based on the use of objects from modern living, such as advertisements, food cans and strip cartoons, which are normally disregarded, or more likely scorned, by the orthodox world of artists, critics, art dealers and purchasers. This movement sets

out partly to shock the art establishment and debunk some of its false beliefs, and partly to re-educate the world to admire and find meaning in a wider range of possible art forms. In this it somewhat resembles the Dada movement of the period around the end of the First World War, which aimed then to deride and destroy the accepted traditions of art and life, as a gesture of despair and horror at the state of the world. However, the Pop Art Movement, for all its cynicism, has been marked in the main by a light-hearted humour and buoyancy, totally unlike the bitterness and despair that underlay the works of the Dada group.

Op-Art (Optical Art) is very different. Here the results of eye fatigue are used to produce surprising and sometimes bewildering effects. It is an art of purely visual sensation and depends to some extent on optical illusion. Its chief exponents are the Hungarian painter, Victor Vasarely and, more recently, Bridget Riley in England, who have both raised this art form into something valuable.

Art Nouveau
At the very end of the nineteenth century, when the Post-Impressionists were making their bid to free painting from an exhausted tradition,

Detail (left) from *Medicine* by the Austrian artist Gustav Klimt (1862–1918). (Above) Stained glass and leaded doors for the Willow Tea Rooms in Glasgow designed by Charles Rennie Mackintosh during the Art Nouveau period.

Lautrec, in his lithographed theatre posters, the expressionist painter Edvard Munch, and especially the brilliant English illustrator, Aubrey Beardsley (1872–98).

The period of the purest form of Art Nouveau was short, from about 1890 to 1910, but in the hands of its most inspired artists works of great originality and beauty were produced. These were based on the importance of flowing lines and curves as seen in the natural growth of plants, or the movement of waves or the spiralling of smoke in the air. To some extent Art Nouveau was a revolt against the machine age and a desire to return to the world of the medieval craftsman. The leading figure in the Arts and Crafts movement in Britain was William Morris, himself an important contributor to the Art Nouveau story. He wanted to encourage everyone to be an artist, to create beautiful things by hand – furniture, pottery, fabrics – which were also functional. Art Nouveau suited the mood of the first years of our own century, for it could be used to express all sorts of opulence and frivolity. But after the tension and suffering of the First World War the mood of the western world changed.

Le Corbusier

Encouraged by the desire for a more straightforward approach to design, the doctrine of Functionalism came into favour. The idea behind this was that, if a building or object is perfectly fitted for its function and constructed with sensible regard for the materials used, it will be pleasing to the eye and satisfying to the mind. The great Swiss architect, painter and writer, Le Corbusier, the pseudonym of Charles Jeanneret (1887–1965) pointed to Greek temples as perfect examples of this, and therefore as expressions of modernism. The Functionalists discarded traditional conventions and superficial ornament, and had a great simplifying and purifying influence on design in every kind of material.

This approach became the basis for the teaching of design and architecture at the Bauhaus in Germany. The help that this college gave in employing some of the greatest refugee artists of the new movements has been mentioned. While at the Bauhaus they succeeded in creating a new, cleaner and more structural tradition of design which spread around the world and is still a strong influence today.

A new method of building construction—reinforced concrete—was perfectly suited to this clean, structural approach. Concrete floors were supported on upright steel girders. This was basically all there was to these new

A montage of images typical of Bridget Riley (top) and Roy Lichtenstein.

a new style of design suddenly appeared. It is called Art Nouveau (the New Art).

A new impulse in design was certainly overdue, as it was in architecture, and this one seemed to appear suddenly without roots in a previous style, though the inspiration certainly came to some extent from the Japanese prints that were then very popular. The Art Nouveau style spread quickly. It penetrated all forms of art and many famous artists were influenced by it. In fact some of them took a hand in creating it. Among these were Gauguin, in his woodcuts, Toulouse-

Figure from *The Great War* by René Magritte (1898–1967), the Belgian surrealist artist.

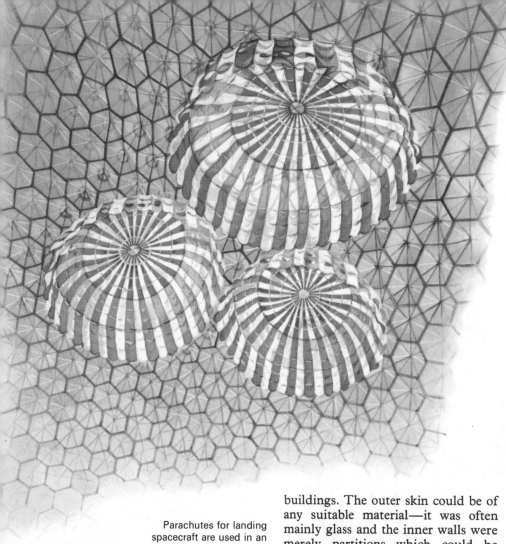

Parachutes for landing spacecraft are used in an exhibition as a decorative feature against the background of a structure made from closely packed hexagons.

Detail from *Coming from the Mill* by L. S. Lowry.

approach is favoured which allows the personality of those who design the building, and those who live in it, the respect that is their due. Buildings which are the chosen creations of gifted architects, who are given freedom to express their ideas, are naturally very costly to design and erect. They can usually only be considered for such special buildings as national theatres, art galleries, churches and city halls.

The Artist-Craftsman

There seems to be a growing rift between the mechanised, mass-produced object and its counterpart, the article designed and made by an artist-craftsman. The first is less expensive, but tends to be impersonal in character; the second must usually be costly because it is given individual attention. This rift is seen in every branch of art, architecture and design – in objects made of every kind of material. In fine art we see it in the contrast between an original painting and the printed reproduction.

Last century it was the rows of identical terrace houses and now it is the new tower-block flats which seem to threaten the way of life of those who live in them. In such conditions men are in danger of becoming like robots—behaving, thinking and feeling alike. Most people long to live in individual dwellings: an old farm cottage, a wandering barge, or at any rate a house which is distinct from its neighbours. In the same way, off-the-peg clothes offer fewer and fewer opportunities for their wearers to express their individualism. But already there is a movement away from the sameness of mass-produced objects, particularly among young people, and in this thought lies the future of art and design.

In this account of western art it is inevitable that many interesting and important aspects of it have been crowded out. This is particularly true of what are sometimes called the minor arts, such as needlework, ceramics, furniture and interior design. Nor has there been much space to consider the influence of art on such things as posters and advertisements. Another subject which has enormous importance in modern society is industrial design, which has brought the work of artists and designers into every home. In the remaining pages we look at the art of lands which have their own forms and traditions outside those of the western world.

buildings. The outer skin could be of any suitable material—it was often mainly glass and the inner walls were merely partitions which could be placed and re-placed wherever required as they played no part in supporting the building. This has become the present-day tradition of the tower-block.

The many opportunities afforded by this building method were demonstrated by Le Corbusier as early as 1915. Although he was a pioneer in this very functional approach, he later showed the way to free architecture from too rigid a repetition of verticals and horizontals. His revolutionary design for the church of Notre Dame du Hart at Ronchamp in France, which he planned forty years later in the 1950s, contrasts strongly with the earlier, impersonal approach. With its boldly unusual curved surfaces and an absence of straight lines and right-angles, architecture becomes here almost a form of sculpture. Le Corbusier's church at Ronchamp has been a great influence on the designers of other unconventional buildings in more recent years.

Today architecture seems to be suffering from a kind of tug-of-war. The need to economise pulls it towards the featureless, tower-block type of construction, where mass-production and mechanisation are possible. On the other hand there is a desire to avoid regimentation. A more personal

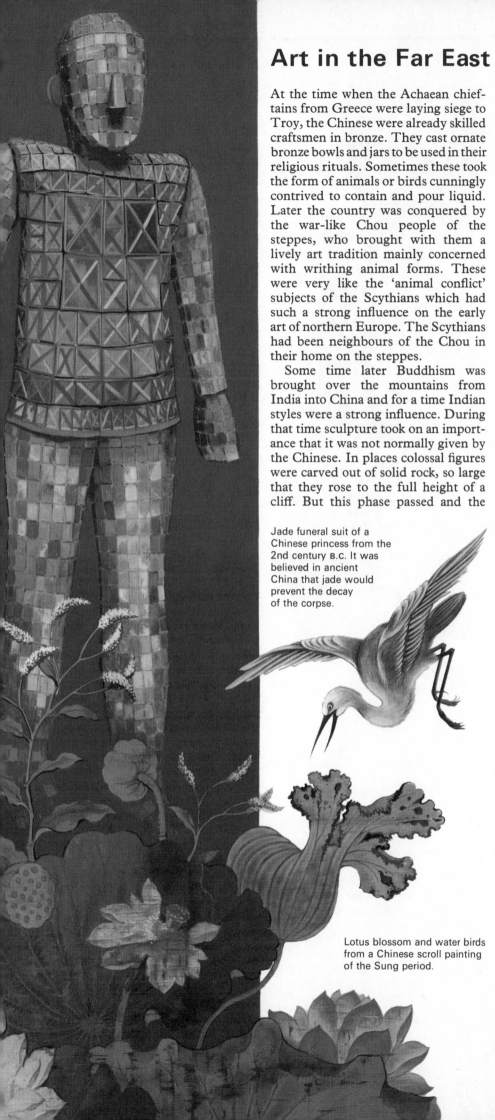

Art in the Far East

At the time when the Achaean chieftains from Greece were laying siege to Troy, the Chinese were already skilled craftsmen in bronze. They cast ornate bronze bowls and jars to be used in their religious rituals. Sometimes these took the form of animals or birds cunningly contrived to contain and pour liquid. Later the country was conquered by the war-like Chou people of the steppes, who brought with them a lively art tradition mainly concerned with writhing animal forms. These were very like the 'animal conflict' subjects of the Scythians which had such a strong influence on the early art of northern Europe. The Scythians had been neighbours of the Chou in their home on the steppes.

Some time later Buddhism was brought over the mountains from India into China and for a time Indian styles were a strong influence. During that time sculpture took on an importance that it was not normally given by the Chinese. In places colossal figures were carved out of solid rock, so large that they rose to the full height of a cliff. But this phase passed and the

Jade funeral suit of a Chinese princess from the 2nd century B.C. It was believed in ancient China that jade would prevent the decay of the corpse.

Lotus blossom and water birds from a Chinese scroll painting of the Sung period.

Chinese philosophy of Taoism reasserted itself and Chinese art resumed its native character.

How different this was from the art of Europe at that time. In the early Middle Ages European art was concerned almost entirely with the Christian story and teaching. Chinese artists were then painting quiet scenes of everyday life and landscapes steeped in silence and stillness. It was not for another seven or eight centuries that Europe realised that such subjects were worthy of the artist's attention.

To understand Chinese art properly it is important to understand the idea behind Taoism. It is not really a religion, for there is no deity to worship. The basis of Taoism is the belief in Tao (the Way) which is defined as 'the indescribable universal principle'—the force pervading all nature. The aim of a good Taoist is to become attuned to the Tao—to be completely at one with nature, without ambition or aggression, but quietly receptive. Painting, together with poetry, was a means of attaining this state. This philosophy determined the nature of Chinese art, its emphasis on landscape, on stillness, on mood rather than story, on atmosphere rather than description.

Chinese Painting

Chinese writing was done with a brush, and to excel in and to practise calligraphy (beautiful writing) was the ambition of every educated Chinaman. With his brush he would express his oneness with the Tao in words, in the form of a poem, or in art, as a painting. Thus Chinese painting was closely linked with calligraphy and resembled it. The work was done in ink on silk or paper, which the Chinese made long before either was known in Europe. Paintings were often done on a long scroll which was kept on rollers. To view it one unrolled and rolled it up continuously, seeing only a section at a time. This produced an approach to landscape quite unlike that which developed in Europe, where a picture was considered as a single, concise unit, complete and perfect within the fixed rectangle of its frame.

In south-west China, white mist often hangs among the mountains, and the forests and rivers are then partly revealed and partly hidden in the mist. The landscape artists often used this effect to infuse a sense of infinite mystery into the still scenes that they re-created with their brushes. But Chinese painters did not paint only

57

landscapes. They delighted to show details from their environment, scenes observed in their daily life; a bird on a spray of fruit blossom, a cat hidden among flowers preparing to pounce, an old man fishing in a boat, a groom in charge of a horse. The simplest subject would suffice to inspire the artist to produce a small masterpiece.

The inks used by the Chinese painters could never be removed or changed once they had been placed on the silk or paper. The painters had to observe their subject very intently, then go away and record their observations swiftly and deftly without making any mistakes. This method encouraged the utmost simplicity and economy in obtaining the fullest expression with the least effort, in getting straight to the heart of a subject. In this tradition there are no shadows, no chiaroscuro.

Porcelain and Lacquer

Chinese artists have used many different techniques besides sculpture and painting. Some glazed pottery figures and animals can rank with the world's best sculpture, and carvings in jade—a smooth green stone—produced

Chinese porcelain of the Ming period (above) and Ch'ing period (right).

charming miniature pieces of sculpture. Porcelain was developed by the Chinese with exquisite results, and the word china is used in English to mean the finest earthenware. In embroidery Chinese craftsmanship excelled, also in lacquer. Movable screens adorned with fantastic landscapes in lacquer were favourite items for furnishing a wealthy Chinese home.

There has never been a grand architectural style in China comparable to those of some western cultures, but Chinese buildings have great interest and charm, and there are many gems of architecture of a modest kind. Most buildings were of timber or brick, even where good building stone was plentiful. The chief feature of a Chinese building has always been its roof, or roofs, for sometimes they are multiplied. In important buildings these are given great attention. Tiles are coloured and even glazed, and the ridges and the characteristic upturned corners are adorned with ornamental cresting and fantastic dragons in glazed earthenware. These roofs are supported on timber uprights, for the walls play no part in carrying their weight.

The most characteristic buildings in China are the temple pagodas. These are towers of numerous storeys, each storey having its own overhanging roof, so that the whole building looks like a number of houses each standing on the roof of the one below. Another structure typically Chinese is the Pai-Lou, a roofed gateway on which is lavished the most elaborate ornament. These gateways were erected as memorials to important people.

Japanese Art

Japanese architecture, and for that matter its art as well, is very like Chinese, for Japanese culture has been developed on a Chinese basis. Because of frequent earthquakes in Japan the buildings there have usually been made of very light material, principally timber and even very light bamboo. A lightness and delicacy in design has followed from this and is typically Japanese. The older, traditional buildings of Japan have the same upturned angles to the roofs that we find in China, and the roofs often jut out even further. Buddhism was brought to Japan from China about the time of the break-down of the Roman Empire in the west, and with it came the Budhist temple and the pagoda. In Japanese pagodas the roofs often project out, one above another, to a great height. The gardens surrounding Japanese buildings have always been carefully designed to resemble small gems of natural landscape, with little lakes, bridges and standard lanterns

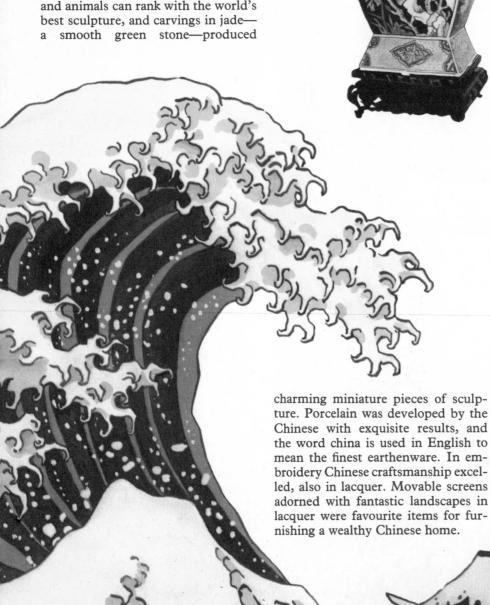

Hokusai's famous picture *The Great wave off Kanazawa* is a colour print from wood blocks.

exquisitely placed to provide charming compositions when viewed from any angle.

The traditional Japanese house is of one storey only. The framework is of timber and the outer walls boarded. The inner walls are sliding partitions made of paper on timber frames. There are usually two living-rooms adjoining each other, the inner one raised slightly and containing two recesses. One recess contains a picture and a flower-arrangement, the other some of the family's art treasures, only a few at one time, for the rest are stored in a clay-lined cellar, safe from earthquakes and fire.

Sometimes Japanese art has followed the Chinese style very closely, but at

Japanese house in the old tradition with typical upturned angles to the roofs.

other times it has shown an independence, even when keeping to Chinese technical methods.

Prints and Woodcuts

Perhaps the most remarkable phase of Japanese art was the development of the coloured woodcut in the eighteenth and nineteenth centuries. For a long time wood blocks had been cut to produce single-colour prints, both in China and Europe. In Japan it became fashionable to colour such prints by hand. But it was found that the various colours could be added by cutting further blocks, one for each colour. The inks were transparent, and where they overlapped many interesting mixtures could be obtained, and very rich results were achieved in the final print.

Many very gifted artists were employed by the publishers of colour prints. Their designs were submitted on paper, then cut by qualified engravers and printed in their hundreds. It was a splendid example of teamwork which provided pictures of the finest quality at a price low enough for everyone to afford.

Naturally, in a popular art the subjects too were of a popular kind —actors in their most famous stage roles, beautiful women, scenes of everyday life. In the figure subjects the noble boldness of Kiyonobu and Kaigetsudo set the standard. Hiroshige excelled in landscapes with small figures, rendered with his own sensitive charm, while Hokusai seized on any and every subject with his eager, vivid imagination, achieving a stirring masterpiece in every painting. He delighted in striking designs which depicted the effects of hurricane-force winds or raging water, or equally of calm, still landscapes.

Group of Kabuki actors attributed to Hishikawa Moronobu (17th century).

Indian and Mohammedan Art

In the lands between the Bay of Bengal and the Mediterranean five of the world's greatest religions were born. Religion played a large part in the lives of the people in this region, and most great art and architecture were produced in the service of religion.

In India the Hindu religion grew with the beginning of civilisation. The earliest important examples of art and architecture that still survive there, however, are not Hindu, but Buddhist, for Buddhism began in India and was the dominant religion for over 1,000 years. Prince Gautama, the Buddha (the Enlightened One), was born in north India about 600 B.C. He urged and taught his followers to discard all inner conflicts and selfish desires and so gain Nirvana, which is perfect peace and stillness of spirit.

Buddhism encouraged a reverance for holy relics and wherever such relics were preserved shrines were established and there pilgrims congregated. Some of the shrines were in the open air, just large, stone, dome-shaped erections called stupas. The relic was preserved at the top of the stupa and a high stone railing, pierced by richly decorated gateways, encircled the whole area.

Temple-caves
Another kind of shrine was the chaitya or preaching hall. We usually think of architecture as a process of addition—the adding of stone to stone or beam to beam. But the earliest of these Buddhist temples that survive were created by a method of subtraction—by patiently carving out a temple-cave in the face of a rock cliff. These chaityas are large, lofty halls flanked by rows of columns. In a central position is a mass of rock carved to form a stupa which housed the relic of the shrine. Other rock-cut halls had many small cells leading off them. These were the living quarters of the monks who attended the shrine. At the great Buddhist holy place at Ajanta there were 27 rock-cut halls, four being chaityas and the remainder having cells leading off them. Several of these man-made caves contain some

of the most beautiful mural paintings of all time.

The rainy season in India is so very wet that almost all the paintings of those early days, and even the buildings they adorned, have perished. It seems certain that there were then large halls built above ground, and they were almost certainly of timber, because the forms of the rock-cut chaityas, which were built as reproductions of free-standing buildings, suggest the timber construction of the originals.

In time Buddhism declined and disappeared in the land of its birth, having produced much magnificent sculpture and architecture—doubtless much painting also, if it had survived. Then the ancient Hindu religion reasserted itself in a more advanced form known as Brahminism, and both architecture and sculpture were dedicated to providing temples and their adornments. In doing so they expressed symbolically the faith and subtle philosophy of these Hindu beliefs. For instance many temples in the north of India were based on the idea of the sacred mountain. The deep base represented the world and was decorated with carved scenes that took place on earth. The temple hall above, which was approached by a stairway, represented Heaven, and its images were of the immortal inhabitants of Heaven. Above this, the central spire and its smaller supporting spires symbolised 'unrepresentable truths' beyond the frontiers of Heaven.

These northern temples curved inwards at the top, whereas those in the south were more square. Both kinds were richly decorated with carvings, but the southern examples tended to be smothered with an exuberant array of figures and animals.

Indian sculpture is characterised by a subtle suggestion of lithe movement. It seems that we can almost hear the music to which the figures and animals sway as though in a smooth, graceful dance. This art came to a great peak about A.D. 1000 in south India and Ceylon in the free-standing bronze figures of gods and goddesses which reached a peak of refinement.

Throughout her history India has been open to invasion from the northwest. From about A.D. 1200 onwards there were a number of such invasions by Mohammedan nomads—violent, ruthless horsemen intent on plundering the rich land of India. It was one of

Decoration from a Persian Minai ware painted bowl (late 12th–early 13th century).

Part of the design for an Oriental carpet.

these onslaughts that virtually destroyed Buddhism in northern India.

The Art of Islam

No two religions could be more strongly contrasted than that of the Hindus with their many gods and goddesses and that of the Mohammedans who were ardently fanatical in their belief in only one god. The Hindus believed that each individual returns again and again in the continuous stream of reincarnation, whereas the Mohammedans staked all in a single lifetime. Mohammed died in A.D. 632 and in little more than a century the rule of his followers stretched from Spain in the west to western India in the east. Over this vast area the new religion was supreme, and the beliefs and art forms belonging to it were firmly established. We will first consider these in this whole region and then return to the subject of India.

The Mohammedan religion rejected the representation of people or animals in art. Painting and sculpture in the European sense are seldom found in the arts of this area, which are mainly restricted to architecture, decoration and calligraphy, and often brought to great perfection.

A Mohammedan mosque is basically a large hall with a courtyard. Many are also tombs of famous people and are therefore domed, for a dome is the mark of a tomb. Arches are pointed or horseshoe-shaped and are often used simply as features of design to provide recesses in a surface. Just as the many-roofed pagoda is the mark of a temple in the Far East, so the slender minaret is the mark of a mosque. From the top of a minaret the muezzin's call goes out to the faithful below when it is time for prayer.

Because the depicting of any person or animal is forbidden, mosques are decorated with purely geometric or floral patterns, or by the art of calligraphy. Exquisite designs are made using texts from the sacred book, the Koran. Every kind of surface and material provided an opportunity for this art, which was aided by the flowing elegance of the Arabic script and the great freedom with which it can be adapted to many techniques.

The Mogul School

Some of the most beautiful mosques and tombs were erected in India in the Mogul (Mongol) period, when a family of rulers descended from Mongol invaders brought unity and peace to that troubled land. This encouraged the development of one of the finest art traditions of all time—the Mogul school. The greatest of these Mogul emperors was Akbar (1542–1605).

In architecture the Mogul school produced mosques, palaces and tombs of noble proportions and exquisite quality and craftsmanship in decoration. Perhaps the greatest masterpiece of all was the Taj Mahal. Like other buildings of its kind it served as a pleasure pavilion during the lifetime of its builder—in this case Akbar's grandson, Shah Jehan—and after his death became the tomb-monument of his queen, Mumtaz Mahal. It is built of white marble on a high marble platform and its image is reflected in artificial lakes that are grouped around. Avenues of dark cypress trees flank these still pools and four tall minarets mark the corners of the base platform.

By Akbar's time the feeling against representing men and animals in art had become less strong, especially in the luxurious court of Baghdad. There the rulers (caliphs) came to employ many illustrators to decorate the beautiful books that were fashionable, and a most excellent tradition of book illumination developed. This Persian style of illumination used a smooth, thin line to define the forms and no shading or shadows. Clear, rich colours were used and Persian artists excelled in combining many bright colours into schemes which were both stimulating and harmonious. The use of the flowing shapes of the Arabic script added to the joyous and vigorous effect of these pages.

Persian Illumination

In India the Mogul emperors followed the fashion of Baghdad. They gathered the best artists from all over

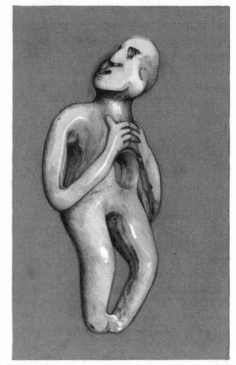

India and set them to work under the supervision of illuminators from Persia, sending abroad for the most perfect pigments in order that the work of their Mogul school of illumination might be the best in the world. Their contact with Europe by means of trade led them to modify the purity of the Persian style. This permitted a greater sense of freedom in their work while preserving the beautiful qualities of colour and pattern of the original tradition. Akbar used these beautiful books in his attempt to bring about a real unity in India. He would send translations of illuminated Hindu books to the Mohammedan rulers of his empire, and the Mohammedan works were translated and sent to the Hindu rulers.

The Mogul tradition influenced all the pictorial art of India. To the traditional mural work was added the painting of sets of small pictures. Often these deal with the love of the god Krishna for the cowherd girls (Gopis), and incidents from other romantic poems and legends. Others represent real-life scenes such as hunting or hawking, or small portraits. A favourite theme was to echo in shapes and flat colours the various set modes of Indian music, changing the colour harmonies in keeping with the mood of the melodies of sound. Sets of such paintings, which usually depict love scenes, are called Ragamalas (Garlands of Modes). This art of the seventeenth to the nineteenth centuries is known as the Rajput school.

Courtyard in a style typical of Islamic architecture.

Art Traditions in America, Africa and Oceania

We have now looked at the art and architecture of the old world of Asia and Europe, but what of the traditional arts of North and South America? What of Africa and Australia and the countless islands of the South Seas?

In these lands communities have been isolated and primitive as far as science and technology are concerned. But this does not mean that their art too is backward. Unfortunately the benefits that have come from contact with the so-called civilised countries have often brought with them a loss of artistic excellence. Europeans and white Americans have tended to despise the unfamiliar art of primitive peoples, who in their turn, often come to despise their own art traditions when they come under the influence of European art. So their ancient traditions, which are often of great value, are gradually lost.

American Indians have always

Aztecs and Incas

The whole Indian culture of North America produced remarkable art in many forms, including some of the world's finest pottery, made in prehistoric times in the south-west of the United States. But the highest points of American native art were reached in Mexico and Peru. When white men discovered America they found there two civilisations that were barbaric in some ways, but which produced superb work in sculpture, goldsmiths' work, pottery, embroidery and architecture. In these two areas there existed the only really advanced examples of architecture outside the old world.

In Mexico a number of tribes followed each other in dominating the land. At the time of the Dark Ages in Europe the Maya people were in control. They excelled in sculpture. They could render figures realistically when they chose, but most of their

of each a small temple stood, in front of which slaves and captives were sacrificed to its god. Toltec gods were nature deities. There was the sun god, the goddess of the maize crop, Tlaloc, the rain god and the great god Quetzalcoatl, the Feathered Serpent, and many more. At the foot of such pyramids a large area would be covered by other religious buildings, courtyards and processional roads. Much later, when the Spanish discovered Mexico they found the Aztecs in control of the land, having overthrown the Toltecs.

The Aztec civilisation flourished from about A.D. 1330 to 1520 at a time when most other ancient Mexican

Painted driftwood and wooden mask from Eskimo cultures. (Opposite page) Eskimo figure carved from bone.

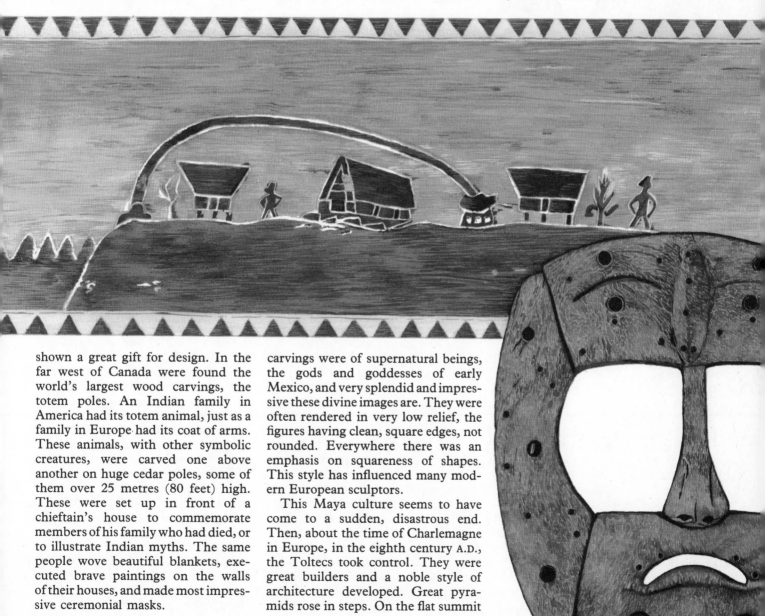

shown a great gift for design. In the far west of Canada were found the world's largest wood carvings, the totem poles. An Indian family in America had its totem animal, just as a family in Europe had its coat of arms. These animals, with other symbolic creatures, were carved one above another on huge cedar poles, some of them over 25 metres (80 feet) high. These were set up in front of a chieftain's house to commemorate members of his family who had died, or to illustrate Indian myths. The same people wove beautiful blankets, executed brave paintings on the walls of their houses, and made most impressive ceremonial masks.

carvings were of supernatural beings, the gods and goddesses of early Mexico, and very splendid and impressive these divine images are. They were often rendered in very low relief, the figures having clean, square edges, not rounded. Everywhere there was an emphasis on squareness of shapes. This style has influenced many modern European sculptors.

This Maya culture seems to have come to a sudden, disastrous end. Then, about the time of Charlemagne in Europe, in the eighth century A.D., the Toltecs took control. They were great builders and a noble style of architecture developed. Great pyramids rose in steps. On the flat summit cultures were in decline. They were an aggressive and warlike people and their art is filled with violent and terrifying figures, such as the fearsome mosaic-covered skulls. They did not make objects for their beauty alone, but employed great craftsmanship in producing work in honour of their gods. Religion was the strong motive for creative output, as it has been so often in the histories of other cultures. The Aztecs produced powerful architecture and sculpture but little worthwhile painting or drawing.

In the same way, when the Spaniards discovered Peru and destroyed the highly organised Inca Empire, they found great works of art, although the greatest periods of Peruvian art were much earlier than that of the Incas. The period known

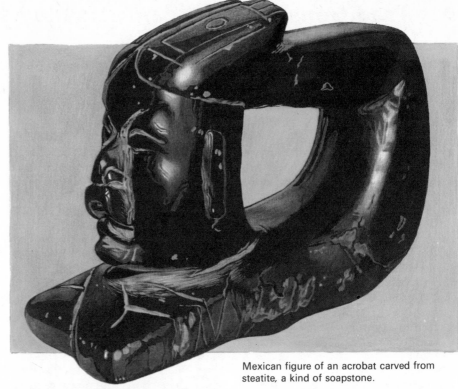

Mexican figure of an acrobat carved from steatite, a kind of soapstone.

(Above) The Mayan observatory at Chichen Itza, one of the best preserved buildings of ancient Mexico. (Left) Mexican carved figure from Vera Cruz.

as the Peruvian Golden Age began somewhere about the time of Christ, when Peruvian potters, goldsmiths, weavers and embroiderers produced superb work. Fortunately the coastal strip of Peru is largely desert, and many pieces of beautiful embroidery have been preserved by the extremely dry conditions there. They would have rotted away long ago in the moist climate of the Andes Mountains in the interior.

Feathers have played a large part in the adornment of many American tribes. The feather war headgear of the North American Indians is familiar, and Maya carvings tell us that elaborate feather head-dresses were also worn in ancient Mexico. The early Peruvians produced what are known as feather mosaics. Small feathers of different colours were fixed to fabric, one row overlapping the next, to form rich patterns and simple pictures. Such feather work is sumptuous in its rich softness.

Ancient Peruvian architecture was not entirely religious in its purpose. Imposing fortresses, watch-towers, stairways and terraces were constructed, as well as tombs and temple pyramids. Some walls are of squared stones, but others are of polygonal shapes, their sides so exactly shaped that they fit together perfectly. Enormous stones, some weighing many tons, were used in the buildings, the best remains of which may be seen today at Cuzco in Peru. These sometimes twelve-angled blocks join snugly together with their neighbours without mortar or any other binding agent. The construction methods used by the people of South America are similar to those employed by others in the ancient world in Egypt, Greece and China, but there is no firm evidence that the Inca had any contact with these lands.

African Art
In Africa we find a native art that has not been appreciated by Europeans until recently. It was once considered the work of crude and ignorant savages, but it has been a great inspiration to some modern European artists. It inspired Pablo Picasso and Georges Braque to make their first experiments in Cubism, for African artists were expert cubists long before the movement arose in Europe. It has also been a powerful influence on modern sculpture.

Primitive peoples—Africans and others—have a firm belief in the presence and power of wandering spirits, who have to be kept in a good mood for fear they may bring trouble to the living. Wandering hunters fear the spirits of the animals they hunt, and settled cultivators fear the spirits of their dead ancestors, who may become resentful, or even revengeful, and do them some injury. They provide carved figures as homes for these wandering spirits, to give them a physical resting place and so make them happy and grateful. They also fear the powerful spirits that seem to live in the forces of nature—the sun, the wind, the rain and so on. They make images called fetish figures and perform magic ceremonies to give these figures a soul with power to act

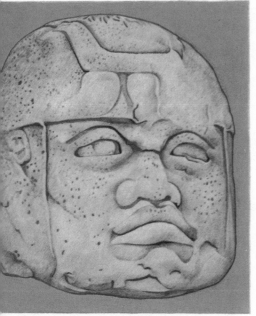

Massive stone head, Olmec culture.

animals, with enormous emphasis on this or that characteristic, they achieve the powerful effect required. Their distortions are necessary to their purpose and are not at all due to incompetence on the part of their creators. Art of this kind is typical of Africa, but is found in many other places as well.

In the state of Benin in West Africa quite unusual and unexpected skills were developed. Benin was once a highly organised kingdom and its art was largely produced to enhance the fame and prestige of the royal authority. Amazing skill in bronze casting was evolved for this purpose. Most of the subjects created in bronze by the artists of Benin are scenes of court life. The kings and their officials and soldiers are shown in stylised and

sculpture resulted in a continent where such realism is almost unknown. The best of these portraits can rank in serene beauty with the highest work of ancient Greece or Renaissance Italy.

Oceanic Art

Moving eastwards to Oceania we reach a region rich in art, infinitely varied and complex. The grotesque masks and carved figures of supernatural beings in New Guinea and the Solomon Islands rival those of Africa. Bold designs of great richness were printed on tree-bark cloth, called tapa, in islands such as Fiji and Hawaii. On tree-bark too the natives of Australia make their lively paintings, as they do also on protected rock walls. The wood-carvings of the Maoris of New

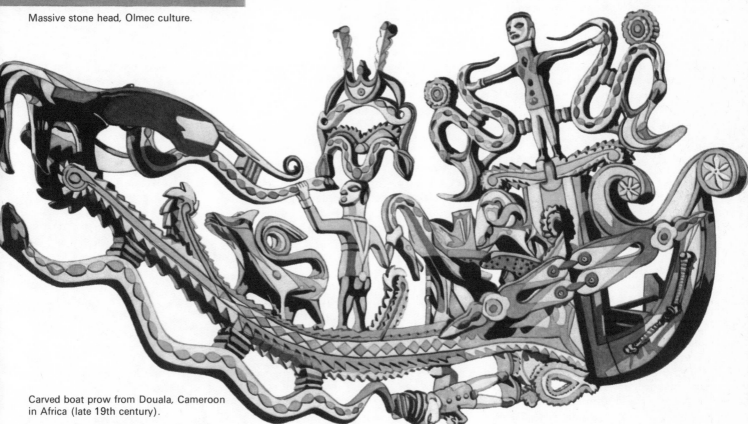

Carved boat prow from Douala, Cameroon in Africa (late 19th century).

as go-betweens with the spirit world, and so obtain benefits or prevent disasters for their owners.

Such carvings and the masks worn in magic rituals do not represent anything of this world. They were never intended to do so. They are symbols of the powers and personalities of the spirit world. If they were representations of real men and animals they would not serve their purpose. On the other hand, if they were just abstract forms, however striking, they would mean little. But by giving them something of the form of men or

decorative form, mostly as adornments for the royal palace and its surroundings.

This kind of art is unusual in Africa. So also is the portrait art of the Ife tribe. They had a custom of holding a second funeral for a very important person some time after his death. To represent the dead person's body they made a framework on which they placed rich clothing, but the head was a very realistic likeness in copper or terracotta. Great care was taken to make these portrait heads true to life and a splendid tradition of realistic

Zealand are the most intricate and delicate in the world. Those on the prows of their canoes are often like lace in their frail delicacy. What a contrast to the giant stone figures that once gazed out to sea on remote Easter Island, probably raised by the islanders as memorials to important members of their community. These figures, averaging about 9 metres (30 feet) in height and originally crowned by red-coloured stone hats, were first seen by Dutch seamen in the eighteenth century and have remained a mystery ever since.

Music and Drama

Of all the arts, music, dancing and drama are the most natural, the least artificial. They are not just pastimes, filling in our leisure hours. They are essential elements in the human condition. Nor are they confined to human beings only. We have inherited them from the other animals behind us in the chain of evolution. In a real sense, it is the practice of these three arts that provides our only communication with other animals.

We react instinctively to bird song. We feel the thrill of pleasure the bird expresses through its melody. We sense its agitation when its territory is invaded and the note changes. We recognise the patterns of a dance in the mating behaviour of many animals. We can watch an understanding develop between male and female of species other than our own when they dance together. We can teach a pet dog to understand the pantomime of our gestures so that it knows when we are angry or pleased with it, or when we are ready to take it for a walk.

At an early age, a human baby is soothed by a lullaby, excited by a tinkling bell. Almost as soon as it can walk, it enjoys the pattern of movement involved in a 'ring-o'-roses' dance. As it grows older, it develops what we call its personality by copying the gestures, voice inflexions and facial expressions of its parents and other adults around it. Our earliest years are very much involved with music, dancing and drama, both as audience and performer.

The First Instruments
Early man invented the percussion instrument by clapping his hands or slapping different parts of his body or hitting different objects with a stick. But he had not produced music until he had regulated these haphazard actions into a rhythmic beat. The primitive hunter who could make a bow to shoot his arrows, could equally well make a simple stringed instrument. Perhaps the one derived from the other, though which came first is something we shall probably never know. The first wind instrument was the voice, both animal and human. It must have been a very early man who learned to whistle in imitation of a bird. Babies and primitive people tend to test strange objects with the mouth. The first sequence of 'woodnotes wild' reproduced by a musical instrument must have emerged from experimental blowing into a conch shell, a hollow reed or some similar object.

It is a common experience to feel the need to rock the body or stamp the feet in time to music. From the invention of music, the invention of the dance could not be far behind. Even to us nowadays, music has a magical quality. To the primitive imagination, it is the voice of the gods. Playing music and dancing to it are a means of communicating with those mysterious forces that seem to rule our lives. From the very beginning, music and dancing have appealed to man's religious instincts.

If music and dance are communication on the abstract or even supernatural plane drama is involved in the day-to-day traffic between man and man. A kind of acting is used by many

The auditorium at Epidaurus (*c.* 350 B.C.) is the best preserved of all Greek theatres.

animals whose vocabulary of sound is limited. A wolf will bare his teeth to indicate a readiness to fight if attacked. When the battle is lost, he will turn his head to expose his throat to the enemy as a gesture of submission and a plea for mercy. Human beings must have acted out their feelings or the news they wished to impart long before the formulation of recognisable language. Even today, mime can be a necessary instrument of communication between

two people lacking a common language. Mime and language together are the instruments of the actor.

In this twentieth century, we live in a particularly exciting time for the arts of music and drama. For 5,000 years, the invention of writing has allowed mankind to pass on ideas from one generation to the next, to build up and store a body of knowledge. For 500 years, the invention of printing has allowed us to reproduce those ideas many times over and spread them around the world. Now at last, science has given us the ability to reproduce

and store both sound and movement. For the first time in history, we can preserve performance.

We shall never hear a Chopin Polonaise played by the composer. We shall never see Shakespeare acting in one of his own plays. But from now on, the musician, the dancer and the actor have become immortal. Their artistry will remain available to the generations that follow ours. At last, the oldest arts of all have a life beyond the fleeting moment. Today's performer can pass on his achievements to posterity.

Performers and Audience
Of all the arts, music and drama are always with us. With the inner ear of memory, we can listen to a popular

tune within our heads. In a crowded room, we can watch the little dramas of human conflict. Some of us will not be content with a seat in the audience, but will learn to become performers ourselves. Through the miracle of modern electronics, a few will reach an audience of many millions, perhaps many more as yet unborn.

There is a performer within us all who responds to the performance of others. It is not only pleasure we gain from this communication, but a greater understanding of our own emotions. The emotions all people share today are the same as those experienced by our forebears. To listen to their music and to watch performances of their

plays is to forge a real link with the past. To watch and listen to the creations of our contemporaries from all parts of the world helps to strengthen the links of common humanity.

This section gives a brief outline of the progress mankind has made in music, drama and the dance, together with a background to what is being produced today and by what means.

Though we may read about the composer, the instrumentalist and the dancer, though we may study the plays of the great dramatists, remember that the aim of their work is achieved only in its performance. There is no substitute for performance, and there is no performance without an audience. Each of us belongs to one or the other, and the bond between the two brings us all closer together.

Terracotta figures of a musician and a character from Greek comedy.

The Story of Music

Music can be defined as the organisation of sound to convey a meaning to or provoke a reaction from the listener. Everyday speech is a kind of music. To form words, we organise the vibrations of sound emerging from our mouths. Their frequency, the number of vibrations per second, give the pitch or note of each sound. A sequence of sounds of varying pitch produces a melody. A particular note carries with it vibrations of a higher pitch called overtones or harmonics which give the note its tone or colour. The speed at which one note follows another is called tempo. Variations in the volume or intensity of the notes within a melody can produce the system of stresses called rhythm.

These four qualities of melody, tone, tempo and rhythm are common to both music and speech. By changing one or more of them, the same word can be given a different meaning. For instance, a word may be spoken in an angry, a sarcastic or a plaintive tone. In some languages, the melody, tone, tempo and rhythm are all important to the meanings of many words. We tend to call such languages 'sing-song'. In all languages there is a considerable overlap between speaking and singing.

There are languages with a limited number of different sounds and a comparatively small vocabulary which are capable of imitation by a musical instrument. The Yoruba, Ibo and Bantu tribes of Africa, for instance, have devised sets of drums which copy the sounds of their languages. These so-called 'talking drums' carry sound farther than the human voice, and so the 'bush telegraph' has developed.

Language and Music

It would seem, therefore, that language, song and simple musical instruments probably developed together. Yet even the most primitive people living today have had thousands of years to create their language and music. Surprising skills, passed on through the generations, go into the making and performing upon the crudest of musical instruments still in use today. Their beginnings can only be guessed at.

Among all people of the world, what separates music from everyday speech is the magical quality we ascribe to it. The great musician has a talent we can all appreciate, though few of us have it. Not even the musician can explain it. From the dawn of mankind, music has been thought to have the power of direct communication with the gods. It has always played a part in religious observances.

With the earliest civilisations, music emerges already in a state of high sophistication. The earliest written references to it come from the city states of Sumer in ancient Mesopotamia. Their temple priests, also the scientists or guardians of knowledge, worked out the first musical theory. More than 5,000 years ago, each god had his own hymn or psalm to be chanted at the temple service performed in his honour. By the twenty-first century B.C., these chants included responses between solo voice and choir, or between one choir and another, accompanied by reed-pipes, flutes, drums and tambourines. Discoveries in the royal tombs of the ancient city of Ur include also the lyre and two kinds of harp dating back to the twenty-eighth century B.C. No doubt, music was not only a means of communicating with the gods in the next world, but also an entertainment for kings and common folk alike.

Between the nineteenth and thirteenth centuries B.C., Mesopotamia was ruled by the Babylonians whose temple services included up to 27 different hymns and psalms interspersed with instrumental pieces, with both male and female musicians taking part. The Assyrians of the thirteenth to the seventh centuries B.C. used music in festivals outside the temple, and their royal households employed musicians. The Chaldaean King Nebuchadnezzar (604–562 B.C.) had his own

Musicians of · ancient Egypt.

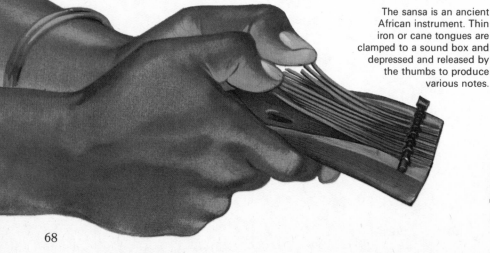

The sansa is an ancient African instrument. Thin iron or cane tongues are clamped to a sound box and depressed and released by the thumbs to produce various notes.

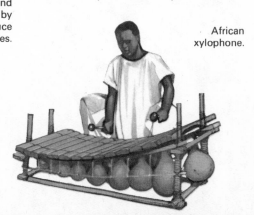

African xylophone.

orchestra. By the time of the Persian Empire (from 538 B.C.), there are records of both sacred and popular music.

The ancient Egyptians thought of the human voice as the most powerful instrument for communication with their gods. We have the words, though not the music, of some of their temple chants, suggesting that both solo voices and dialogues between two priestesses were used. The Pharaohs were priest-kings, so there was a strong link between religious and court music. The most revered instrument was the harp.

The Music of India

In southern India, the earliest of the high cultures worshipped nature. There is still a tradition in the subcontinent that the seven notes of the Indian scale each represent the cry of a different animal. Between 1500 and 1000 B.C., the Aryan people from western Asia came into India from the north-west. Their religious books, called Vedas from the word for knowledge, contain hymns to their gods. Their earliest known chants made use of only three notes which followed closely the pitch and rhythm of ordinary speech. Such chants, hardly changed after 3,000 years, are still heard in India today.

As in other ancient civilisations, the human voice was paramount in the temple, though the Vedas mention several musical instruments. More than any other, Indian music has its basis in song. Even instrumental pieces aim to capture a mood as it would be expressed vocally. From this basis has developed the classical Indian melodic system called the *raga*, meaning colour or feeling. Raga music has three elements: the raga itself which is the melody provided by a voice or an instrument such as the sitar; the *tala*, a drum rhythm; and the *kharaja*, a drone note maintaining the central tone as in bagpipes, but usually provided by a stringed instrument. The player embellishes the raga-melody with improvisations to match his own mood or that of the audience, or to fit the time of day and season of the year.

These improvisations eventually harden into compositions to be passed on from father to son.

Chinese Orchestras

Ancient China uniquely developed the stone-chime, a series of 14 to 24 stone plates hung from a frame, a similar bell-chime and the reed mouth-organ comprising a gourd wind-chest with a mouthpiece and a number of bamboo pipes rising from it. Their earliest stringed instrument was the zither, and more than 200 other instruments are known to date back some 3,000 years. Orchestras were organised by the emperors, and noblemen maintained private bands. The Chinese adopted a five-note scale, developed from each of twelve foundation notes representing an hour of the day or a month of the year.

The Spread of Ideas

Musical ideas and instruments were dispersed around the world in ancient times by the migrations of people, expansion of empires and spread of religions. The five-note or pentatonic scale of China found its way across the Bering Straits to become the basis of music in the early civilisations of Central and South America. It also became the fundamental scale of European folk music. The spread of Buddhism carried Indian music and its instruments into South-east Asia. The ancient Greeks inherited the

The sitar is an Indian instrument. It has seven main strings and eleven or twelve 'sympathetic' strings tuned to the scale of a particular melody.

Chinese musicians with (below) the koto, Japan's national instrument

69

An illuminated music manuscript of the Middle Ages.

musical traditions of the Middle East and handed them on to the Romans.

Ancient Greek society was based on a citizen élite served by slave labour. Slaves tended to be the singers and instrumentalists. Greek philosophers concentrated on the mathematics of music. In the sixth century B.C., Pythagoras and his followers defined the ideas first put forward by the Sumerian priest-scientists, showing that harmonious notes are produced only when a vibrating string is divided by whole numbers into exact parts. Greek poets introduced music into their drama. With the collapse of the Roman Empire, the guardians of musical theory were the Arabs, who delighted in mathematical precision. Islam's most famous musician, Ishaq al-Mausili (A.D. 767–850), was not only a great singer but an important musical theorist.

The Christian Ritual

Meanwhile, a force had arisen that was to become the greatest single influence on western music—organised Christianity. The first Christians were Jews, and early Christian music was adopted from the rites of the synagogues where full-time singers and instrumentalists were employed. The psalms attributed to King David, though mostly of a later date, were sung to a simple chant. The Christian ritual, developing in the Middle East and North Africa before crossing the Mediterranean, included many chants from Palestine and Syria.

From the start, hymns were given a freer treatment of both words and music than psalms. There is an Egyptian papyrus dating back to the third century written by a Greek-speaking Christian with Greek letters inscribed below the words of a hymn to indicate the rise and fall of the melody. These letter signs were called neumes, and various systems were devised over the centuries, leading eventually to our modern musical notation.

The pattern of each verse of a psalm is of two balanced but contrasting halves. This led to chants sung in antiphonal fashion, with one group singing the first part and another group the second. By the sixth century, there were morning and evening services and a Mass based on the Gospel story of the Last Supper led by priests living a monastic life at each place of worship. Singing was often in Greek or Latin for the benefit of mixed communities. Indeed, the Church was early divided between east and west, respectively with a Byzantine and Roman rite, and there were many local variations.

Gregorian Chant

By the end of the sixth century, the situation was so confused that Pope Gregory the Great decided to formalise all Church observances. He sent missionaries to convert the heathen and to direct established churches into a common mode of worship. For this

This medieval painting of singers and musicians depicts typical instruments of the period—lute, viol, trumpet, cymbals and bells.

reason, medieval psalm-singing has been given the name Gregorian chant. Countries like Ireland and Wales, remote from the upheavals following the end of the Roman Empire, had developed sacred music of their own which so impressed Gregory's missionaries that it was absorbed into the Roman rite. Some chants or plainsong survived Gregory's reforms. Ambrosian chant is still sung in Milan. French Gallican chant was suppressed by Charlemagne in the eighth century. The Visigothic or Mozarabic chant of Spain survived into the eleventh century. The Eastern Church continued the Byzantine rite still in use today.

Nevertheless, Gregory and his successors encouraged Church musicians to establish rules for sacred music. At first, instruments were frowned upon for their secular associations, but by the eighth century, the organ, an instrument that reverberates, like the human voice, was permitted. So too, a little later, was polyphony, the harmonising of different parts within a single composition. Greater elaboration followed, with the chant sung slowly to allow soloists or choirs to

develop an independent melody. This kind of music was given the popular name *organum*. Free compositions with no basis in existing words or music were called *conductus*.

The Troubadours

Meanwhile, popular music outside the Church was taking its own course. A marriage between poetry and music had taken place. Tales of mighty deeds, of love and passion, had long been told in verse since it is more easily memorised than prose. In the twelfth century, the troubadours of southern France, the *trouvères* of northern France and the *Minnesingers* of Germany set the old verse tales to music, providing a popular entertainment for kings and nobles. A century later, these balladeers influenced the creation of the motet (from the French *mot*, a word). Perhaps at first, this was just a single word or short phrase given a melody of its own as part of the organum. It soon became more elaborate, and motets were composed for both secular and sacred use. The same melody often had different sets of words for each purpose.

Supported by the educated aristocracy, the new music began to influence the Church. New hymns, called Laudi spirituali, resembled troubadour songs. Francis of Assisi, bringing joy into the Christian message, urged his followers to be 'God's minstrels'. Composers began to achieve personal fame. Guillaume de Machaut (*d.* 1377), composer, poet, priest and civil servant

Wood carving of medieval musicians.

to the King of France, wrote the first complete setting, by any single composer, of the Mass. Francesco Landini (1325–97), blind organist and songwriter, became famous beyond his home town of Florence. John Dunstable (*d.* 1453) wrote settings for the Mass, songs and motets, spending most of his life away from his native England, and using, since music and the composer's work were international, the universal language of Latin.

From the writings of Philippe de Vitry (1291–1361), composer and theorist, the new music was termed *Ars Nova* as distinct from *Ars Antiqua*, the ancient art. By the fourteenth century, music had changed in form and style to march with the other arts into the great period of the Renaissance.

The Schools of Music

The Renaissance was a long process which reached its peak about the beginning of the sixteenth century. It sprang from the rediscovery of ancient science, using that word in its broadest sense to cover all knowledge. The works of the ancient Greek philosophers had long been preserved in Arabic throughout Islam. They began to be translated into Latin. The invention of printing dispersed them throughout Europe. Men began to realise their own powers of creativity and invention. The idea developed of the complete man—soldier, scientist, poet, artist and musician.

The best music, as always, was expensive to produce. The training and employment of composers, teachers, choirs and instrumentalists had

The first printed collection of music for the virginals was *Parthenia* (1611). Portraits of the English composers (left to right) Byrd, Bull and Gibbons.

member of the papal choir. Jacob Arcadelt (*d. c.* 1567) became singing-master of the papal choristers in Rome. Another Fleming, Adriaan Willaert (*d.* 1562), held the same post at St Mark's Cathedral, Venice. Willaert composed music for psalms arranged to be sung by two groups of choristers placed in different cathedral galleries to create a stereophonic effect. This stimulated other composers to orchestrate their music for different voices and instruments.

Music for Pleasure

What was new in all this was that people began to appreciate music for its beauty rather than for its obedience to mathematical rules. Even Church leaders of this period appreciated the same luxuries demanded by wealthy aristocrats and merchants. More than this, the educated classes began to play music themselves for the sheer joy of it. Renaissance musical composition can be divided between church music

for choirs and organ, festival music for open-air performance, usually by professionals, and chamber music for domestic entertainment.

This led to an industry of musical instrument manufacture. For indoor and private use, viols and recorders were made in different sizes for each member of the family, so that a group could reproduce the same notes their voices would sing. Any group of instrumentalists became known as a consort. The young Renaissance man became skilled on the lute, much as modern young people struggle with the guitar. Young girls learned to play the keyboard instruments, the virginals and the larger harpsichord. Instrument-makers vied with each other in the beauty of design and elaborate decoration of their products.

Books of instruction were written, such as Thomas Morley's *A Plaine and Easie Introduction to Practicall Musicke* published in London in 1597. Music was printed, first from wood-blocks and later from engraved plates. Ottaviano dei Petrucci of Venice became the first famous music publisher. The commercial music industry had arrived.

In Italy, composers set Renaissance poems to an old form of part-song

The term virginal was often used in England to include all domestic keyboard instruments.

long been a monopoly of the Church, with just a few kings and nobles able to compete. Improvements in farming and the growth of international trade created wealthy communities. Such were the Flemings of what is now Belgium, who used their wealth to patronise the arts. Alongside the great Flemish painters appeared a new school of composers, notably Gilles Binchois (*d.* 1460), Guillaume Dufay (*d.* 1474), Jean de Ockegham (*d. c.* 1495), Jacob Obrecht (*d.* 1505) and Josquin des Prés (*d.* 1521).

These composers were employed not only by the Church, but also by private patrons. They enjoyed a standard of living that gave them great freedom. They composed Masses often based on folk music, and *chansons* or part-songs for private entertainment. Their work spread and grew in popularity. Obrecht's setting of the Passion story had a great influence on a new school of Passion music that developed in Germany. Des Prés was, for a time, a

A 16th-century group or 'consort' of viols.

called the *frottola*. This developed into the madrigal as exemplified in the work of Luca Marenzio (*d.* 1599), Carlo Gesualdo (*d.* 1614) and Claudio Monteverdi (1567–1643). Madrigals were written to complement the feeling in the words of a poem. Sometimes they were accompanied by instruments, sometimes played by instruments only, so that the music alone expressed the mood. The idea grew up that music could be sad or happy. The madrigal was introduced into Britain by Thomas Morley (*d. c.* 1603) and perfected by him and by Thomas Weelkes (*d.* 1623), John Wilbye (*d.* 1638) and Thomas Tomkins (*d.* 1656). Another great writer of madrigals was the Italian master of Catholic Church music who spent most of his life in the service of the pope in Rome, Giovanni Pierluigi Palestrina (1525–94).

Palestrina's Masses and other liturgical works were proclaimed as the perfect religious music during the Catholic Church's campaign known as the Counter-Reformation. The opposite movement, the Reformation, had begun in 1517 when Martin Luther nailed his complaint against Church abuses to the door of the Castle Church in Wittenberg. It was Luther himself who wrote the battle hymn or *chorale* of the German Reformation, *Ein' feste Burg* ('A sure defence'). Jean Calvin, another Protestant leader, preferred simpler music, settings of the psalms published in the *Geneva Psalter* in 1542. Both the chorale and these psalm settings were meant to arouse the populace and drew freely from the folk music of the time.

Popular Music
The Reformation also produced translations of the Bible from Latin into the languages of everyday speech. Services were similarly held in the vernacular. Composers of Protestant Church music were encouraged to write to words in their own languages. Church and secular music were moving ever closer together. After the death of Palestrina, this became increasingly true even in the Catholic Church.

Music was reborn in the Renaissance, taken from the mysteries of pure worship into the realms of human emotion. Dance movements and imitations of vocal forms were introduced into instrumental works whether for solo performance or chamber ensemble. Compositions for keyboard instruments reached new heights of expression, for example, in the toccatas

Giovanni Palestrina, seen here presenting his music to the pope, was choirmaster of the Julian Chapel in the Vatican.

The great organ was at its most popular and achieved its highest importance both artistically and technically in the 17th and 18th centuries.

of Antonio de Cabezón (1500–66) in Spain and Andrea Gabrieli (*d.* 1586) in Italy, which were intended to display the instrument's power and the player's skill.

The Reformation encouraged national literature and popular forms of Church music such as the German chorale and its English equivalent, the anthem. The Counter-Reformation launched the arts into even more extravagant realms in the style known as Baroque. From our own perspective of history, the sixteenth century produced music that speaks directly to us today. Popular consorts are now reviving it, often on modern copies of the instruments of those times.

Early Opera
Much sixteenth-century music had been contrapuntal, that is to say, a note or melody was contrasted and combined with another note or melody in counterpoint to the first. In the seventeenth century, a simple line of melody, the tune in fact, became more important. This gave the individual instrumentalist or vocalist greater freedom to express personal emotion. Verbal

In later life Handel's health failed and by the age of 68 he was completely blind.

by strengthening the choral element in his oratorios. In Germany, Heinrich Schütz (*d.* 1672) combined Venetian opera with German Passion music.

Italian opera spread throughout Europe. Only in France was another national style founded when Jean-Baptiste Lully (*d.* 1687) combined it with ballet by including minuets, gavottes and sarabandes. In England, Henry Purcell (*d.* 1695) produced dramatic works such as *Dido and Aeneas,* but received little financial encouragement.

Meanwhile, improvements in the manufacture of keyboard instruments had created a school of composers in Germany, including Johann Jakob Froberger (*d.* 1667), Johann Pachelbel (*d.* 1706) and Dietrich Buxtehude (*d.* 1707) for the organ, and Johann Kuhnau (*d.* 1722) for the harpsichord. Italy retained its lead in compositions

ideas were presented in the form of speech-music called recitative and this developed into the lengthened form of melody called the aria.

The Renaissance stemmed partly from the rediscovery of ancient Greek philosophy. In music, attempts were made to revive the Greek combination of music and drama. This led eventually to the form of musical drama called opera that has survived into our own times. Its first exponents were the Florentines, Giulio Caccini (*d.* 1618) and Jacopo Peri (*d.* 1633), but the first great master was Monteverdi, writing as a court musician in Mantua. Not unnaturally, Monteverdi went back to Greek literature for inspiration, and his first operatic work was based on the legend of Orpheus, poet and musician beloved by the gods. The story was written for him by another Mantuan court musician, Alessandro Striggio, thus establishing the operatic combination of composer and librettist. The arts of the painter and designer were also co-opted to provide the settings.

The first performances of *The Story of Orpheus* were sponsored by societies, called academies, of aristocratic enthusiasts for the arts. The spread of these sponsoring bodies became an important source of income for musicians and encouraged expensive productions of new works. Monteverdi became Music Director at St Mark's Cathedral in Venice where the first opera house, the S Cassian Theatre, was opened in 1637. The Theatre of St John and St Paul, opened two years later, was the one for which Monteverdi composed his greatest opera, *The Coronation of Poppea,* the first to have an historical rather than mythological subject.

Oratorio
Already, during the Counter-Reformation, the Catholic Church had encouraged music-drama based on sacred subjects. The new Church equivalent to secular opera became known as oratorio. It evolved from the incidental music to mystery and miracle plays based on Bible stories and began in Rome with the composer Emilio de Cavalieri (*d.* 1602). At first it was staged like an opera. Giacomo Carissimi (*d.* 1674) distinguished between the two

The upright piano was invented in the 18th century.

for string instruments, thanks largely to the wonderful violins manufactured in Cremona, notably by the Amati family and Antonio Stradivari (1644–1737). The sonata, an instrumental work in three or four movements, and the concerto, a sonata-form for solo instruments and orchestra, began to be developed by such composers as Arcangelo Corelli (*d.* 1713) in Rome and Antonio Vivaldi (*d.* 1741) in Venice. In Naples, Alessandro Scarlatti (*d.* 1725) perfected a stylised form of the aria which became the standard pattern for composers of both opera and oratorio. Scarlatti was the greatest Italian opera composer of his time, perhaps his best work being his last, *Griselda* (1721).

Bach and Handel

All this music-drama was reflected in the dramatic style shown by the other arts of painting, literature and architecture, usually called the Baroque style, which lasted roughly between the years 1600 and 1750. The greatest composers of this period, who brought all the trends into their own works, were Johann Sebastian Bach and George Frederic Handel. Both were born in the same year, 1865, within a month of each other and about 80 miles apart, Bach in Eisenach, Thuringia, and Handel in Halle, Saxony. Both made the most of their musical opportunities though they lived very different lives. Handel was born the son of a prosperous surgeon in a city with a long musical tradition. He left Germany to work first in Italy and then in England. Bach came from a family of town, court and Church musicians and remained all his life in Germany. Handel acquired a great reputation and much wealth. In 1759 he was given a state funeral in London. Bach had to struggle for his living all his life and was recognised as a fine organist and as a master of composition by only a few in the last years of his life. He was buried in 1750 in an unmarked grave. It was left to succeeding generations to recognise that both men were equally great, the works of each complementing those of the other.

Handel studied law at Halle University and became organist of the Calvinist Cathedral. He then went to Hamburg as violinist in the opera orchestra, succeeding in having two of his own operas produced. In Venice, he had great success with his opera *Agrippina*, written in the heroic, Italian style. He repeated this success in London with *Rinaldo*, produced at the new Haymarket Theatre designed by John Vanbrugh. Since the accession of George I, Elector of Hanover, to the British throne, German music had become the vogue. Handel settled in London where he wrote music for state occasions, operas, chamber and orchestral works, settings of the Te Deum and Church anthems and pieces for the harpsichord and organ which he performed himself. In 1726, he became a naturalised British subject and was appointed composer to the Chapel Royal. With his music publisher, John Walsh, Handel prospered and soon became an established figure in court circles.

The old type of heroic opera from which Handel received a good part of his income began to wane in popularity and was satirised in *The Beggar's Opera* by John Gay and J. C. Pepusch. Handel saw that there could be a place in the theatre for the Church's form of music-drama, the oratorio, with words specially written in English. To compensate for the lack of action, he wrote his oratorios with an extensive part for a large chorus. Of his 20 or so oratorios, some with purely secular subjects, outstanding is the *Messiah*, one of the most widely admired musical compositions ever written.

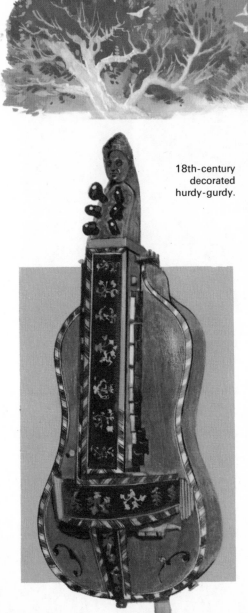

18th-century decorated hurdy-gurdy.

Vivaldi's *The Seasons* (1725) was an early example of programme music.

While Handel was becoming rich and famous, Bach was struggling to make a living as a humble organist. He joined the musical staff of the Duke of Weimar and later became musical director to the Duke of Anhalt-Köthen. In 1723, he became cantor of St Thomas's School in Leipzig, a post already turned down by two better-known musicians. Yet Bach had already composed many of the works that were to win him lasting fame. Lutheran Church ritual required large-scale choral works and motets, and cantatas—in Italy secular works with alternating recitative and aria, but in Germany based on the hymn-like chorale. Choral melodies also formed the basis for a kind of organ music called the chorale prelude. Bach composed in all these forms and also in the contrapuntal organ pieces called fugues which, with their ingenious design and texture, allowed him to display his great talent as a performer. He also composed orchestral works, notably the six Brandenberg Concertos, and much violin and clavier music.

Programme Music

Towards the end of the Baroque period, a new spirit was stirring, especially in France. François Couperin (1668–1733) composed a great deal of delicate harpsichord music and was an early writer of what is called programme music which tells a story in sound. Jean Rameau (1683–1764), whose works included 24 operas, wrote on musical theory and laid the foundation for its study in our own day. Christopher Gluck (1714–87), the Bavarian composer working in Paris, so reformed the stilted Italian heroic opera as to give it a new dramatic power. His *Orpheus and Eurydice* and *Alcestis* are among the earliest operas still performed today.

Johann Sebastian Bach, considered by his contemporaries as the greatest organ and clavier player that ever lived.

The opera house had traditionally developed new orchestral techniques, but the eighteenth century saw the growth of concert performances. In Mannheim, Duke Carl Theodor, the Elector Palatine, founded a great orchestra under the leadership of the Czech violinist, Johann Stamitz (1717–57). It was Stamitz and the Mannheim orchestra who did most to establish the four-movement symphony much as we know it today. Meanwhile, J. S. Bach's second son, Carl Philipp Emanuel Bach (1714–88) was finding new realms of expression in his keyboard sonatas. It is largely the development of the symphony and the sonata which covers the Classical period of musical history and brings us to the great names of that period: Haydn, Mozart and Beethoven.

It was a period of political revolution, especially in France, and it was matched by as great a revolution in the arts. It was known as the Age of Enlightenment, when the rising middle classes were demanding that control of their destinies should be wrested from the all-powerful aristocracy. Courts, nobles and high churchmen had been associated with the extravagant dramatic display, both in architecture and music, which characterised the Baroque style. The new movements were therefore anti-Baroque. They shunned ostentation and demanded a new naturalism, appealing to ordinary human emotions.

This was particularly true in opera. From Italy came the new *opera buffa* or comic opera, as distinct from the *opera seria* or heroic and generally tragic opera. *Opera buffa* was not entirely comic, having its tragic moments, its tears among the joys expected of the new realism. It took France by storm, sweeping away the heroic melodrama exemplified by the operas of Rameau. In orchestral work, the equivalent became the sonata form and the symphony.

Sonata means literally 'sound piece' as opposed to cantata or 'sung piece'. In the eighteenth century, it became the word for a piece of chamber music in three or four movements written for one or two instruments. Similarly, the word symphony originally meant merely any piece of music for instruments. For a time, it referred to the operatic overture, played not only before the opera performance began, but also separately as part of a concert programme. In the Classical period following the Baroque, it was based on the sonata form and came to dominate the orchestral concert. The sonata and the symphony had both begun, like *opera buffa,* in Italy, but their development soon spread elsewhere. C.P.E. Bach developed the keyboard sonata in Germany. Domenico Scarlatti (1685–1757), son of Alessandro, working in Spain, wrote some 600 single-movement sonatas. The mainly Austrian and Czech musicians of the Mannheim orchestra, with their soaring arpeggios and crescendos, brought a new dynamism to the symphony.

Haydn

All this impressed the young Josef Haydn (1732–1809). He was born of peasant stock in the village of Rohrau

managed to remain true to his musical genius. He lived most of his life close to the place of his birth and never forgot his origin or the folk music of his boyhood. His work displays a love of life, compassion and humour, a sense of the open air and truth to nature unsurpassed until his time.

Mozart

Meanwhile, his brother Michael was organist to the Archbishop of Salzburg where one of his colleagues was the violinist and composer, Leopold Mozart, father of the two infant prodigies, Marie Anna and Wolfgang Amadeus Mozart (1756–91). Both gifted performers, they were ruthlessly exploited by their father who took them on tour and to all the most important European courts. The young Mozart soon showed a great facility for composition in all the styles of the period. Wolfgang's early success created jealousy, and he had difficulty in his later and tragically short life in obtaining posts suited to his talents. At the age of twenty-five, he left a minor post in Salzburg and went to Vienna. Though a prolific composer, he earned barely enough to feed his growing family and died in poverty. Yet he raised *opera buffa* to a new height

The young Mozart at the harpsichord with his father Leopold playing the violin.

near Eisenstadt in the Croatian part of Austria. With his brother Michael, he joined the Imperial Choir in Vienna and became a pupil of the cathedral school. When his voice broke, he maintained himself in all sorts of jobs that allowed him to continue his musical studies and to compose works of his own. At last, in 1761, he took service in the household of Prince Paul Anton Esterhazy, head of the wealthiest and most influential family in the Austrian Empire, where he was to remain for almost thirty years, becoming their director of music. As a servant in livery, Haydn gave up much of his personal freedom, but always

Schubert (second from right) admired Beethoven (far left) and often drank in the same café, but never spoke to the great composer.

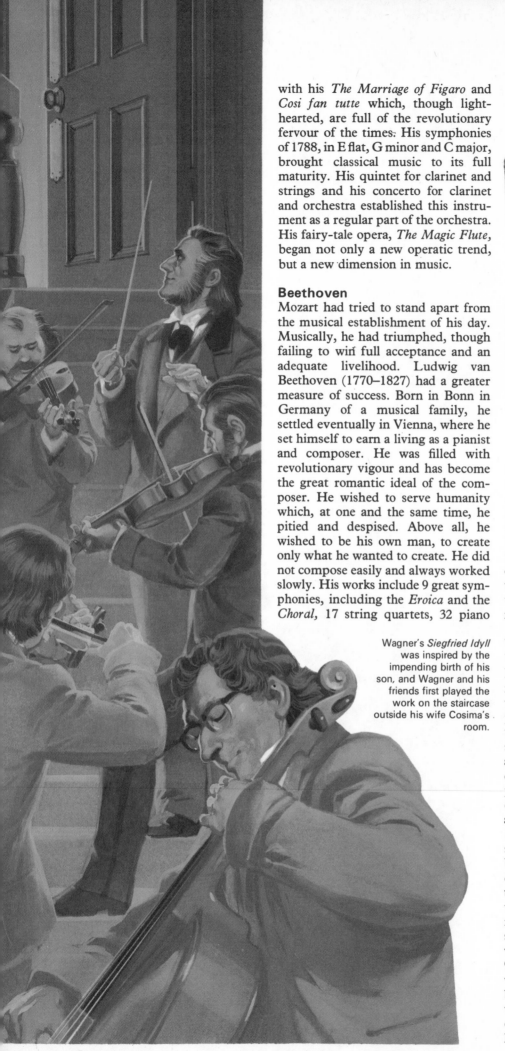

with his *The Marriage of Figaro* and *Cosi fan tutte* which, though light-hearted, are full of the revolutionary fervour of the times. His symphonies of 1788, in E flat, G minor and C major, brought classical music to its full maturity. His quintet for clarinet and strings and his concerto for clarinet and orchestra established this instrument as a regular part of the orchestra. His fairy-tale opera, *The Magic Flute*, began not only a new operatic trend, but a new dimension in music.

Beethoven

Mozart had tried to stand apart from the musical establishment of his day. Musically, he had triumphed, though failing to win full acceptance and an adequate livelihood. Ludwig van Beethoven (1770–1827) had a greater measure of success. Born in Bonn in Germany of a musical family, he settled eventually in Vienna, where he set himself to earn a living as a pianist and composer. He was filled with revolutionary vigour and has become the great romantic ideal of the composer. He wished to serve humanity which, at one and the same time, he pitied and despised. Above all, he wished to be his own man, to create only what he wanted to create. He did not compose easily and always worked slowly. His works include 9 great symphonies, including the *Eroica* and the *Choral*, 17 string quartets, 32 piano

Wagner's *Siegfried Idyll* was inspired by the impending birth of his son, and Wagner and his friends first played the work on the staircase outside his wife Cosima's room.

Mendelssohn was a child prodigy and died when he was only thirty-eight.

sonatas, the magnificent Mass in D, a number of concertos and one opera, *Fidelio*, a deeply emotional plea for freedom and love. He began to go deaf in his twenties and never married. He was a lonely, fiercely independent man, regarded as the last and greatest of the Classical composers and first of the Romantics, the group of musicians which followed him and that he did so much to inspire.

The Romantic Era

While Beethoven was ushering in the Romantic era with his great instrumental works, contemporary poets were turning to nature, to country pursuits and folk song, and to antiquity for inspiration. The old solo songs, sung to the accompaniment of a lute, had faded from popularity. The development and popularisation of the pianoforte provided a new, ideal accompanying instrument. All this found a focal point in the genius of Franz Schubert (1797–1828), the first of the so-called Viennese composers to have been born there. Like Beethoven, he devoted his life to composition, a life that was short and hard, supported by the devotion of a few friends. He wrote more than 600 songs, many of them still regularly sung today. He also wrote chamber and piano music, and 9 symphonies of which the B minor was unfinished. His lead was followed by Robert Schumann (1810–56) who wrote more than 200 songs and a quantity of piano music inspired by his wife Clara, one of the greatest

pianists of her day. The tradition was carried on by Johannes Brahms (1833–97) who also composed symphonies, concertos, overtures and choral works. Operatic singers began to fill concert halls with programmes of songs only.

Opera in the eighteenth century had been composed to librettos in Italian to be sung in the brilliant Italian style called *bel canto*. The beauty of the melody had often outweighed the sense of the words. Mozart's *The Magic Flute* and Beethoven's *Fidelio* were written in German and gave opera new depths of feeling that spoke directly to the popular audience. The first great opera in the true Romantic mould was *Der Freischütz* by Carl Maria von Weber (1786–1826). Based on an old German legend it embodied the new national pride and regard for the simple qualities of the working man, which also inspired the German songs called *Lieder*.

Wagner and Verdi

Following Weber came one of the greatest of all composers, most of whose work was in the field of music-drama, Richard Wagner (1813–83). He began as a conductor in various obscure opera houses and by 1842 had produced his own opera, *The Flying Dutchman,* in Dresden. This was followed by *Tannhaüser* and *Lohengrin,* both from medieval stories. These were conventional operas, but Wagner had the idea of remodelling opera with a new unity of design inspired by the symphonies of Beethoven. The result

was the *Ring of the Nibelungs,* four music-dramas based on German and Norse mythology, which took twenty years to complete. For the last twenty years of his life, Wagner was under the protection of Ludwig II, King of Bavaria, who preferred the arts to affairs of state. He fulfilled Wagner's great ambition to have a national theatre devoted to music-drama. This was built at Bayreuth.

Contemporary with Wagner was Giuseppe Verdi (1813–1901) whose life spanned the period of Italy's struggle for unification and nationhood. Both composers were to become national symbols. Whereas Wagner's work was contrapuntal (combining melodies) in texture, and philosophical and literary in ideas—in fact essentially German—Verdi followed the Italian tradition of flowing melody and vocal beauty. He ranged widely for his subject matter. *Il Trovatore* is a Spanish story, *La Traviata* is based on a novel by Alexandre Dumas the Younger, *Aida* was an Egyptian story commissioned to celebrate the opening of the Suez Canal, *Otello* and *Falstaff* are taken from Shakespeare's plays. Yet Verdi spoke always to the ordinary man. His tunes were hummed and whistled in the streets. For this, he was often classed as vulgar, particularly in Paris where the grand opera of Gioacchino Rossini (1792–1868) was preferred. France produced the operatic composers Charles Gounod (1818–93), whose rather sentimental works include *Faust* and *Romeo and Juliet,* Jules Massenet (1842–1912), who wrote melodius operas as well as oratorios, orchestral works and songs, and Georges Bizet (1838–75), whose most successful work was *Carmen.*

Beethoven's symphonies, particularly the Ninth, made great demands on the orchestra. Mozart wrote concertos, not only for the clarinet, but also for oboe, horn, flute, organ and violin. The individual instruments of the orchestra were becoming important, as also was the whole orchestra as a single gigantic instrument. Techniques of playing improved and instruments became more expressive. The modern concept of orchestration was emerging, as illustrated in the *Fantastic* Symphony of the French composer, Hector Berlioz (1803–69), one of the most colourful of all symphonic works. The *Hebrides* Overture and *Italian* Symphony of Felix Mendelssohn (1809–47) and the symphonic poems of Franz Liszt (1811–86) are other examples of the use to

Characters from the popular
Savoy operas of Gilbert and Sullivan.

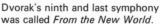
Dvorak's ninth and last symphony was called *From the New World*.

which the greater variety of an enlarged orchestra could be put. Mendelssohn, Schumann and Liszt were also producing work that did much to popularise the piano. Liszt was himself one of the greatest piano virtuosi of his day, filling concert halls wherever he went and incidentally popularising the piano works of Beethoven.

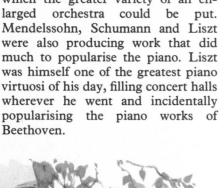

National Music

The Romantic era was, above all, a time of fierce national pride. Protest was all against foreign oppression and in support of the national identity. Liszt was a Hungarian and proud of it. He was inspired by the dance rhythms and folk songs of the Magyar people and the gypsy musicians of his country. His symphonic poem *Hungaria* is one fine result of this.

In Russia, Michael Glinka (1803–57) was angered by the fashion for French and Italian music in the capital of St Petersburg. He wrote the opera *A Life for the Czar*, full of Russian and Polish folk songs and patriotic choruses. His *Russlan and Ludmilla* was based on a poem by the Russian writer, Alexander Pushkin. His inspiration was followed in the instrumental works of Mily Balakirev (1837–1910) and Alexander Borodin (1833–87), and in the operas of Modest Mussorgsky (1839–81), such as *Boris Godunov*, and of Nikolay Rimsky-Korsakov (1844–1908). With Cesar Cui (1835–1918), these formed the so-called 'Five', all amateur musicians earning their living in other professions. Peter Tchaikovsky (1840–93) was influenced by Balakirev and Rimsky-Korsakov.

Frédéric Chopin (1810–49), born in Poland though with a French father, composed many works based on national dances, such as the polonaise and the mazurka. *The Bartered Bride* by Bedřich Smetana (1824–84), the Czech composer, was a folk-opera displaying aspects of national life and based on national music. Another Czech, Antonín Dvořák (1841–1904) used folk song, folk dance and even negro idioms within the conventions of classical music and became the most celebrated nationalistic composer of the period. A distinctively Spanish school grew up around the works of Isaac Albéniz (1860–1909), Enrique Granados (1867–1916) and Manuel de Falla (1876–1946).

The symphonic tradition of Austria was continued by Anton Bruckner (1824–96) and Gustav Mahler (1860–1911). Meanwhile, in France, Claude Debussy (1862–1918) was writing music to complement the paintings of the Impressionists as exemplified by his *L'après-midi d'un faune*, a composition of the open air and sunlight. Maurice Ravel (1875–1937) was another member of this Impressionist school. The Norwegian, Edvard Grieg (1843–1907), in his short piano pieces and songs, found the spirit of his native land, as did Jean Sibelius (1865–1957), born in Finland, with his symphonies. In Britain, Edward Elgar (1857–1934) gave a personal and national flavour to his work, whereas Frederick Delius (1862–1934) belonged more to the Impressionists, though with his own individual harmonies. Gustav Holst (1874–1934) and Ralph Vaughan Williams (1872–1958) both turned to folk music and past modes for inspiration, combining them with modern forms in large-scale works.

Edward Elgar.

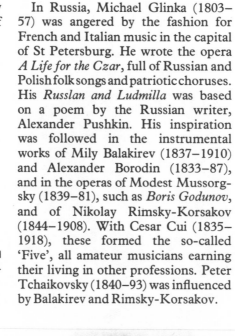

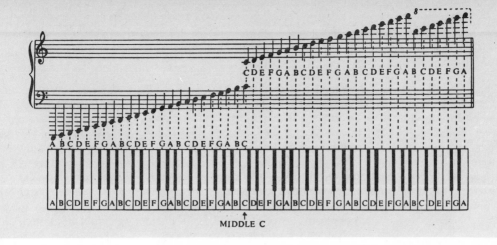

Materials of Music

Music is not only an art: it is a physical science with a precise and mathematical language of its own. The material of music is sound, which is produced physically by movement in the form of vibration. When the vibrations in the air are regular, what we hear is musical. When they are irregular, we hear only noise. One vibration source can set up a sympathetic vibration in physical objects that are in tune with the original source. This phenomenon is called resonance. Thus, the sound of the human voice is produced not only by the vocal chords, but also by sympathetic vibrations set up within the cavities of the skull. Similarly, the sound-box of a musical instrument vibrates sympathetically with the first movement imparted to the instrument by the player. For instance, the belly of a violin resonates with the vibrations of the bowed string, reinforcing the tone produced.

The frequency of vibration, the number of vibrations per second, determines the pitch of a sound. The more vibrations per second, the higher the pitch. The human ear is extremely sensitive to differences in pitch and has a range between about 20 vibrations per second and 20,000. A mixed choir produces frequencies between about 64 and 1,500, whereas a concert piano can manage a range between 20 and 4,176. When a group of musicians plays together, they tune their instruments to a standard pitch of 440 vibrations per second.

Notation

From ancient times, it has been found desirable to give music a written language. Though the ancients knew little about the science of musical sound, they understood its mathematical nature, and they could recognise a wrong note when they heard it. Music could be taught, passed on from composer to performer, but a lack of a written language meant that much

music was forgotten or became altered from generation to generation. The first musical symbols called neumes were little more than aids to memory, giving a rough idea of the rise and fall of the notes in a melody. About the ninth century A.D., the staff appeared, at first a single horizontal line, later two and later still three or four. Gregorian chant still uses four horizontal lines, but music today is usually written on a staff of five horizontal lines.

In modern notation, the first seven letters of the alphabet are used to indicate pitch. For historical reasons, this musical alphabet starts at C, thus: C D E F G A B. The next seven notes begin at C, and the interval between the first C and the next one, comprising eight notes in all, is called an octave. The eight notes of the octave are represented by the white notes of the piano keyboard (see the diagram on this page). An octave can, of course, start at any note, providing it covers an interval of eight notes in all. An interval is the difference in pitch between one note and another. Thus, an interval of five notes is called a fifth, an interval of four notes a fourth, and so on. Pianos usually comprise seven octaves. The first C in the middle

octave is called middle C and has a vibration frequency of 256. The C below has half that number, 128, and the C above twice the number, 512.

For convenience, music is not written in the letters of the alphabet but in symbols positioned on a staff of five horizontal lines. One staff is used for the notes from middle C upwards and another, placed below the first, for the notes from middle C downwards. Notes are positioned either on the lines or between them. As two groups of five lines are not enough for all the notes, short extra lines are added above and below to accommodate higher and lower notes. These extra lines are called ledger lines. To indicate which staff of five lines covers which range of notes, the staff is marked by a clef. There are three kinds of clef, the G clef, the F clef and the C clef, of which the first two are most commonly used. The G clef is known as the Treble clef, and the F clef as the Bass clef. The centre of the Treble clef rests on the second line of the staff, the line for note G, and the head of the Bass clef is on the fourth line (together with dots above and below this line) to indicate that this is the position for the note F. Thus we have this arrangement:

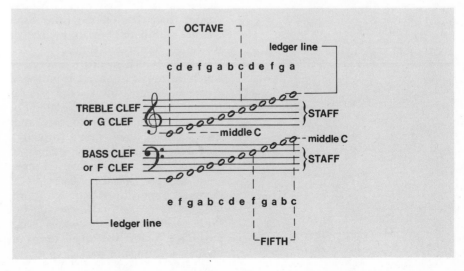

As well as pitch, notes have duration. At present, the longest note in general use is the semibreve. This is divided in terms of duration into 2 minims, 4 crotchets, 8 quavers, 16 semiquavers, 32 demisemiquavers and 64 hemidemisemiquavers. The actual duration of a note is indicated by the addition of stems and tails to white or black notes thus:

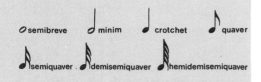

Sometimes a note is held for twice the duration of a semibreve. This note is called a breve. When several notes occur together, sometimes their tails, which can be on rising or falling stems, are joined together thus:

When both words and sounds are written together for song music, it is general practice to write a separate note for each new syllable. Prolonging the time value of a note can be indicated by the addition of a dot beside it, giving the note an extra duration exactly half its own time value. Sometimes, two notes of the same pitch are linked with a tie, a slightly curved line, to indicate that the note should be held for the time represented by the two notes together. There is also a set of symbols for periods of rest or pauses between notes, equivalent to the length of duration of the notes themselves, thus:

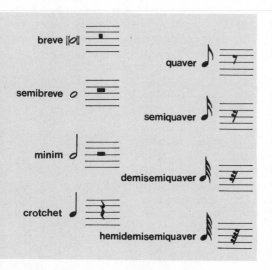

Rhythm is an element present in all kinds of movement, not least in music. Ordinary speech has its rhythms produced by the stressed and unstressed syllables of the words. This pattern of stress is systemised in poetry. Stress applied to notes in a piece of music is called the beat, which occurs in groups of two, three and multiplications of these numbers of notes. Written music is divided into these groups by means of a vertical line drawn through the staff. These lines are called bar-lines, and they divide the music into bars which are the equivalent of the metrical feet into which the words of a poem are divided. Bars are separated by single bar-lines, and the end of a piece of music is completed by a double bar-line.

If there are two beats to a bar, one stressed and the other unstressed, then the figure 2 is placed after the clef and between the fifth and third lines of the staff. To indicate the kind of note which is the basic unit of the bar, a second figure is written below the first between the third and first lines of the staff. A figure 4, for example, in this position indicates that the basic note is a quarter-note or crotchet. The piece of music then begins like this:

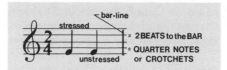

The bar-line is usually placed before the stressed note of the bar. The two numbers together form the time signature of the piece of music. Music with two beats to the bar is called duple time. Music with three beats, such as waltz time, is called triple time, and with four beats quadruple time which is really double-duple time except that the stress on the first beat is usually greater than that on the third beat. Greater numbers of beats to the bar are called compound time.

Tempo, which means the speed at which the music is played, is indicated at the beginning by a word usually Italian, written above the staff. The most important ones are: *Grave* (very slow), *Lento* (slow), *Largo* (broadly), *Larghetto* (rather broadly), *Adagio* (in a leisurely manner), *Andante* (at moderate walking speed), *Moderato* (at moderate speed), *Allegretto* (fairly fast), *Allegro* (fast), *Vivace* (lively), *Presto* (very fast), *Prestissimo* (as fast as possible). There are other terms to indicate a change of pace.

Letters, written usually below the staff, indicate the volume of sound when the notes are played. These letters are called dynamic marks and are, in descending order: *fff* (*molto fortissimo*, extremely loud), *ff* (*fortissimo*, very loud), *f* (*forte*, loud), *mf* (*mezzo forte*, fairly loud), *mp* (*mezzo piano*, fairly soft), *p* (*piano*, soft), *pp* (*pianissimo*, very soft).

To complete this brief introduction to the language and written symbols of music, tones and semitones must be described. On the diagram of a piano keyboard shown above, it will be seen that between some of the white notes there are black notes. Playing eight white notes in succession, C D E F G A B and C, produces an octave where the pitch of each note has an equal interval between itself and the next note. These intervals are called whole tones or just tones. If the black notes are included, between a black note and a white there is an interval of half the value which is called a half-tone or semi-tone. Symbols used to indicate the raising or lowering of a note by a semitone are called sharps and flats respectively. Thus the black note above C on the piano keyboard is C sharp and is written ♯C. But the same black note is also immediately below the white note D and is therefore D flat and can be written ♭D. Notice that the symbols for sharps (♯) and flats (♭) are always written before the letter indicating the note. Notes which are neither sharps nor flats are called natural. To readjust sharpened or flattened notes to the natural or basic pitch, the symbol ♮ is used. Thus F sharp readjusted to F natural is written ♮F.

Music often has a keynote to which all the other notes gravitate. This recurring keynote may be a sharp or a flat. To avoid repeating the symbol each time the note occurs, it is usual to put it in at the beginning of the piece in the position on the staff where the note would be written and between the clef and the time signature, thus:

In this example, the sharps indicate that, until further notice, all the Fs and Cs are to be played sharp. This is called the key signature. The key signature above indicates that the piece of music is written in the key of D major.

Glossary of Musical Terms

Aria A composition for solo voice with instrumental accompaniment, though built on a larger scale than a simple song. The *da capo* (from the beginning) aria has a three-part structure with a repetition of the first part after a contrasting second part. There are many other forms.

Anthem English church composition based on the antiphon and motet (*qq.v.*)

Antiphonal A method of performance using two alternating groups of singers. The antiphon, for which this kind of performance is devised, is a scriptural text set to a plainsong (*q.v.*) melody.

Arpeggio The playing of the notes of a chord in succession instead of simultaneously.

Ars Antiqua Literally, the 'old art' as opposed to the 'new art' or *Ars Nova*. For convenience medieval music of the thirteenth century and before is classed as *Ars Antiqua*. From the fourteenth century onwards, music becomes *Ars Nova*. Apart from the development of new styles, there was a different method of notation, particularly of motets (*q.v.*).

Bel canto The dominant style of singing in the Italian school of music, with the emphasis on beauty of tone with the words taking second place.

Cantata An extended vocal piece consisting of alternate recitative and arias (*qq.v.*), originating in Italy.

Chamber music Compositions for small groups of instrumentalists, sometimes with singers, mainly for private performance. Works for string quartets are typical chamber music.

Chanson Song for solo voice or part-singing, developed in France and Flanders.

Choral Prelude An organ piece used in the German churches in the seventeenth and eighteenth centuries to introduce and elaborate on the hymn to be sung by the congregation.

Chorale Hymn used in the German Evangelical or Lutheran church.

Colour In music, this refers to the sound-quality or tone, apart from the tempo, rhythm and melody which make up the other parts of a musical work.

Concerto A composition for solo instrument and orchestra in which these two complement each other (from the Latin *concertare*, to fight side by side). When the solo instrument is replaced by a group of instruments, it is called Concerto Grosso. A concerto is commonly in three movements, corresponding to the first, second and fourth movements of the sonata (*q.v.*). As part of the first movement, and sometimes of the other two, a cadenza is added to give the solo instrument a chance of displaying its virtuosity. At one time, the cadenza was improvised by the soloist, but since Beethoven's time it has been included by the composer.

Conductus A chant with a consistent rhythm throughout its parts, sung during the procession of priests and deacons from the altar to the choir steps and back again in medieval churches.

Consort A group of instruments in sixteenth- and seventeenth-century England and the music composed for them. Instruments of the same family, such as recorders, were called a whole consort. Instruments of different families, such as mixed recorders and viols, were called broken consorts.

Crescendo A passage of music getting louder and louder.

Frottola An Italian song for several voices, often of a popular character, a forerunner of the madrigal (*q.v.*).

Fugue A contrapuntal composition usually, but not always, with three or four simultaneous melodic lines moving independently but with harmonious progression.

Gavotte A four-beat time dance form with each phrase beginning on the third beat, once one of the lively movements of a suite.

Harmonic One of a series of sounds subsidiary to the fundamental sound produced by a vibration, also called an overtone. There is a mathematical relationship between a fundamental sound and its harmonics.

Kharaja In Indian music, the drone note which acts as a tonal centre to guide the musicians through the piece.

Laudi spirituali A hymn of praise.

Libretto, librettist The libretto is the words of the opera or oratorio (*qq.v.*) written by the librettist, usually someone other than the composer of the music.

Lied (pl. **Lieder**) A song, particularly a German song of the Romantic period. *Lieder ohne Worte* are songs without words.

Madrigal A part-song for several voices, polyphonic (*q.v.*) in style and concerned with the beauty of the words, though madrigals were played without voices. Madrigals date from the fourteenth century, but were particularly popular in the sixteenth.

Mazurka Three-beat time Polish dance form with the second beat tending to be the one accented, dating from the sixteenth century or earlier.

Melody The tune of a piece of music, the arrangement of rise and fall in pitch of a sequence of notes.

Minnesinger German equivalent of the troubadour (*q.v.*).

Minuet A three-beat French country dance which became popular, in a modified form, throughout Europe. Sometimes used in old suites, it also became part of some classical sonatas (*q.v.*).

Motet A church anthem, usually unaccompanied, the term applying nowadays to similar secular works.

Neumes Signs used in the old manuscript copies of Gregorian chant to indicate rise and fall of pitch. They were also used for the songs of the troubadours (*q.v.*) and other secular as well as church music. Present-day musical notation derives from neumatic notation.

Note In English usage, this word can be taken to mean a single sound, the written symbol of that sound in music or the key on a piano or other instrument. Care should be taken in distinguishing between the three meanings from the context in which they are used.

Opera A presentation on stage of a drama with music, with the use of singers, orchestral accompaniment, costumes, scenery and dramatic acting. Formerly, opera was divided between the two styles, *opera buffa* or comic opera and *opera seria* or tragic opera. These terms are unsatisfactory, since the former often means realistic opera and the latter melodramatic opera. A better term for modern opera with a convincing plot and characters, where the drama is as important as the music used to heighten it, would be music-drama.

Oratorio A music-drama, often of a religious subject, but without stage movement and acting. Developed during the Counter-Reformation to compete with secular entertainment and attract people back into the Catholic Church.

Organum The technique of singing in unison with voices pitched at intervals from each other, developed in medieval chant.

Overtone A harmonic (*q.v.*) developed from a fundamental note by sympathetic vibration. The overtones of a particular instrument give it its individual character.

Pentatonic scale A scale of five notes which can be produced on the piano by playing the black keys only, beginning with F sharp. It appeared as early as 2000 B.C. It has been popular in many parts of the world and forms the basis of much folk music. *Auld Lang Syne* is an example of pentatonic tune.

Pitch The level of a particular note, created by its frequency or the number of vibrations per second.

Plainsong The traditional form of melody developed for the Catholic Church liturgy, often called Gregorian chant though it exists also in the Greek Orthodox Church rites.

Polonaise A Polish dance form in three-beat time, popularised in modern times by Chopin.

Polyphony Contrapuntal music written in many interweaving parts, usually for voices.

Programme music Music which tells a story in sound, a synopsis of which is usually printed in the concert programme. It became popular in the nineteenth century.

Raga The melodic part of Indian music, often improvised but crystallising into a composition becoming part of the instrumentalist's repertoire and passed on by him to younger members of his family.

Recitative A musical setting for

words in which the speech rhythms are allowed to prevail, rather than the melody taking them over.

Rhythm The pattern of stresses that gives a musical composition its vitality or tension.

Sarabande Originally a slow solo dance in three-beat time with the accent on the second beat, often found in seventeenth- and eighteenth-century suites.

Sonata This has developed over many years into a work of three or, more often, four movements. The

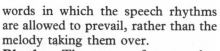

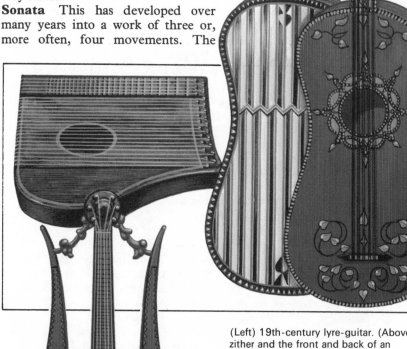

(Left)
18th-century serpent and an early form of trumpet called a labyrinthine.

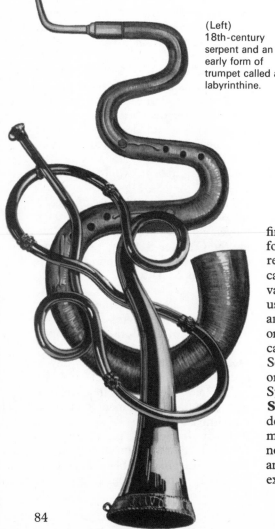

(Left) 19th-century lyre-guitar. (Above) zither and the front and back of an 18th-century decorated guitar.

first movement is the so-called sonata form of exposition, development and recapitulation. The second movement can be another sonata form, a rondo or variations. The third movement is usually a minuet and trio or a scherzo and trio. The last movement is a rondo or sonata form. What we nowadays call a String Quartet is usually a Sonata for Strings. When the full orchestra is involved, we speak of a Symphony (*q.v.*).

Symphony A work for full orchestra, designed on sonata-form lines. It is the musical equivalent of the large-scale novel in literature with room in it for anything from delicate lyricism to the expression of heroic struggle. It is the

mainstay of the classical orchestra's repertoire.

Symphonic poem This is a one-movement work, but of symphonic proportions, often telling a story in sound like programme music (*q.v.*).

Tala This belongs to the drums in classical Indian music and to hands clapped in unison with them. It maintains the rhythm in raga-music (*q.v.*).

Tempo The speed at which a piece of music is played.

Toccata A rapid, brilliant piece of music, originally designed for keyboard instruments.

Tone An interval between two white notes on a piano keyboard containing two semitones; often used to describe the sound quality of an instrument (see Colour).

Troubadour A poet-musician in medieval southern France, usually a member of the ruling class, but the term is often used to describe an itinerant entertainer.

Trouvère A troubadour of northern France in medieval times, but more usually a professional musician and entertainer.

Musical Instruments

Nowadays, when we talk about the strings of an orchestra, we usually mean the modern violin family. There are four members. In order of increasing size, they are the violin, the viola, the violoncello—usually just called the cello—and the double bass. The smallest of these is tuned to the highest range of notes and the largest to the lowest range, with the other two, also in size order, taking the intermediate ranges. All four instruments are basically the same shape. The violin and viola are held under the

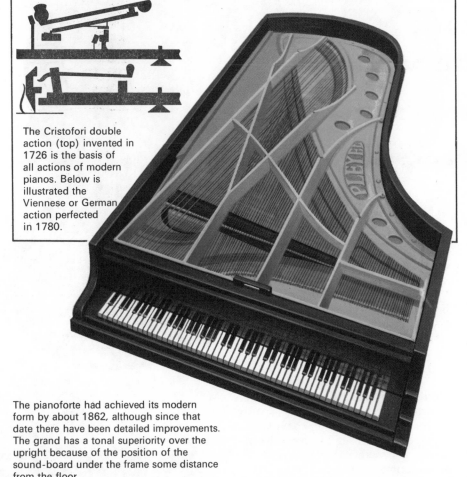

The Cristofori double action (top) invented in 1726 is the basis of all actions of modern pianos. Below is illustrated the Viennese or German action perfected in 1780.

The pianoforte had achieved its modern form by about 1862, although since that date there have been detailed improvements. The grand has a tonal superiority over the upright because of the position of the sound-board under the frame some distance from the floor.

chin, while the cello and double bass have a spiked foot for standing on the ground to play them in an upright position. All four are played by drawing a bow across the strings.

The violin was derived from the rebec, a medieval instrument that came originally from the East. It was made from a single piece of hollowed-out wood covered by a flat board of pine to form the resonator. It had only three strings and was played with a bow. The final shape of the modern violin was arrived at in Italy during the seventeenth and early eighteenth centuries in the superb instruments produced by the Amati, Stradivari and

Guarneri families. The cello and double bass are derived from the viol, early versions of which were in use in the eleventh century. During the fifteenth century in Italy, it took the shape still in use today, together with its six strings. Viols are played with a bow and held between the legs. The smaller viols were ousted by the violin during the seventeenth century.

One of the oldest stringed instruments of all is the harp, examples still being preserved from ancient Sumer and Egypt. In recent times, it has been regarded as a lady's instrument, perhaps because of its elegant shape. The strings are plucked by the fingers and their vibrations amplified by a sound-board. The pitch of all the strings can be altered by a system of seven pedals, worked by the player's foot. Terms specially applied to the harp are the arpeggio, the notes of a chord played in succession instead of simultaneously, and the glissando, a fast scale passage played by gliding the hands up and down the strings.

The Pianoforte
The other important stringed instrument is the piano which has derived from the harpsichord. Though both are keyboard instruments, they produce their sounds by quite different means. In a harpsichord, depressing a key operates a jack to which is attached a quill or small piece of leather which plucks the string. A smaller version of the harpsichord was the virginal, an instrument favoured by the ladies of the sixteenth and seventeenth centuries. It was superseded by the spinet, the most noticeable difference of which is its winged shape compared with the rectangular virginal. The strings of the spinet are set at an angle of 45 degrees to the keyboard, whereas the strings of the virginal are in line with the keyboard. Modern versions of both instruments are popular again today.

The great difference between the piano and other keyboard instruments is that the former has its strings struck by little hammers and not plucked. The principle was first applied about 1709 by the instrument-maker Cristofori in Florence. For the first time, the loudness or softness of the notes played could be controlled by the force applied to the keys by the player's fingers, hence the full name, pianoforte, meaning 'soft-loud'. The upright piano, with the strings mounted

The baryton is a bass stringed instrument belonging to the viol family and first appeared in the 17th century.

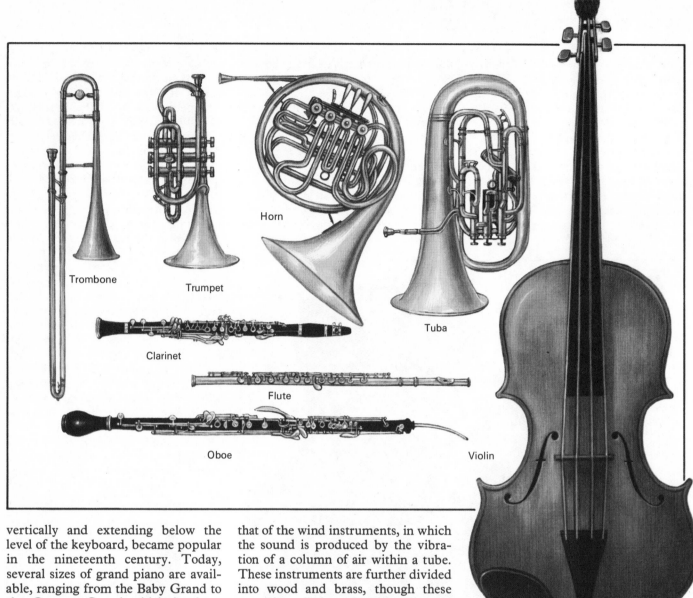

Trombone

Trumpet

Horn

Tuba

Clarinet

Flute

Oboe

Violin

vertically and extending below the level of the keyboard, became popular in the nineteenth century. Today, several sizes of grand piano are available, ranging from the Baby Grand to the Concert Grand which is about 2·5 metres (8½ feet) long.

Though not usually a part of the orchestra, the modern guitar has a long history. A popular medieval solo instrument was the lute which, by the seventeenth century had acquired up to thirty strings. Similar instruments were the mandoline and the cittern, the former with eight strings tuned in pairs, plucked with a tortoiseshell plectrum, the latter also with eight strings tuned in pairs, made of metal and plucked with the fingers. Other stringed instruments worth mentioning are the dulcimer, with strings stretched across a shallow wooden box and struck with small wooden hammers, and the psaltery, a similar instrument except that the strings are plucked by the fingers or a plectrum. The dulcimer can be said to be the forerunner of the piano, whereas the psaltery was the forerunner of the harpsichord.

Wind Instruments
The next division of the orchestra is that of the wind instruments, in which the sound is produced by the vibration of a column of air within a tube. These instruments are further divided into wood and brass, though these terms have little to do with the materials from which they are made. The distinction is concerned with vibrations set up by vibrating a thin piece of reed fixed in the mouthpiece of the instrument, or with vibrations set up by vibrating the lips of the player within a cup-shaped mouthpiece. Reed instruments, with either one reed or two vibrating against each other, are called woodwind. Instruments without reeds are called brass. Also included in the woodwind section are the flute and its smaller relative, the piccolo, where the vibrations are set up by blowing across a mouth-hole.

A typical single-reed woodwind instrument is the clarinet. The oboe, the lower pitched alto oboe or cor anglais and the basson are all double-reed instruments. Brass instruments are the horn, often called the French horn or valve horn, which is a long tube wound round and ending in a bell shape, with a valve system for varying the effective length of the tube; the trumpet which is the soprano brass instrument and also includes a valve

system; the trombone, the length of which is varied by sliding one tube inside another; and the tuba which is an instrument between a large trumpet and a horn and provides the lowest range of pitch in the brass section.

There are, of course, many other wind instruments ranging from the simple recorder to the mighty church organ. Their history includes the tabor, the flageolet, the bagpipe, the hunting horn, the Roman buccina (a kind of tuba), the sackbut (a kind of trombone) and many more. They all derive ultimately from primitive man's attempts to make music out of a conch shell or the horn of an animal.

Percussion

The last section of orchestral instruments is the percussion. The timpani or kettledrums are tuned to a definite pitch. They are composed of a bowl-shaped kettle, usually made of copper, across which a calf-skin head is stretched and held by a metal ring which is adjustable with screws. The pitch can be varied by loosening or tightening the screws and therefore the tension of the skin. Kettledrums are normally used in sets of two or more. The bass drum has stretched skin on either side of a cylindrical body and is of indefinite low pitch. The side drum is similar but smaller and has strings of catgut called snares stretched across its lower head. These give it its characteristic rattling sound. The tambourine is a small drum with only one head and with small metal plates or jingles set loosely around the shell. Cymbals are two slightly concave brass plates with leather handles. They are perhaps the noisiest instruments of the orchestra and can be sounded by

30 violins divided into two groups, the First and Second, about 10 violas, 10 cellos, 4–8 double basses and perhaps 2 harps. Woodwind instruments are usually in pairs: 2 flutes (with one piccolo), 2 oboes (with one cor anglais), 2 clarinets and 2 bassoons. The brass section is usually 2 trumpets, 2–4 horns, 3 trombones and one tuba. Percussion instruments are added as required by the music to be played. If a choir is included, it is usually ranged behind the orchestra, whereas soloists, both instrumental and vocal, are generally in front.

The Modern Orchestra

A modern orchestra, with or without a choir, can be looked upon as one gigantic instrument. It is for the parts of this instrument that the composer composes and, nowadays, the interpretation of his work is the responsibility of the conductor. In the eighteenth century, a composer more or less led the performance of his work from a keyboard instrument. The principal violinist also had a disciplinary function. In Germany and America,

Orchestral plans, or the seating arrangements for the different sections of players, have developed considerably over the years. A modern example is shown, but the actual placing will vary according to the individual conductor.

this member of the orchestra came to be known as the concertmaster, in Britain as the leader of the orchestra. The interpretation of music by a conductor was pioneered in Britain by Sir George Smart (1776–1867), in Germany by Louis Spohr (1784–1859) and in France by François Habeneck (1781–1849). These conductors regarded the proper interpretation of Beethoven as their greatest duty. Richard Wagner was also greatly influenced by the way in which Beethoven used the total instruments of an orchestra to express his ideas.

Nowadays, the whole science of sound and the technology that goes with it needs to be understood by players and most of all by the conductor. The science of sound is called acoustics. We have now discovered how to provide the best acoustical environment for the performances of orchestras. Buildings are designed with their acoustic qualities in mind. Old concert halls are fitted with sound baffles to absorb echoes and yet leave the right mixture of overtones undisturbed.

Electronic Recording

The electronic recording of music has likewise become a new science. It is not only concerned with equipment but also with the placing of that

clashing together or by hitting one of them with one or two sticks. Finally, the triangle is a steel rod bent into a triangular shape and struck with a steel beater to make a bright, clear, ringing sound.

The total number of instruments in and the exact composition of an orchestra can vary considerably. A full symphony orchestra usually has about

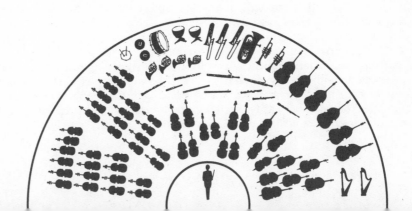

Much of Bartok's music has its origin in the Magyar folk songs of the Hungarian people. Here he is shown recording the unaccompanied voice of a peasant woman.

Modern Music

At the beginning of the twentieth century, music seemed to have arrived at a set of rules which henceforth would remain for all time. Above all, music was intended to give pleasure and not to make the listener uneasy. The best music had already been composed, and any new music, if it were to be good, had to follow well-established lines. The term classical came to be applied to all music of acceptable quality. Popular forms were regarded as trivial.

But music is a living force and cannot be fossilised. Debussy was one of the first composers to turn away from the accepted tonal system. He revived some of the scales and modes from medieval times and from folk music. He used a scale without any half-tones called the whole-tone scale. His harmonies were intuitive, rather than based on a set of rules.

After Debussy, Arnold Schoenberg (1874–1951) was free to introduce atonality, to dispense with tonal values altogether. He arrived at the twelve-note scale in which all twelve notes of the chromatic scale are given equal value. Themes contain all twelve notes, each appearing once, but with the use of any rhythm. The same twelve notes were also grouped together to form chords. Schoenberg's methods were followed by the American Charles Ives (1874–1954) and by Alban Berg (1885–1935) and Anton Webern (1883–1945). Their work was followed by the so-called serial method of composition in which a limited series of sounds and rhythms are repeated in an increasingly complex manner. Masters of this style are Pierre Boulez and Karlheinz Stockhausen.

Apart from tonality, an important ingredient of music is rhythm. Beethoven used powerful, insistent rhythms, sometimes sounding almost primitive, to impress his ideas upon an audience. In his lifetime, complaints were made that his music was too loud. The nationalistic movement of later composers made use of the insistent rhythms of popular or folk music. This development of often disturbing rhythmic patterns reached its culmination in the early ballet music of Igor Stravinsky (1882–1970) and in the work of the Hungarians, Béla Bartók (1881–1945) with his strange new harmonies and Zoltán Kodály (1882–1967).

Thus in recent times, there has been much experimentation and innovation in the modes and rhythms of

equipment in relation to the members of the orchestra. Some music is orchestrated by the blending of several tape-recordings at different times and brought together only on the final master tape. Composers are even making music without the aid of performers at all, producing the sounds entirely electronically. The recording industry is concerned with the reproduction of orchestral concerts in the ordinary home and has produced various stereophonic systems to turn the living room into a concert hall.

The new technology has completely changed the economics of music-making. No large orchestra, or solo instrumentalist for that matter, can exist without the revenue from record sales. This wholesale distribution of recorded music has, on the whole, been entirely beneficial to musicians. It is comparable with the invention of printing in the fifteenth century when writers' ideas could be easily and cheaply dispersed around the world.

The availability of broadcast music and inexpensive recordings has rather increased attendance at concerts than otherwise. Nor has the home music-maker disappeared from the scene. Sales of instruments have never been higher. The invention of simple-to-play electronic instruments has awakened a new interest in family entertainment, and everywhere the music teacher flourishes.

In the search for new musical experiences, the past is being explored. Copies of long redundant instruments are being manufactured again, and music of the distant past is once again being heard on the instruments for which it was originally composed. The whole range of musical possibilities has never been wider nor more international. The East is hearing and enjoying the music of the West, and the traditional forms from the remotest corners of the globe are winning acceptance everywhere. It would be hard to imagine a modern civilised country without readily available music. In an increasingly noisy world, sounds pleasing to the ear have never been more needed.

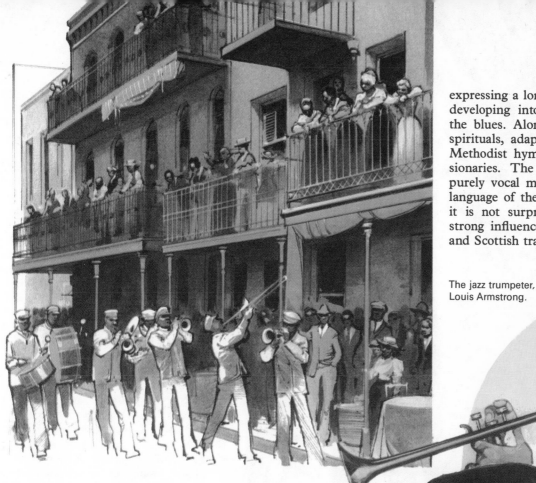

expressing a longing for freedom and developing into the style known as the blues. Alongside these were the spirituals, adapted directly from the Methodist hymns of the white missionaries. The language of all this purely vocal music was English, the language of the adoptive country, so it is not surprising that there is a strong influence from English, Irish and Scottish traditional ballads.

The jazz trumpeter, Louis Armstrong.

Musical accompaniment to a funeral procession in New Orleans.

modern music. In Germany, Paul Hindemith (1895–1963) had a large and varied output. In France, the Swiss Arthur Honegger (1892–1955) did much work for films, and Darius Milhaud (1892–1974) has worked on polytonal lines. In Britain and America, Arnold Bax (1883–1953) has introduced a Celtic influence, Ernest Bloch (1880–1959) used Jewish themes, Arthur Bliss has composed for unusual instrumental combinations, Aaron Copland has shown both Jewish and jazz influence, Edmund Rubbra has written five symphonies, concertos and choral works, William Walton has written sparingly but with high quality, Lennox Berkeley has made full use of a direct style and harmonic innovation, Samuel Barber has ranged over ballet, choral, orchestral, military and chamber music as well as songwriting, and Benjamin Britten has followed his own path to international reputation and influence.

stemming from a means of communication between field and field, gang and gang, in a special language and sing-song voice that would not be understood by the overseers. Worksongs helped the rhythm of the work itself and kept up the spirits of the workers. Similar to these were the ballads of the convict chain-gangs,

The singer
Billie Holliday.

Jazz and Ragtime
One dynamic form of music to emerge in the twentieth century is jazz. It has a mixed origin, yet its development has been confined almost exclusively to one country, the United States, and to one ethnic group, the American Negro. Its rhythmic basis certainly comes from Africa where the slaves of the southern states originated. Its vocal character was a new development from the slaves themselves,

The Glenn Miller Band

Elvis Presley

the hot tone. This includes an excess of vibrato and also a general thickening of the tone which has become a feature of jazz ever since.

Meanwhile, a new form of piano music had appeared, written in march-time but with the left hand always slightly behind or ahead of the right hand melody. This became known as ragged time which was soon shortened to ragtime. The great exponent of this kind of carefully composed music was

The Beatles

Bob Dylan

It is the vocal aspects of jazz that have this early connection with slavery and convict labour. When the slaves were freed after the American Civil War, there happened to be available a lot of cheap instruments from defunct military bands, mainly brass and woodwind. It was on these instruments that Negro musicians began to copy the vocal characteristics of the old slave songs. From this has come the particular distortion of the normal tones of the instruments, known as

One of the greatest figures in modern music, Igor Stravinsky, was the most cosmopolitan of composers. Born in Russia, he became successively a citizen of France and then of the United States. Much of his music bridges the gap between that of his more traditional contemporaries and modern experimental styles.

Scott Joplin whose work is under-going a present revival. Ragtime, however, was composed music, sub-ject to its own restrictions. It had a short period of popularity before the First World War, associated with a style of Negro dancing attempted also by whites. Jazz was based on a much freer mode of expression and, indeed, was not composed at all but extem-porised. Almost by definition, jazz is improvised by the soloist or group and only hardens into composition after continued playing. At this point it imposes a harmonic restriction upon the group as a whole, within which each instrument is allowed a passage of extemporisation.

Jazz in its classic form began in New Orleans with such great pioneers as Ferdinand La Menthe, known as Jelly Roll Morton, and Joe 'King' Oliver. When the places of entertain-ment were closed down by civil decree, the centre of jazz moved to Chicago. A commercialised version of jazz called swing emerged about 1935, largely from white and highly-trained musicians who formed the big bands of the period. The next generation, again led by black musicians, broke away with a form called bop or bebop which dispensed with the bar breaks and other rhythmic conventions, changed the basic harmonic chords and allowed the soloists greater free-dom of extemporisation. Bop relied heavily on the virtuoso ability of the soloist as exemplified by that genius of the alto sax, Charlie Parker.

Pop Music

Today, jazz has become a musician's music which has largely lost its audi-ence to the continually varied develop-ments of so-called pop music. Pop music is a highly commercialised form drawing on all the aspects of folk music, ballads, blues, hymn-tunes, even Eastern music, and depends for much of its success on the personality of the performer. It follows public taste and seems to have no discernible permanent trends. It makes full use of the possibilities of electronic re-cording and is open to almost any influence, though it has not as yet attracted a very high degree of musi-cianship. All branches of music, how-ever, continue to fertilise each other as never before. And technology, furthered by commercial interests, puts the modern composer in closer contact with the individual members of his audience in a new and exciting way.

The Dance

The material of music is sound, produced physically by vibrations of the air. The material of the dance is the human body and the physical movements produced by the muscles. The word dance comes from an old German word, *danson*, meaning to stretch. But it is not just the limbs that are stretched. Eye, head and finger movements are just as important. As man has learned to produce improved musical sounds by the design of instruments, so he has learned to enhance the expressive movements of the body with the aid of costume, make-up and scenery.

So closely related are music and dance that it is impossible to distinguish which aspects of each art came first. Perhaps the stamping of feet gave primitive man the idea for percussion instruments, or perhaps a foot-stamping dance was inspired by the rhythm of a drum. So much is dancing an expression of feeling that the desire to dance has been described as instinctive. Certainly, human beings are not the only animals to perform expressive movements. Many others produce movement patterns for purposes of display and communication, such as the courtship dances of birds. There are patterns even to inanimate objects such as crystals and ritual movements of the circling planets. Rhythm is a part of the bodily functions, as in the heartbeat, for example, or the regular need for sleep and food.

Primitive Dancing

Physical movement is affected by environment, so different kinds of dancing have tended to develop in different parts of the world. For instance, people who live in mountainous districts have long been herders of animals or hunters. They tend to develop a springing step with the weight on the toes, head held high to look up at the hillsides. Their dances thus tend to involve leaping. The plainsman, concerned with the cultivation of crops, has his attention directed more to the ground. His dances involve a heavier step with much stamping as though urging the earth to bring forth its riches. A popular form of dancing in the Bavarian mountains is called *ländler* and involves the throwing of partners high in the air. The Plains Indians of America gather in circles, looking down and stamping their feet, addressing the earth from which they believe all life springs.

Like early music, primitive dancing has an element of magic, of communication with the gods who determine mankind's success. Hunters dance in simulation of the hunt and of the animals who provide them with the necessities of life. By sympathetic magic, they hope that a dance will bring success in the hunt. Primitive farmers simulate the natural phenomena of sun and rain in the hope that the gods will provide these in their due season for the production of bumper

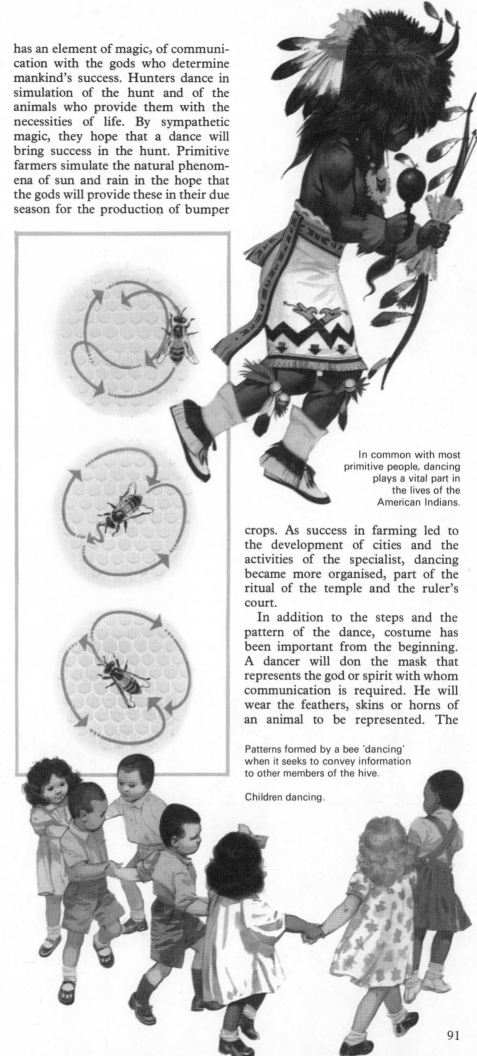

In common with most primitive people, dancing plays a vital part in the lives of the American Indians.

crops. As success in farming led to the development of cities and the activities of the specialist, dancing became more organised, part of the ritual of the temple and the ruler's court.

In addition to the steps and the pattern of the dance, costume has been important from the beginning. A dancer will don the mask that represents the god or spirit with whom communication is required. He will wear the feathers, skins or horns of an animal to be represented. The

Patterns formed by a bee 'dancing' when it seeks to convey information to other members of the hive.

Children dancing.

Medieval court dances were often stately affairs, not least because of the elaborate costumes in which they were performed.

local peculiarities of everyday dress affect the dance itself. Heavy clothes suggest slow dances, skirts can be whirled by spinning on the spot, even the shape and weight of weapons suggest the sort of arm movements to go into a war dance.

The Professional Dancer

Civilisation soon produced professional dancers. Temple priests used them to introduce ordinary people to the gods, to tell the imagined stories of the gods' beginnings. Dancers and musicians became a real link between people and the mystical authorities who ruled their lives. The telling of stories and the practice of the art of mime to express the details of the story must have been a very early development. From the beginning, also, there must have been an element of entertainment in such ritual performances. As rulers became more powerful and surrounded themselves with a leisured class of courtiers, they liked to display their power by maintaining troupes of dancers to entertain their guests. Though we shall never know exactly what the dances of early civilisations looked like, there are written descriptions to give us some inkling. Certainly we know that there were dances in a circle, the magical shape representing the continuity of life, foot-stamping dances as appeals to Mother Earth, and processional dances for marriages, funerals and other celebrations.

The rulers of ancient Egypt were priest-kings. They controlled temple dancers and dancers for entertainment. The richest of their subjects were allowed dancing as an entertainment only. We have some very graphic wall paintings showing dancers at private banquets. Similarly, the ancient Greeks used dancing as part of their religious ceremonial which led to the public displays by professional performers and the first specially built theatres in which to hold these performances. We have vase paintings showing us how acrobatic some of this Greek dancing became. But perhaps the oldest continuous dance tradition comes from India. It can be traced back through temple sculpture for some 2,000 years.

Hindu Dancing

The movements of modern Hindu dancing are derived from a book written by the ancient sage Bharata about the time of Christ. It is called Natya Sastra, the science of dancing. It is the only textbook of an art which is also a sacred book. Hindu dancing is perhaps the most completely organised of all forms. Every part of the body has its special movements which are learned and performed by full-time temple dancers. The Natya Sastra lists nine movements of the head, eight of the eyes, six of the eyebrows, four of the neck, and about 4,000 mudras or hand gestures. A mudra can imitate a physical object such as a bird in flight or the opening of a lotus bud, or it can express an emotion, such as fear, love, hate, surprise. A complex story can be told by means of body movements and hand gestures.

There are four distinct traditions of the dance in India. The oldest is the Bharata Natya of southern India, the style shown in temple sculpture and

The waltz had its origins in peasant dances of Europe but was transformed in the gay and glittering ballrooms of the 19th century.

The Village Dance,
after the painting by Rubens.

thought to have been performed only by women, the *devadasis* or professional temple dancers. In recent times, the style has been revived also by men. So expressive are the hand movements that it is possible to speak of dancing hands. Along the south-west coast of India, there developed a dance-drama called Kathakali. Billowing skirts are worn for this style of dancing. Three kinds of characters are involved, the heroic, the devilish and the virtuous, to enact the life-stories of gods and devils. Kathakali performances take place on stages in the open air. Originally only men took part, since the dances required great stamina, and elaborate make-up was worn. In northern India, there is the Kathak style of dancing, which belonged to court entertainment, though including stories of the gods. It is associated with the Moslem conquerors of the north-west, who used dancing more for entertainment than religious purposes. From the northeast, comes the distinctive style of the Manipur district, telling the legends of the god Krishna. It is said that the land of Manipur was created as a dance floor for the gods, and the area is rich in folk dances.

The Indian civilisations moved into south-east Asia and the Buddhist missionaries travelled into China and Japan. The Chinese Lion Dance derives from India, as do the Bugaku masks and dances of Japan. The make-up of the actor in the Chinese theatre stems from Indian Kathakali dance-drama. Though hand gestures are not as highly developed in the Far East as in India, a Chinese actor needs to be an acrobatic dancer, and the Japanese use of the fan as an expressive instrument is similar to the Indian mudra.

Dance-drama

The dance-drama of the ancient Greeks was borrowed by the Romans to overcome the language difficulties inherent in a vast empire. But Roman mime-dances were never much more than fillers between the main spectacles of the arena. With the acceptance of Christianity, authority tended to frown on dancing for the debased art it had become. Yet the Christian Church adopted pagan dances into its own ritual. One form of Greek religion had preached the idea of an after-life and had used a circular dance at funerals to lead the dead spirit into the other world. Early Christians believed that throngs of angels would lead the dead into the presence of God whom they worshipped with dances in a ring. Dancing in church was intended to follow the heavenly rings of the angels. Dancing was also introduced into religious processions. But much of the dancing in churches and churchyards had a pagan origin, and such occasions as the sixth-century Festival of Fools were a curious mixture of Christian and pagan ceremony.

Meanwhile, people continued to dance purely for joy. The medieval village green was the ballroom of its time. Ancient ring-dances became the medieval carole or branle, which in turn became the eighteenth-century

Traditional Morris sword dance.

Vaslav
Nijinsky as
the slave
in the ballet
Scheherazade.

cotillon and quadrille, and eventually the square dance still enjoyed today. Such village dances were often wild affairs, much as dancing to rock music became in our own day. The ruling classes, on the other hand, developed a strict code of etiquette derived from the old codes of chivalry. The dress of the nobles was not, in any case, suited to wild prancings. Women wore long trains, and men often had very long shoes with pointed toes. A more courtly style of dancing for pleasure thus developed, beginning in the twelfth-century castles of France.

As fashions changed, dances changed with them. A book of the sixteenth century, written to teach dancing, described the stately pavane and the lively galliard together with the more intimate volta, ancestor of the waltz. Later still, revolutionary fervour swept away the idle ruling classes. In place of the courtly gavotte and minuet, the people danced the carmagnole around the guillotine itself. The new freedom is perhaps expressed most notably in the waltz. When it became the rage of Vienna, it was danced as much by the parlour-maid as the great lady at court. Rivalling the waltz in other countries were the equally freedom-expressing polka from Central Europe, czardas from Hungary, tarantella from Italy, gopak from Russia and flamenco from Spain. Ballrooms were built to accommodate them and composers produced a flood of music to go with them.

Meanwhile, the freed slaves of America were beginning to introduce their music and dances to a wider public. American Negro dances were not designed for huge ballrooms, but to be performed in small areas. From them, we have inherited the close dancing of the private house or the cellar discotheque. After the First World War, the waltz and the polka were superseded by the Bunny Hug, the Cakewalk, the Black Bottom and the Charleston. In our own times, we have had the jitterbug, the twist and the frug. Modern dancing has derived from the most primitive forms, with the rhythms of the jungle invading the dance halls of civilised society.

Masques and Court Dances

Alongside dancing for enjoyment were the professional entertainers. Travelling juggler-acrobats were often skilled both in the playing of musical instruments and dancing to the music of others. Such performers entertained the townsfolk for the small coins dropped into their collecting boxes. The modern equivalent, the buskers of today's city streets, are pale versions of their medieval ancestors. The wealthy ruling classes could afford something better, spectacles to enliven a banquet. The dancing involved in such masques eventually blossomed into ballet, a word which comes from the Italian *balletti*, court dance displays. A notable early ballet production in France celebrated the betrothal of Margaret of Lorraine to the Duc de Joyeuse in 1581. It was based on the Greek legend of Ulysses and was designed by an Italian violinist, Baldassarino Belgiojoso. Such expensively mounted productions were often danced and designed by the courtiers themselves. Louis XIV appeared in court ballets to dance the principal role.

Cardinal Richelieu built the first

Serge Diaghilev (above left).

Anna Pavlova in three
poses from *The Dying Swan*.

94

theatre in France in 1636. It was not long before courtly entertainments began to move into theatres specially built for them. The introduction of a raised stage made a considerable difference to the style of ballet dancing. The whole figure of the dancer, down to the feet, could be clearly seen by the audience. The lively leaps and expressive gestures of solo dancers replaced the stately gliding of the courtly spectacle. Skilled dancers and ballet masters appeared and only professional and practised performers could reach the required standard.

The earliest ballets have been forgotten, but in 1701 Raoul Feuillet's *Choreographie* or *The art of how to write down a dance* appeared. Since then several systems of ballet notation have been devised. The choreography of a past ballet master can be preserved for future dancers to copy or adapt. Though ballet began in France, the teacher who perfected classical ballet was the Italian Carlo Blasis (born 1797). To begin with, boys had played the female roles, but now the ballerina became even more important than the male dancer. The first ballets were based on classical legend from ancient Greece or Rome. The Romantic period in music coincided with ballets based on folk tales. Greek and Roman gods were replaced by sylphs and fairies from northern folklore. Dancers of the earlier ballets were encumbered by heavy clothing. The ballerinas of the nineteenth century began to wear looser and lighter costumes. Marie Camargo (1710–70) was the first to raise the hem of her skirt and to remove the heels of her shoes. This led to the short skirt called the tutu and to the blocked shoes of today.

Russian Ballet

It was the introduction of French and Italian ballet to Russia that eventually produced the lively dancing we know today. Dancers who were serfs were employed at the court of Catherine the Great. Later, the Imperial Russian Ballet was founded. Its serf dancers were granted their freedom fifty years before the farm-workers achieved theirs. It was these dancers who introduced the vitality of Russian folk dances into ballet. The form was later perfected in other countries: by Marius Petipa (1822–1910) in France, by Christian Johannsen (1817–1903) in Sweden and by Enrico Cecchetti (1850–1928) in Italy. But it was again a Russian, exiled in Paris, who brought all the elements of ballet together and popularised it in the capitals of Europe.

His name was Serge Diaghilev (1872–1929), and he built up a team of dancers, composers, painters and poets such as had not appeared since the days of court ballets and the theatre of Molière. With his Ballets Russes, he toured the world. His most famous male dancer was Vaslav Nijinsky. Artists like Léon Bakst and Pablo Picasso created costumes and

scenery. Igor Stravinsky wrote music for the company. Poets and writers suggested themes from the Arabian Nights, from folklore and from pagan rites. Thanks largely to Diaghilev, modern ballet has experimented with many story themes, with new kinds of music, with exciting stage designs and costumes. No ballet company is now complete without the varied talents of the sort of team he gathered around the Ballets Russes.

Musicals

Music, dance, stage design and story have all combined to make ballet the varied art it is today. The same ingredients have gone into the sort of production that borrows a little from ballet, but is a form of theatre all its own: the stage musical. This has perhaps reached its most elaborate style in films. It is the cinema that has greatly popularised dancing and most often introduces new styles to

A good performance in the theatre depends on many hours of arduous practice in the class room.

the world. Now television has joined in to present also live performance. Though the sheer fun of dancing will remain as a popular pastime and the folk dance tradition will continue, dancing is now firmly in the hands of the professional impresario, choreographer, designer and performer. The commercial exploitation of these skills will keep it firmly in the forefront of popular entertainment.

Drama and the Theatre

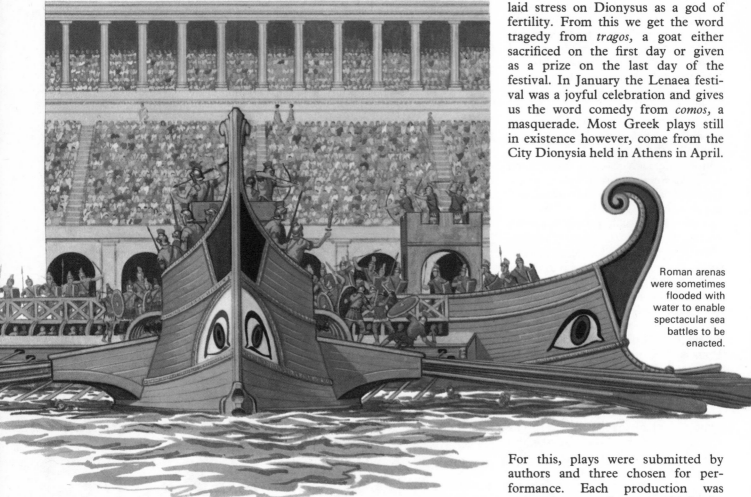

laid stress on Dionysus as a god of fertility. From this we get the word tragedy from *tragos,* a goat either sacrificed on the first day or given as a prize on the last day of the festival. In January the Lenaea festival was a joyful celebration and gives us the word comedy from *comos,* a masquerade. Most Greek plays still in existence however, come from the City Dionysia held in Athens in April.

Roman arenas were sometimes flooded with water to enable spectacular sea battles to be enacted.

Theatrical drama, as we understand it today, requires three components. First, there must be an actor or actors speaking or singing lines independently of any chorus. Second, there must be some dramatic conflict between actors or between a single actor and a chorus. The word conflict here is used to describe a variety of relationships. The two sides may be enemies, they may be friends with a difference of opinion or personality between them, they may be of opposite sex or have other physical differences such as fat and thin, tall and short, clever and stupid, or they may be divided only by misunderstanding. Third, and just as important as the other two components, there must be an audience emotionally involved in the progress of the drama.

The first theatrical performances to fulfil these requirements took place in ancient Greece. Other civilisations had had religious or social ceremonies that were also entertainments, but they were not true theatre. They were events taking place at the particular moment and not recreations of past or fictional events. Indeed, the Greek drama developed from the dithyramb or unison hymn sung before the altar to Dionysus, god of wine and the good life. But it did not become true theatre until its scope was widened to include stories of the other gods and actors to represent them.

The first actor known to us was called Thespis. He was the leader of a dithyrambic chorus who is said to have travelled from his birthplace, Icaria, with a cart that carried all his belongings and could be turned into an improvised stage for performances en route. He arrived in Athens and became the first recorded man to win a prize at the newly founded drama festival known as the City Dionysia. He is also thought to be the first to separate himself from the chorus for the purpose of creating a dialogue with it. He was the first professional performer to dare the impersonation of a god, a role hitherto reserved to priests or kings.

Greek Festivals

In the fifth century B.C. there were three yearly festivals in Greece. The Rural Dionysia, held in the winter, For this, plays were submitted by authors and three chosen for performance. Each production was assigned a cast of actors paid for by the state and a patron called *choregus,* a wealthy citizen who paid all the other expenses. The author was producer, composer of the music, arranger of the dances, and often played the principal part himself.

Though little remains of the earliest Greek theatres, it would seem that they were usually built in a natural bowl in a hillside and close to a temple. As they developed, they consisted of a circular, flat area called the *orchestra* with an altar to the god in the centre. In front of this, the hillside was fitted with tiers of seats in a horseshoe shape, those closest to the orchestra being more elaborate to accommodate priests, rulers and patrons. Behind the orchestra, there was a raised stage with a central entrance and two side entrances leading into buildings used as changing rooms, stores for stage properties and to conceal any stage machinery. The main piece of stage machinery was a crane by which an actor representing the god could be lowered as though descending from heaven to interfere with the affairs of the mortals. There was no scenery as we know it today, but on either side of the stage were the *periaktoi*, triangular prisms that could be revolved to display a drawing of a tree, an architectural column or water to establish the locale of the scene. There were also wheeled carts that could be drawn on with a prearranged tableau at certain moments, and concealed machinery for producing sound effects like thunder.

The chorus usually entered on either side through gaps between the horseshoe of seats and the stage itself. They would be dressed alike to represent soldiers or citizens, and even animals. The musicians would sit throughout around the central altar. The actors would more often perform from the stage which gave them added height for a clear view by the audience. They were dressed in elaborate robes, with thick-soled boots and tall head-dresses to give them extra height and dignity. They wore masks representative of the basic emotions, hate, fear, love and so on, which the particular character was meant to convey. Comic actors wore lighter clothing and masks since they were expected to be acrobatic.

The First Dramatists
The first great dramatist whose plays survive was Aeschylus (525–456 B.C.).

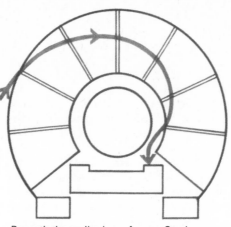

Beneath the auditorium of some Greek theatres there ran a tunnel through which large stones were rolled to create the effect of thunder.

Seven of his 80 or 90 plays with several fragments still exist. They illustrate the early development of dramatic productions. The earliest has a chorus of fifty and only one actor. Later, the chorus was reduced to twelve, and a second and eventually a third actor introduced. His *Oresteia* is the only example of a Greek drama trilogy that has survived in its entirety. The first part, dealing with the murder of Agamemnon by his wife Clytemnestra, is still performed in modern translation.

Younger than Aeschylus was Sophocles (496–406 B.C.) whose plays lack the fine verse and grandeur of the older man, but are more complex in plot, characterisation and subtleties of human relationships. He increased the chorus to fifteen, but integrated

song and dance less into the dramatic action. Notable among his plays and still performed are *Antigone* and *Electra*. Sophocles was followed by Euripides (484–406 B.C.) author of *Medea, Hippolytus* and *Cyclops* among others. He invented the prologue to set the situation at the opening of the play and gave even less importance to the chorus as plays became more realistic. The great Greek writer of comedies was Aristophanes (448–380 B.C.) whose plays are named after the disguises assumed by the chorus in each of them: *Frogs, Birds, Wasps, Knights* and *Clouds*. His topical jokes are difficult for modern audiences to understand, but his plays are still performed, perhaps with some modern adaptation, for their earthy vitality. Finally, Menander (342–292 B.C.) was a writer of the comedy of manners based on contemporary urban life. His plays were polite, inoffensive, superficially realistic and had no place for a chorus.

Roman Theatre
The New Comedy of Menander was the sort of drama found in Greece by the expanding Roman Empire. It influenced the work of the Roman playwrights Plautus (254–184 B.C.) and Terence (190–159 B.C.). Plautus adapted many Greek plays, transferring the action to Rome and introducing aspects of Roman life. He made use of stock characters such as

Reconstruction of a Greek amphitheatre during the performance of a play.

An entertainer since medieval days, the court jester wore a chequered costume.

Mr Punch, the hero of the puppet play 'Punch and Judy' originated in the *commedia dell'arte* character Punchinello.

the braggart soldier, the miser, the idler, identical twins and the ever-present bullied but cunning slave. Terence, though a freed slave from Africa, had been better educated by his old master and showed greater originality. But comedies languished in popularity among the Romans who were more interested in gladiatorial contests and what we would now look upon as circus performances.

At the beginning of the Roman era, theatres were built in all parts of the empire, but they were not like the ancient Greek theatres. Open to the sky, they were surrounded by a high wall of highly decorated masonry and, with the disappearance of the chorus, there was no need for the circular area of the orchestra. The stage was backed by a permanent architectural feature, the *frons scaenae*, often two storeys high and broken by three entrances and window openings. In front of this was a curtain that disappeared into a trough in the floor. Tiers of benches for the audience were ranged across an auditorium with awnings to protect them from the weather. There were stalls for fruit-sellers and showers of perfumed water for hot days. It was, however, the spectacles of the arena that won in popularity during the latter days of Roman power. As the cinemas of our own day have become bingo halls and bowling alleys, so the Roman theatres ended their useful time as supermarkets.

Medieval Drama

The closing of the theatres did not result in the disappearance of the professional entertainer. He merely took to the road or 'went on tour' in the modern theatrical phrase. Comic actors already had the skills of the

17th-century pageant cart from Brussels.

juggler, acrobat, dancer and mimic. Professionals with a literary or musical skill became balladeers and story-tellers. Some even took to animal training. The best of them earned a good living performing in the halls of the rich and powerful. Others entertained the village folk and passed around a collecting cup. The Dark Ages that followed the collapse of the Roman Empire were not short of light entertainment.

Meanwhile, the Christian Church saw the value of the entertaining arts as a means of attracting people to their congregations and of putting over their message. They had a huge fund of good stories from the Bible. At first, the priests played the principal roles in the Bible plays that spread throughout Europe. Soon capable amateurs from the congregation were given a chance to take part. In each area, the stories of Biblical characters or the lives of the saints took on a local character. Laughter was a powerful weapon to deride the ambitions of Satan and his attendant devils. Their parts were taken by comic actors, some of them professional acrobats, jugglers and dancers. The theatre used for these performances was, of course, the church itself. So popular did they become that even the largest cathedrals could not accommodate the available audiences. The performances moved out, first into the churchyard and then to the village greens and town squares.

Such success defeated the original object. Liturgical drama was keeping

98

people out of the church. The clergy began to frown on it and refused to be involved. But the people were not to be deprived of their entertainment. They organised it for themselves. Fit-up stages could be quickly erected on a village green, but there were problems with the scene changes. The solution was to have each scene set up on its own stage. To begin with a number of stages were strung out in a line or set up in a circle, with each scene enacted in turn, often with the audience moving from one stage to

the next. These stages became known as 'houses'. Certain groups got together to produce their own playlet in the house they had built for themselves. These groups were often formed from the trades guilds of the time. The shipwrights, for instance, would specialise in the story of Noah and the building of the Ark. Eventually, the houses were put on wheels and dragged through the town. Audiences would wait at convenient corners for the pageant carts to arrive, one by one, pause to enact their scene and move on to the next audience.

Mystery and Miracle Plays

Theatre of this kind was not as primitive as might be supposed. Specialisation led to great elaboration. The production of a particular town would take place, usually at Easter, sometimes every year but often at intervals of several years. In the intervening period, there would be plenty of time

to prepare the next production. There was great rivalry between the different groups involved. Since they were mostly artisans from the trades guilds, the trades unions of the time, they had many skills to call upon. They devised elaborate stage machinery to produce their effects. Hell's Mouth was a popular scene, with fire and smoke emerging as Satan and his minions thrust the damned souls into it. One such production at Mons in 1501 took seventeen men to work the machinery for this scene alone. The houses had trapdoors in the floor and often were built to the height of

The Norwich dragon, a traditional part of English municipal pageantry in the Middle Ages.

several storeys with cranes for a flying ballet of angels.

Nor were the plays themselves badly written. Individual towns would be noted for their cycles of plays, and as the years went by, the regular addition of improvements built up to a work of art which was magnificently staged and dressed. Alongside religious drama, the Mystery and Miracle plays, there was also the play of ordinary vice and virtue, the Morality play such as the story of *Everyman*. Nor was purely secular drama ignored, much of it dating back to pagan times. Such are the Maytime festivals, the Mumming plays and the Feasts of

Fools. Troupes of full-time, professional actors moved from town to town to join in the general celebrations.

The Proscenium

All this theatrical endeavour was bound eventually to create the need for a more permanent place where the actor could feel at home, where stage machinery could be permanently installed and where an audience could be assembled. The Renaissance began in Italy, and much of it was concerned with the rediscovery of the ancient arts of Greece and Rome. Italian architects designed theatres in what they

Elizabethan travelling theatre.

supposed to be an ancient Roman style. An auditorium with a horseshoe of seats faced a platform stage with an architectural background. This consisted of entrances and windows rather like the *frons scaenae* of the Romans. But it was also a straight row of houses, each one labelled, obviously based on the medieval open-air theatre.

99

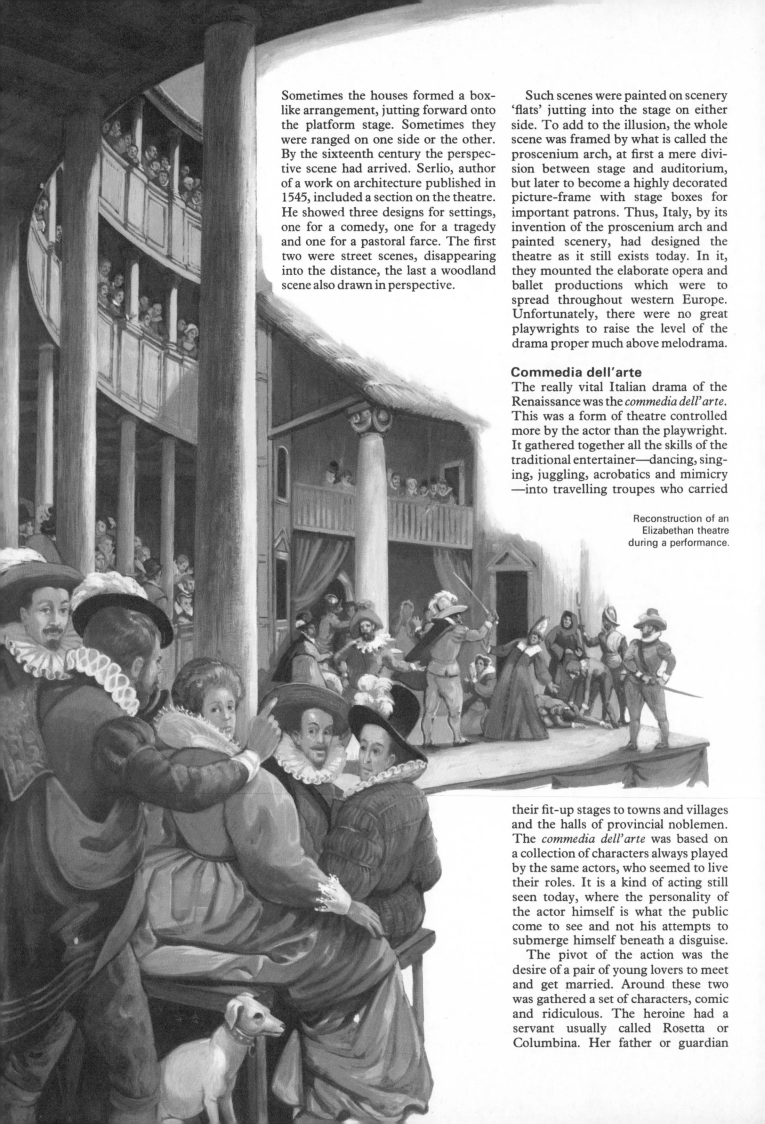

Sometimes the houses formed a box-like arrangement, jutting forward onto the platform stage. Sometimes they were ranged on one side or the other. By the sixteenth century the perspective scene had arrived. Serlio, author of a work on architecture published in 1545, included a section on the theatre. He showed three designs for settings, one for a comedy, one for a tragedy and one for a pastoral farce. The first two were street scenes, disappearing into the distance, the last a woodland scene also drawn in perspective.

Such scenes were painted on scenery 'flats' jutting into the stage on either side. To add to the illusion, the whole scene was framed by what is called the proscenium arch, at first a mere division between stage and auditorium, but later to become a highly decorated picture-frame with stage boxes for important patrons. Thus, Italy, by its invention of the proscenium arch and painted scenery, had designed the theatre as it still exists today. In it, they mounted the elaborate opera and ballet productions which were to spread throughout western Europe. Unfortunately, there were no great playwrights to raise the level of the drama proper much above melodrama.

Commedia dell'arte
The really vital Italian drama of the Renaissance was the *commedia dell'arte*. This was a form of theatre controlled more by the actor than the playwright. It gathered together all the skills of the traditional entertainer—dancing, singing, juggling, acrobatics and mimicry—into travelling troupes who carried

Reconstruction of an Elizabethan theatre during a performance.

their fit-up stages to towns and villages and the halls of provincial noblemen. The *commedia dell'arte* was based on a collection of characters always played by the same actors, who seemed to live their roles. It is a kind of acting still seen today, where the personality of the actor himself is what the public come to see and not his attempts to submerge himself beneath a disguise.

The pivot of the action was the desire of a pair of young lovers to meet and get married. Around these two was gathered a set of characters, comic and ridiculous. The heroine had a servant usually called Rosetta or Columbina. Her father or guardian was a ridiculous old man called Pantalone with an elderly friend called Graziano. There was also often a braggart soldier called Il Capitano. Around these was a troupe of clowns or *zanni* playing the roles of servants and with a particular skill as a tumbler, juggler, singer, musician and so on. Servants were usually more intelligent or at least more cunning than their masters, a fact that delighted a mainly working-class audience. Actors adopted standard names for their roles which became instantly recognisable to the audience. Among them were Arlecchino, Pulcinella, Perdolina Scapino, Mezzetino, Scaramuccia and Brighella. From them, we get the romantic figures of Harlequin and Columbine, the Pierrots of the seaside concert party, and the Punch and Judy of puppet shows.

William Shakespeare
Italy founded the modern theatre, yet the first modern playwright of genius was an Englishman, William Shakespeare (1564–1616). The first

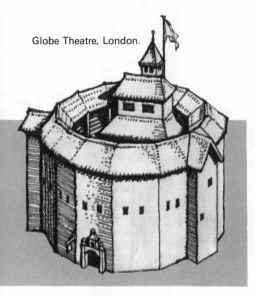

Globe Theatre, London.

English Renaissance play was *Ralph Roister Doister*, written by a schoolmaster, Nicholas Udall (1504–56) for performance by his pupils. The beginning of modern drama in England was mainly amateur. But rich men employed entertainers in their households, and it was from these that the professional English actor emerged. Actors first began performing to the public in inn-yards which, with their surrounding galleries and architectural background, formed a reasonable facsimile of an Italian playhouse.

The first permanent theatre was built by a carpenter and part-time actor called James Burbage (d. 1597).

It was simply called the Theatre and, because of the restrictions in the city of London, it was built outside in Finsbury Fields. Burbage's son Richard (1567–1619) became the country's first leading actor. Other theatres, the Curtain, Rose, Swan, Globe, Fortune and Hope followed. Some

of these were built by a shrewd businessman, Philip Henslowe, (d. 1616), whose stepdaughter married the other outstanding actor of the time Edward Alleyn (1566–1626).

The Elizabethan theatre was an enclosed auditorium open to the sky with a central area for a standing audience. Galleries round the sides provided seats for richer patrons. The stage jutted out into the auditorium and was backed by an architectural set piece with entrances, an inner chamber that could be curtained off and a gallery above. The stage was covered by a canopy painted with stars and called the 'heavens'. There

was a tower to accommodate stage machinery and from which a flag flew when a performance was in progress and a trumpeter summoned the audience.

Elizabethan Theatre
The companies of actors appearing in these theatres, of which Shakespeare was one, were employed by rich noblemen. Shakespeare and Burbage belonged to the Lord Chamberlain's Men, Alleyn to the Admiral's. There were no actresses, young women's parts being played by boys apprenticed to older actors, older women's parts taken by the company's clowns, of whom William Kemp (d. 1603) and Richard Tarleton (d. 1588) are famous examples. All the actors were expected to be musicians and dancers, and a jig, comprising dancing and a sung dialogue, was a feature of every performance.

Poetic drama, based on lines in iambic pentameters, was introduced by Christopher Marlowe (1564–93) who might have achieved as much as

Two designs by Inigo Jones (1573–1652), the English stage designer and architect. It is said that he introduced movable scenery to the English stage.

Shakespeare if he had not been killed in a duel. Another influence on Shakespeare was the work of Thomas Kyd (1558–94), author of *The Spanish Tragedy*. An author who used more classical themes and wrote for the educated audiences of the indoor Blackfriars theatre was Ben Jonson (1572–1637). The choirboys of St Paul's and the Chapel Royal appeared at Blackfriars and in an earlier theatre nearby where their playwright was John Lyly (1554–1606).

Jonson also wrote for the Court Masques which became popular in the seventeenth century, but gave it up because he disliked competing with the scenery and music. These Court productions introduced the Italian theatre to England, with the proscenium arch and painted scenery. Inigo Jones (1573–1652), the architect, had travelled extensively in Italy and became a successful designer of masques. Many of his designs are still in existence and closely resemble the work of Serlio.

The English theatre declined after the death of Shakespeare. The collaborators Beaumont (*c.* 1584–1616) and Fletcher (1579–1625) turned high tragedy and low comedy into a less vital romanticism. A final flicker came from John Webster's (*c.* 1580–*c.* 1625) *The White Devil* and *The Duchess of Malfi*, with their passionate poetry and realistic staging. Then the Civil War closed the theatres for eighteen years.

Spain and France

The development of modern theatre in Spain followed much the same progress as it had in England. The first companies of professional actors played in noblemen's halls or in the space between buildings, called a *corral*, similar to the inn-yards of England. The first theatre buildings in Spain resembled these *corrales* and were open to the sky. Later Italian influence produced roofed-in theatres with proscenium arch and painted scenery. The first notable figure in Spanish theatre was Lope de Rueda (*c.* 1510–65), an actor-manager who controlled a touring company and wrote a number of short farces or *pasos* to be played in the intervals between the acts of more serious dramas.

The great Spanish author of *Don Quixote*, Miguel de Cervantes (1547–1616), wrote a number of plays, but Spain's first great dramatist was Lope

A performance of one of Molière's comedies before his patron King Louis XIV, who is seated in the position of honour directly in front of the stage. Molière is the greatest figure in the history of the French theatre.

interpreted by Mlle Champmeslé, the first great leading lady of the *Comédie Française*. Racine was so severely attacked by a clique of critics and publicists for being a second-rate playwright that he gave up writing for the theatre, his last works being written for the convent school of St Cyr founded by Mme de Maintenon for the daughters of impoverished noblemen.

Molière
The greatest figure of the French theatre, however, is undoubtedly Jean-Baptiste Poquelin (1622–73), known by his stage name of Molière. He was educated at a Jesuit college and may have taken part in the theatrical productions for which such schools were famous. Early in life, he became friendly with a family of actors called Béjart. At 21, he gave up his law studies and appeared with the Béjarts in a production in a converted tennis court in Paris. The indoor courts in which the game of real tennis was played were particularly suited to theatrical productions, but the *L'Illustre-Théâtre* of the Béjarts was not a commercial success. They retired into the provinces, taking Molière with them. For the next thirteen years, he lived the life of an itinerant actor in French plays based on *commedia dell'arte* originals, many of them adapted by himself.

At last, Molière got his big 'break' on the 24th October 1658 when his company appeared at the Court of Louis XIV at the Louvre. The tragedy they first performed was not well received. But then the company performed one of Molière's own comedies, since lost, which was a great success. From then on, the company settled in Paris, sharing a theatre with a *commedia dell'arte* troupe from Italy. To begin with, Molière's company paid a rent to the Italians, but their success was so great that the Italians were soon paying rent to Molière's company. For the next fifteen years until his death in 1673 at the age of fifty-one, Molière's position was assured.

Molière was a writer of comedies which, in translation, lose something of the contemporary spirit of the original. Titles include *The School for Husbands* and *The School for Wives*, *The Enforced Marriage*, *Love as a Doctor*, *The Miser*, *The Bourgeois Gentleman* and *The Imagined Invalid*. Such titles indicate how he pilloried some of the more ridiculous aspects of his own society. With them, he raised the level of comedy to that of the

Corneille
In its concern with *pundonor*, the point of honour whereby morality is treated on a black or white basis with human behaviour being either wholly good or wholly bad, Spanish drama was to influence the first great French playwright, Pierre Corneille (1606–84). From the production in 1637 of Corneille's *Le Cid*, based on the life of Spain's national hero, the beginning of modern French theatre can be dated. Early French theatre was much influenced by visiting troupes of Italian *commedia dell'arte*. The first theatre buildings in Paris, however, were never open to the sky and had stage-lighting by candles from the beginning. The first troupes of professional players also included actresses, an innovation not found in England until the Restoration. These companies soon gave the stock characters of *commedia dell'arte* a distinctively French flavour. The standard of acting was high and quite able to cope with the high drama of Corneille when he appeared.

Corneille was a native of Rouen and first wrote for a travelling company who arrived in that town. He later moved to Paris where *Le Cid* established him as the leading dramatist. Among his other works are *Le Menteur*, a comedy based on a Spanish original, about a compulsive liar who is not believed when he tells the truth, and *Andromède*, a spectacle with a mythological theme written to exploit the Italian scenery and stage machinery introduced into the Paris theatre.

In his later years, Corneille was rivalled by Jean Racine (1639–99) who wrote nine great tragedies, including *Phèdre*, *Bérénice* and *Britannicus*. His works are noted for the great lyric beauty of the dialogue, their psychological depth and tightly woven plots. Many of his female roles were first

de Vega (1562–1635). He is supposed to have written some 1,200 plays of which about 750 survive. His plays cover many subjects, but are usually concerned with an ideal Christian society, with the triumph of good over evil, virtue over vice. In *The Sheepfold*, he wrote perhaps the first play concerned with class warfare, with the theme of a villagers' revolt against a brutal overlord. His successor, Pedro Calderón (1600–81), has left some 200 plays, also concerned with morality and with the concept of honour. At the Coliseo theatre, opened in 1640, he produced plays based on myth and legend intended for lavish production in the Italian style.

greatest tragedies and was himself a link between the two great tragic dramatists of French literature. He first appeared in Paris as an actor in Corneille's *Nicomède* and put on in his own theatre Racine's first play. He was the complete man of the theatre, managing a company, acting in and writing plays. He died a few hours after appearing in one of his own plays, *The Imagined Invalid*, on the stage of the Palais-Royal. He was responsible for many lavish entertainments at the Palace of Versailles and for plays produced at Court. His death was followed by some decline in the brilliance of French drama. But his company was carried on by his widow and her second husband. Eventually, Louis XIV amalgamated it with two other companies to create the *Comédie Française*, France's national theatre. Its second name, in honour of a great pioneer, is *La Maison de Molière*.

English Restoration

When in 1660 Charles II was restored to the British throne, he gave Royal Patents to Thomas Killigrew (1612–83) and William Davenant (1606–68) to restore the British theatre. These Patents are still in force, one belonging to the Drury Lane Theatre which now stands near the site where Killigrew built his first Theatre Royal in 1663, the other inherited by the Royal Opera House, Covent Garden, from Davenant's Duke's House and his later Dorset Garden Theatre. The first Restoration theatres had an apron-stage protruding from behind a proscenium arch with an opening into a music gallery above it. The proscenium framed painted

David Garrick as Hamlet.

Nell Gwynne, English actress and friend of Charles II.

flats with shutters running in grooves in place of the previous solid back wall. On either side of the proscenium were up to three Doors of Entrance leading directly on to the apron-stage.

For the first time, actresses appeared on the English stage. They were untrained and seemed to emerge from nowhere, but they took the public by storm. Towards the end of the seventeenth century a new style of satiric comedy also blossomed in the works of Etherege, Wycherley, Congreve, Vanbrugh and Farquhar. Congreve's *Way of the World* stands well alongside any intellectual comedy from any writer of the time. Mrs Aphra Behn became the first woman in the world to earn her living as a playwright. The leading actor of the time was Thomas Betterton. The leading actresses were Mrs Barry in tragedy and Mrs Bracegirdle in comedy. From the *commedia dell'arte*, Harlequin was adapted to popular characters of the day, such as Harlequin Doctor Faustus and Harlequin Jack Sheppard, beginning a tradition that was to continue in that thoroughly English entertainment, the Christmas pantomime.

Stock Companies

New theatres began to be built early in the eighteenth century, both in London and the provinces, and lighting became a more important feature of the productions in them. Plays began to match the public taste for

sentiment and pathos. Provincial companies appeared, touring repertoires of plays from one town to another within limited areas which soon developed into circuits. Such were the Tate Wilkinson stock company of York and the Sarah Baker company of Kent. These stock companies provided fine training grounds for young actors and actresses before they appeared in London. Though this was a poor period for plays, it produced some great acting talent. David Garrick (1717–79), who had his training in the Ipswich circuit, changed the English acting style to one of greater freedom of movement and natural speech as opposed to the stiffly standing declamation of former times. His great rival was Charles Macklin (1697–1797) who first played Shakespeare's Shylock as a believable and pathetic figure instead of a snivelling clown. Leading actresses of the eighteenth century were Kitty Clive and Peg Woffington, the latter appearing in young men's parts.

Garrick was actor-manager at Drury Lane Theatre. He was succeeded as manager by the playwright Richard Brinsley Sheridan (1751–1816) who was also a politician. The plays of Sheridan and Oliver Goldsmith (1728–74) were written in revolt against the sentimental theatre of their times. Goldsmith's *She Stoops to Conquer* revives Elizabethan styles, and Sheridan's *The School for Scandal* and *The*

Rivals go back to Congreve and Restoration comedy. All three are still revived in modern times. Sheridan also wrote the first pantomime of *Robinson Crusoe*.

Germany and France

In Germany, the medieval style of theatre lingered on longer than elsewhere in Europe. The guilds of Mastersingers took over the production of much secular drama. Hans

Sachs, famous for his appearance in Wagner's opera, *Die Meistersinger von Nürnbĕrg*, was a cobbler by trade who wrote many comedies and tragedies and short Carnival plays to be presented on an improvised stage in an abandoned Nuremberg church. He trained his own actors and produced the plays with the simplest of costumes. He was active in the 1550s and died in 1576.

The next impact on German theatre was made by groups of strolling players from England. Their performances were full of action with some *commedia dell'arte* acrobatics, and they were a useful antidote to the wordiness of much native drama. They led eventually to the popularity of a kind of melodrama full of dark deeds in high places called *Haupt-und Staatsaktionen*. Early in the eighteenth century, attempts were made to introduce a more serious drama, especially by Germany's first leading actress and theatre manageress, Carolina Neuber (1697–1760). She produced the first comedies of Gotthold Lessing (1729–81) who also worked as a dramatic critic and was involved in the first attempt to establish a national theatre in Hamburg.

Though the Hamburg venture was a failure, the company introduced a more natural style of acting and produced, among others, the actor Friedrich Schröder who introduced Shakespeare in translation and produced

work by the ageing Lessing and the first play by the young Johann Wolfgang Goethe (1749–1832). Schröder moved to the Vienna Burgtheater where Joseph II was creating a national home for serious drama. Schröder trained Johann Brockmann, the leading actor at the Burgtheater.

Goethe and Schiller

It was Goethe, however, with his plays influenced by Shakespeare and by French dramatic literature who began a trend to be followed by all young German dramatists, especially Friedrich Schiller (1759–1805). For a time, Goethe and Schiller shared the management of the Court Theatre at Weimar. Goethe was a poet, novelist, dramatist and actor and carried on scientific research. His most famous work is *Faust* which has been performed in its entirety, though its breadth of conception is really too great for the ordinary playhouse.

Elaborate effects using ingenious stage machinery were popular in the 18th-century theatre.

Schiller was a poet, philosopher and dramatist whose works for the stage include *The Robbers*, *Wallenstein*, *Maria Stuart* and *Wilhelm Tell*.

The early nineteenth century was to see a decline in the literary standards of the German theatre. In standards of production, in acting, scenery, costume, music and stage effects, however, it had come a long way and found its national heritage.

In France, meanwhile, the *Comédie Française* had become too hemmed in by tradition. Tragedy sank to melodrama, and comedy to contemporary trivialities. The Italian company, inheritors of the *commedia dell'arte* tradition, received permission to perform in French. They evolved a new technique combining Italian improvisation with French elegance and wit. These were exemplified in the production of plays by Pierre Marivaux (1688–1763). Marivaux retained the *commedia dell'arte* tradition of using the actor's own name for the part he was playing and based all his plays on a single theme of the difficulties encountered, often through their own fault, of young lovers.

Voltaire
Meanwhile, tragedy received its final flowering from that universal genius Voltaire, the pseudonym of François Marie Arouet (1694–1778). He devoted

much of his time to the theatre, building a number of private theatres, and was himself a good amateur actor. His dramatic works include *Oedipe*, *Zaire*, *Mérope* and *Semiramis*, and are mainly neo-classic in form. He mingled comedy and tragedy and used spectacular stage effects which were quite new to French tragedy. They required the removal of members of the audience from the stage itself, a reform effected by Garrick in London soon afterwards.

It was Garrick's natural style of acting that influenced Voltaire's friend and protégé, the great actor Lekain. Voltaire took Lekain into his own home and converted a room there into a theatre where the young man learned his acting technique in a company composed of Voltaire's friends and relations. Lekain went on to a career of unbroken success at the *Comédie Française*. He was returning home from a performance there in 1778 when he caught a chill and died a few weeks before his famous patron. He was the first actor to attempt historical accuracy of costume in the parts he

It was Voltaire (left) who finally banished members of the audience from the stage in the 18th- century.

Friedrich Schiller

played. He abandoned the plumed head-dress and flowing cloak of the tragic hero and dressed himself in more classic simplicity. The minor actors were also dressed in costumes suitable to the period of the play.

Before the upheaval of the French Revolution, there emerged one last great dramatist in the person of Beaumarchais, pen-name of Pierre Augustin Caron (1733–99). He was the author of two fine plays, *The Barber of Seville* and *The Marriage of Figaro*, remembered now principally as the sources of the operas by Rossini and Mozart. The original comedies were attacks on society as it existed at that time. They predicted the coming Revolution. The first, performed in 1775, amused an audience who still felt safe from the upheavals to come. But by the time of the production of the second in 1784, the audience was beginning to sense the dangers that lay ahead. Both plays were produced at the *Comédie Française* which had moved to a new building on the present site of the *Odéon*.

By this time, one more change had taken place in the theatre. The long supremacy of Italy in stage design was over. The baroque style of architectural columns and neo-classical form was over. The more flowing and flowery decoration of the rococo had become the fashion. This was the style of the French theatre, and it was a Frenchman, Garrick's designer de Loutherbourg, who became responsible for the design of the new London playhouses at the end of the eighteenth century.

American Theatre

While the countries of Europe were establishing their national theatrical traditions, the first theatres in America were being built. Plays in Spanish had been presented on the West Coast in the sixteenth century, and French plays appeared in Quebec by the eighteenth. But it was companies of English actors and actresses that were to establish the first lasting theatres in the East Coast states. Williamsburg had a theatre by 1716. Charleston's Dock Street Theatre was presenting London hits by the 1730s. Philadelphia had its 'Virginia Company of Comedians' by 1749. A temporary playhouse was opened in Nassau Street, New York in 1750. There was, however, a strong Puritan tradition among American settlers and, after independence, the new states tended to prohibit theatres on the grounds that they encouraged undesirable passions.

Drama has too universal an appeal for its banning ever to submerge it for long. The first comedy by an American-born author, Royall Tyler's *The Contrast*, appeared in New York in 1787, though it had to be disguised as a moral lecture to get a showing in the author's home town of Boston. The first notable man of the theatre to be born in America was William Dunlap who, with the English actor John Hodgkinson, opened the Park Theatre in New York in 1798. The leading centre for American theatre alternated between New York and Philadelphia where the Walnut Street Theatre, the oldest still in use in the United States, was opened in 1811. But the policy of importing expensive talent from Europe eventually bankrupted the Philadelphia theatres, and the lead passed permanently to New York where it remained until recent times.

The first great American actress was Charlotte Cushman (1816–76), famous for her Lady Macbeth. She was tall and rather plain and had a great struggle to establish herself. She often played male parts, notably Romeo and Hamlet to her beautiful younger sister Susan's Juliet and Ophelia. The first great American actor was Edwin Forrest (1806–72), famous for his role as Spartacus in *The Gladiator* by Robert M. Bird. There was bitter rivalry between him and the English actor, William Macready (1793–1873), which led to the Astor Place riots when twenty-two people were killed and Macready had to be smuggled out of New York.

In 1853, the Irish actor and playwright Dion Boucicault (1822–90) first visited the United States. From then on, he divided his time equally between New York and London, producing and acting in his own plays, especially at Wallack's Theatre in New York. One of his plays was the first to treat the American Negro seriously. It was called *The Octoroon or Life in Louisiana*, and a principal role was played by the American actor Joseph Jefferson who became famous as Rip Van Winkle in Washington Irving's story adapted for the stage by Boucicault. Jefferson created the role of Asa Trenchard in *Our American Cousin* by the English playwright Tom Taylor. It was first produced in America by the actress-manager Laura

Contemporary print of John Kemble in *Pizarro*.

A popular pastime in Victorian England was the Toy Theatre, or Juvenile Drama.

107

Keene whose company was appearing in this play at Ford's Theatre in Washington, DC, when President Abraham Lincoln was murdered in 1865 by the actor John Wilkes Booth. He was the younger brother of Edwin Booth (1833–93), a great tragedian and the first American actor to win a European reputation.

Another American actress-manager, this time of the Arch Street Theatre in Philadelphia, was Mrs John Drew. Her son was an actor, and her grandchildren were the famous Barrymores. Succeeding generations of American actors and actresses moved westward with the pioneers. At the time of the great gold rush, Charlotte Crabtree, known as Lotta, toured the mining camps from the age of ten. A London actor, William Chapman, pioneered the showboats of the Mississippi river with melodramas and pantomime to entertain the passengers. A craze for Negro minstrel troupes swept the continent and even reached England. Variety shows and later vaudeville became popular.

Though there was no shortage of American acting talent in the nineteenth century, there was as yet no outstanding American playwright. Augustin Daly wrote about ninety plays, mostly adaptations, but is principally remembered for the theatres he opened in New York and London. Bronson Howard was the first American to make his living as a playwright.

Anna Cora Mowatt wrote the first American social comedy in *Fashion, or Life in New York*. David Belasco, who built his own New York theatre, was a prolific playwright, but is remembered for his spectacular productions with their subtle use of stage lighting.

European Theatre

Even in Europe no great playwrights appeared for the greater part of the century. There were very gradual changes in the theatres themselves. The apron stage receded and was replaced by the orchestra pit. Theatres became larger, which resulted in the declamatory style of voice and gesture that robbed much drama of its realism. Pixérécourt wrote, as he said himself, for an audience who could not read. One of his plays in translation was the first in England to be called a melodrama, a form that was to dominate the theatre for many decades. The spectacular production was common, with much use of elaborate stage machinery including representations of fire, flood and earthquake.

Yet there was plenty of fine acting talent. John Philip Kemble (1757–1823) and his sister, Mrs Sarah Siddons (1755–1831), were highly thought of in Shakespearian tragedy. Their younger brother Charles was good in comedy and excelled in Shakespeare's young heroes and the gentlemanly roles of Sheridan. The Kembles went to considerable trouble to mount their productions with accurate settings and costume and with subtle gaslit

Music-hall in England provided entertainment as a background to eating and drinking.

by a mixture of magic, farce and parody not unlike English pantomime called *Zauberstück*. The great comic actor Ferdinand Raimund wrote his own plays concerning humans who learned the truth about life from magic beings and in which spectacle, transformation scenes, music and singing all intermingled.

France had plays by Alexandre Dumas, Victor Hugo and Alfred de Vigny, but Dumas was essentially a novelist and the other two poets. The comedies of Alfred de Musset had to be rediscovered in Russia by a French actress before they were performed in Paris. Amid all the vaudeville and melodrama, Eugène Scribe continued to turn out a prolific flow of well-made dramas, setting a pattern for playwrights everywhere with their carefully constructed plots. Meanwhile, companies like the *Comédie Française* were finding rivals in the new theatres such as the *Odéon*. Emile Augier wrote for them plays of greater realism than his contemporaries, the best-known of whom was Dumas's son, known as Alexandre Dumas fils, who created the character of Marguerite Gautier in *La dame aux camélias*. This play has provided a splendid vehicle for actresses ever since. The actor who first played the hero of the play, Armand Duval, was Charles Fechter, half English, half French, who achieved an international reputation.

The Actor-manager
In London, the actors William Macready and Samuel Phelps carried on in the tradition of the Kembles and the Keans, while the actress-manager Mme Vestris (born Eliza Bartolozzi) introduced the burlesque plays of James Robinson Planché and the first work of Dion Boucicault. In 1871, Henry Irving became the leading man at the Lyceum Theatre at the age of thirty-three. With his harsh voice and ungainly movements, he was not a natural actor. But at the Lyceum, which he later managed, he created London's leading company, with Ellen Terry as his leading lady, and became the first actor to be knighted. Ellen's sister Kate was also a fine actress whose eldest daughter became the mother of Sir John Gielgud. Their younger brother Fred had great success as a romantic hero with his wife, the beautiful Julia Nielson, as his leading lady. Other famous actors who appeared in the second half of the nineteenth century were Willian Terriss, Seymour Hicks, Johnston Forbes-Robertson and John Martin-Harvey.

It was the period of the actor-manager, with the Shakespeare companies of Frank Benson and Ben Greet leading eventually to the Shakespeare Memorial Theatre at Stratford-on-Avon and the Old Vic in the Waterloo Road which was to house the first British National Theatre Company. Other actor-managers were George Alexander at the St James's Theatre,

John Wilkes Booth leaps from the theatre box in which he assassinated Abraham Lincoln.

effects. Edmund Kean (1789–1833) and George Frederick Cooke (1756–1811) were two erratic but brilliant actors, the former especially as Shylock and the latter as Richard III. Kean's son Charles, with his wife Ellen Terry as his leading lady, ran a successful company for many years.

In Germany, George, Duke of Saxe-Meiningen who married a niece of Queen Victoria and was a keen theatre-goer on visits to London, founded a Court theatre company called the Meiningers. The duke himself produced the plays and designed the settings and costumes. In Austria, Franz Grillparzer's plays brought new vitality, but mainly in the popular theatre. The extempore farce in *commedia dell'arte* tradition had been replaced

Edwin Booth as Hamlet.

109

LA·DAME·
AUX·CAMELIAS

SARAH BERNHARDT

THÉÂTRE DE LA
RENAISSANCE

IMP. F. CHAMPENOIS. PARIS

London in the same play, one performing in French, the other in Italian, and both travelled extensively throughout their careers. A rapidly expanding form of theatre in Britain was the music-hall with which the straight drama had to compete with the exploitation of the individual performer's personality and a good deal of advance publicity. This situation created the star system. Music hall artistes such as Marie Lloyd, Vesta Tilley, Little Tich, the clown Grock, Harry Lauder and George Robey aroused public interest in their private lives as well as their stage personalities. Though the music-hall was based on the individual acts of the performers, artists attempted straight acting in the annual Christmas pantomimes into which their popular routines were incorporated.

for the Bergen Theatre, which he managed, but little of them remains. It was not until he left Norway for Rome that he wrote the verse-plays *Brand* and *Peer Gynt* which established his European reputation. Then, in the third phase of his career, he produced the prose dramas, searing satires on contemporary society, which shocked the complacent theatre-going public. Such plays were the *Pillars of Society*, *A Doll's House*, *Ghosts* and *An Enemy of the People*. At the age of seventy, he wrote his last play, *When We Dead Awaken*, which has been compared with Shakespeare's *The Tempest* for its depth of poetic thought and form. He was followed in Sweden by August Strindberg (1849–1912) whose plays deal less with society than with the evil inherent in the individual.

Three great dramatists of the European theatre (from left to right) George Bernard Shaw, Henrik Ibsen and Anton Chekhov.

Beerbohm Tree at Her Majesty's and Charles Wyndham who built the theatre named after him in 1899.

A new school of realistic playwriting was emerging with the so-called cup-and-saucer drama of Tom Robertson. His plays required a much more naturalistic style of acting and realistic settings, as did those of Arthur Wing Pinero which have survived more readily than those of H.A. Jones which equally shocked their contemporary audiences. At the same time, Oscar Wilde was producing highly mannered witty comedies, W. S. Gilbert was writing the libretti for light operas derived from the burlesques of Planché and, in France, Victorien Sardou had taken over from Scribe as the creator of well-constructed melodramas.

Many of Sardou's plays were written for the French actress Sarah Bernhardt (1844–1923), whose Italian rival, Eleonora Duse (1859–1924), appeared in the plays of d'Annunzio. At one time, the two actresses appeared in

Political Drama

Perhaps because of its religious origins, the theatre every now and again shrugs off its role as an entertainer of the public and takes itself more seriously. Then it deals with matters of social importance and political propaganda. This can lead to plays of very poor literary merit, but the end of the nineteenth century produced three playwrights of high quality and serious intent. They came from unexpected quarters, the first of them being Henrik Ibsen (1828–1906), a Norwegian. His first plays were written

In Britain, Ibsen's great disciple was George Bernard Shaw (1856–1950) whose plays deal with difficult subjects with a wit and elegance that disarms prejudice.

Meanwhile in Russia, Anton Chekhov (1860–1904) was writing the plays which established the influence of the Moscow Arts Theatre. *Ivanov*, *The Seagull*, *Uncle Vanya*, *The Three Sisters* and *The Cherry Orchard* deal with ordinary provincial people in such a way as to reveal the inner truths of universal human aspirations. They embody a high degree of stagecraft and a blend of melancholia and humour that is very Russian. These plays and Chekhov's short stories have had a great influence on European literature in the twentieth century. From his work, and that of Ibsen and Shaw, has stemmed the Theatre of Ideas which still, in one form or another, dominates the more literary output of the modern theatre.

Model of the stage set by the Japanese designer Noguchi for a production of Shakespeare's *King Lear* at the Shakespeare Memorial Theatre at Stratford in 1956.

A Kabuki actor from the Japanese theatre.

Modern Theatre

Everywhere, the Theatre of Ideas and the realistic interpretation of its plays gained the ascendancy. At the Moscow Arts Theatre, the plays of Chekhov were subtly interpreted by Stanislavsky (1865–1938) who trained his actors in the form of emotional expression which was to lead to the Method style of acting in America. In Spain, attempts were made to introduce Ibsen at the *Teatro Intim* in Barcelona founded by Adria Gual. The project was a failure but it did influence some contemporary playwrights such as Echegaray. The Spanish theatre remained firmly planted in its sentimental past until the plays of Garcia Lorca, *Blood Wedding*, *The House of Bernard Alba* and *Yerma*. Lorca was unfortunately killed in 1936 at the age of thirty-six in the Spanish Civil War.

Italy produced the playwright Luigi Pirandello (1867–1936), who directed his own plays at the *Teatro Odescalchi* in Rome. They expressed a negative philosophy concerned with life's illusions and the impossibility of perceiving reality. They have had a lasting influence since their first impact on the disillusioned generation of the 1920s and 30s. In Ireland, the remarkable theatre manager, Miss Horniman, founded the Abbey Theatre in Dublin in 1904 which was to mount the plays of poetic realism by J. M. Synge (1871–1909) and Sean O'Casey (1880–1964). It was Miss Horniman who brought the idea of repertory theatres to Britain from the Continent. She ran a company at the Gaiety Theatre in Manchester which created its own playwrights, a policy much followed in the main urban centres ever since.

The new realism was to have its effect on stage design. In the United States, the Swiss artist Adolphe Appia produced settings which were more than a background to the actor, but provided a total environment heightened by dramatic lighting made possible by the introduction of electricity into theatres. Ellen Terry's son, Gordon Craig (1872–1966), went even further in his insistence on simplicity of stage design. He evolved a system of screens, rostra and flights of steps, constantly changed by the direction, colour and strength of lighting applied to them. Within such a setting, the performance of the actor was bereft of all distraction and his emotional expression communicated directly to the audience. Much of this desire for simplicity was through the influence of the East, though its ancient forms of drama were largely misinterpreted and misunderstood in the West.

111

China and Japan

The Chinese theatre, chiefly the Peking opera, has been concerned more with the actor than the play. There is a mingling of dialogue, song, dance and acrobatics, telling old legends and stories from national history. Costume, make-up and gesture are all highly stylised. There is little or no scenery and props have symbolic values. In Japan, the *Noh* play is derived from religious ritual. There are only two actors, the principal one being masked. There is little action, the drama unfolding mainly through soliloquy. Miming and clowning is introduced into the *kyogen* or comic interlude. The theatre of *kabuki* is

this came in the form known as expressionism, in which the action had a dreamlike quality. Such were the plays of Wedekind and Kaiser in Germany, O'Casey's *Silver Tassie* and *Within the Gates* in England, and O'Neill's *The Hairy Ape* and *Emperor Jones* in America. A further reaction to realism was constructivism, a more theatrical approach which put the actor in a position of primacy over the play. In a completely different direction were the romantic dramas of Rostand, the fantasies of Maeterlinck and James Barrie, and the mannered, cynical comedies of Noel Coward and Somerset Maugham. Austria had its

1943). If Craig was the first to envisage a theatre dominated by one man, Reinhardt was the person who came nearest to achieving that ideal. He refused to be confined to the ordinary theatre, setting his plays in ballrooms, circuses, cathedral squares and exhibition halls. He introduced huge crowd scenes, manipulating his casts with consummate ease. His most permanent influence, however, has been in the cinema for which he directed a number of films. It seemed that his spectacular productions needed to use modern technology to confine them in a manageable form and reproduce them on film in a theatre building where the audience could feel more

Typical scene from a light comedy of the 1930s.

composed of singing and dancing, and has a more popular approach. Nowadays, particularly in Japan, the East is coming under the influence of the West's realistic theatre of conflict.

The super-realism of Émile Zola's *Thérèse Raquin* (1873) and Gorki's *Lower Depths* (1902) was followed in America by Eugene O'Neill's *Anna Christie* and *Desire Under the Elms* (1924). Such plays produced the convention of an audience peering through the 'fourth wall' at a rather remote action which appeared to go on without reference to them. A reaction to

own cynic in Arthur Schnitzler, though its best playwright of the period was Hugo von Hofmannsthal, who was also librettist for Richard Strauss. France's reaction to realism is perhaps best represented in the works of Giraudoux, for example *Ondine*, the story of a mortal in love with a water nymph.

The Director

A phenomenon of the modern theatre is the rise in importance of the director, sometimes called the producer. The first of these was Max Reinhardt (1873–

comfortable. Too close a contact with a massive army of performers seemed to threaten the spectator in a way that the director did not intend. Nevertheless, in modern times, directors have sought to involve the audience by direct contact with the performer planted among them. Even the medieval presentation, with the audience wandering from one acting booth to another, has been recently reintroduced.

Whatever form the theatre takes, however, there seems no substitute for the author. In Germany, Bertold

112

Brecht created an impressive kind of ensemble playing, but it is for his plays that he will finally be remembered. The theatre of protest has been firmly established by such plays as John Osborne's *Look Back in Anger* and Samuel Beckett's *Waiting for Godot*. The theatre of the absurd has produced the works of Jarry and

Scene from Samuel Beckett's *Waiting for Godot*.

Ionesco. The theatre of cruelty has derived from the work of Artaud and is perhaps best known from Weiss's *The Marat/Sade*. All these have appeared in productions enhancing the reputations of directors, yet all are dependent for their originality on their authors. Drama will continue to have its great players, directors and designers, but it will always be firmly based in literature.

Theatre Design
Perhaps one of the most noticeable changes in the theatre of recent times

is the abandonment of the proscenium arch and the front curtain. Even older theatres have been altered to accommodate a large protruding apron stage, and new theatres have been built in such a way that they can be adapted to suit each production or the demands of the set designer. Much experiment has recently taken place with theatre-in-the-round where the action goes on in an arena surrounded by spectators. Scenery has largely been supplanted by a system of acting levels created by structures that only loosely represent the locale of the play.

There have always been fringe activities around the main trends of theatre, but today this is probably more than ever so. The cost of mounting a production in one of the principal theatres of an urban centre is such that companies often play safe with star

actors and actresses, popular authors and conventional production. The young unknown, eager to try out new ideas, has difficulty in getting the opportunity from established managements. This has led to much fringe theatre. In New York, the established theatres are along a stretch of Broadway. Experimental theatres have mushroomed in off-Broadway locations. These, in their turn, have become well known, so that a new off-off-Broadway theatre has developed.

Nowadays, the most exciting theatrical experiment at any given time in

any city may be taking place in a cellar, in the back room of a public house, in a tent in the park or, in at least one case, in an old disused railway locomotive shed. Often the comfort of the audience is entirely disregarded. Much of this back-alley activity achieves considerable publicity through the media of television and radio and the newspapers. Much of it is really only semi-professional, but the professional has never had the monopoly of the theatre. In an age of increasing leisure, ordinary people are becoming less willing to sit back and be entertained by others. Amateur theatricals are as popular as they ever were and are reaching ever greater heights of sophistication. In the interests of attracting tourists, whole communities are reviving ancient pagan festivals, mock battles and knightly tournaments, and

all manner of pageants. Theatre is even coming back into the churches where much of it began at the beginning of the Christian era. Plays are being published, not only in acting editions, but in ever-increasing numbers for reading by the general public, just as in Roman times the plays of Terence had a reading public.

All these fringe activities eventually have their effects on the established theatre, as do the technological advances of the films and television. But in the final analysis, it is the professionally mounted and performed work of real literary merit, exciting a large audience to new emotional reaction and intellectual thought, which constitutes the real theatre. There seems every indication that such theatre is going to continue with renewed vitality.

Theatre Life

The theatre of the western world is broadly speaking administered in two ways. There are in every country the national, subsidised theatres, and there are the commercial managements operating for profit. The national theatres are usually self-contained, with their own theatre buildings, often including rehearsal rooms, wardrobe departments, scene-building studios and schools for students of theatre. The commercial managements rarely have more than the offices from which they control their projects. Let us follow the progress of a commercial production from its inception to the final excitement of the opening night.

It begins with the written play. The author usually entrusts his work to a professional literary agent who, for a percentage of the money made, handles all the business dealings with theatre managements, publishers and such things as film, television and radio rights. Often a commercial management will commission a play from a well-known author, but they also receive many new plays submitted to them by literary agents. Once a play has been accepted by the management in principle, discussions will take place between them, the author and his agent and a contract will be drawn up. This usually promises payment of a certain percentage of box-office receipts to the author's agent. From these payments, the agent will deduct his percentage and pay the remainder to the author. The discussions may also include matters such as the casting of the play, the sort of settings required and who will design them, and the choice of director. Often management will ask for adjustments to be made to the original play, either

The production company will employ, for the run of the play, its own specialist technicians—electricians, carpenters, scene-shifters, property master, wardrobe mistress and so on —all of whom come under the stage director, also employed for the run of the play. All the people named have their assistants according to the complications of the particular production. The play's producer, now more often called the director, is employed to mount the production for the opening night. Thereafter, he might go on to directing other productions, spending only part of his time checking the standard of performance during the run and perhaps rehearsing a replacement actor with the rest of the cast. The same applies to the stage designer who is no longer involved once the original settings have been designed and approved unless perhaps when the

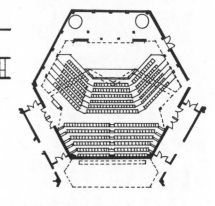

Modern theatre design not only allows a more scientific seating plan so that all may have a good view of the stage, but provides patrons with comfort and safety.

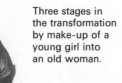

Three stages in the transformation by make-up of a young girl into an old woman.

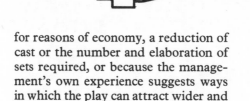

for reasons of economy, a reduction of cast or the number and elaboration of sets required, or because the management's own experience suggests ways in which the play can attract wider and larger audiences.

Casting the Play

Once the management has gained control of the play's first production from the author, it becomes the management's responsibility to cast the play and find a theatre it can lease for the performances. Some managements own their own theatres, but more often they must make a deal with a theatre management. Those who manage the theatre itself may also receive a percentage of box-office receipts in return for the use of the theatre building and certain specified services. These include provision of front-of-house staff, box-office clerks, bar and restaurant staff, cleaners, programme sellers, firemen and so on, and also certain backstage staff such as the stage-door-keeper, a stage manager and other technicians like electricians and maintenance men, and sometimes the call-boy.

production moves to another theatre and design alterations are required.

Once the cast has been chosen, in the first instance usually by the director, though with the approval of the management and sometimes the author, rehearsals can begin. Star players are usually selected according to their suitability and availability, but auditions might be held for the lesser parts. Rehearsals take place for the most part in special rehearsal rooms hired by the management. The size and shape of the setting can be chalked out on the floor and rough representations of the furnishings placed in position. During the rehearsal period, usually about three weeks unless the production is very complicated, the members of the cast are required to attend costume fittings at the costumiers. There are studios that both design and build scenery and others that both design and make costumes.

Often, however, the designer is an individual artist.

In the theatre, though this is not true of films and television, the actor or actress is responsible for his or her own make-up. Performers become very skilled in this art, but they can also receive help from cosmetics firms who employ their own theatrical make-up experts. During the run of the play, members of the cast are usually expected to arrive at the theatre half an hour before beginners are called to appear on the stage, which is five minutes before curtain-up. The call-boy is responsible for seeing that everyone is there on time. If an actor has a particularly complicated make-up or costume to put on, he will arrive perhaps even an hour or two earlier.

The First Night
There is usually a day or two before opening night available to fit the sets into the stage area and rehearse scene changes. A lighting engineer is brought in to establish the levels of lighting and to prepare a list of lighting cues. The stage director and his staff are also busy collecting props for use in different scenes and in organising sound effects and their cues. Final dress rehearsals bring together all these elements and provide an opportunity for last minute alterations and to get rid of unnecessary delays.

On the opening night, performers and staff arrive in good time. The 'call-boy'—nowadays more often a loud-speaker system linked to every dressing-room—calls the 'half-hour'. The front-of-house staff begin to receive the audience, to sell them a drink, a box of chocolates, a programme. The stage director checks the set and the readiness of the stage staff to make the first changes. The cast begin to make up and get into their costumes with the help of dressers who already have the costume changes waiting in their correct order. The house lights are on, the stage lights dimmed. The electricians are ready with their cues. 'Beginners' are called and those performers who open the play make their way down to the stage to take up their positions. Music from a record-player begins to flood the auditorium. The footlights go on, lighting up the curtains or 'tabs' as they are called in the theatre. The first lighting pattern for the stage is already set. The switch is thrown. The players lick their lips, clear their throats, make final adjustments to their clothing. Everybody stands by. There is a moment as though time has stood still. The music fades, the curtain rises, there is an expectant cough and shuffle from the audience. Someone makes the first move or speaks the first line. The play has begun . . .

Cinema

The mechanism of the eye and its system of nerves to the brain work in such a way that an image is retained for a split second. If, therefore, a progressive series of still pictures is presented to the vision, for example the movements involved in a walking figure, the retention of one image while the next is being assimilated fills in the gap between the two so that the brain comprehends a smooth-flowing movement. We actually see a moving figure rather than a series of jerks from one position to the next. This principle was described as early as the second century A.D. and demonstrated by Dr Peter Roget in 1824. The first device to make use of it appeared in 1826 and was called a thaumatrope. You can make your own thaumatrope. by attaching two threads to a cardboard disc and making drawings on both sides of the disc between the threads. When the disc is held by the threads and they are twisted so that the disc revolves, the two drawings will appear to be superimposed upon each other. For instance, one drawing could be of a parrot and the other of the parrot's cage. Spinning the disc appears to put the parrot in the cage. Remember that one drawing must be upside down in relation to the other so that, as the disc revolves, the second drawing turns the right way up.

The thaumatrope involves only two drawings. J. A. Plateau's phenakisto-

Zöetrope, or Wheel of Life.

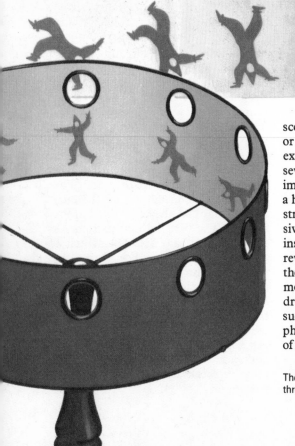

scope of 1833, and Horner's zoetrope or Wheel of Life of the following year, extending the principle to the use of several drawings to create a moving image. The Wheel of Life consisted of a hollow cylinder with slits cut in it. A strip of drawings showing a progressive cycle of movement was placed inside the cylinder which was then revolved. Viewed through the slits, the figure in the drawings appeared to move. The next step was to replace drawings with photographs in rapid succession, a process called chronophotography, developed by a number of scientists. What brought the pro-

The magic lantern was an early device for throwing still pictures onto a screen.

duction of motion pictures to its final successful outcome was the printing of images on a continuous roll of celluloid film. This was devised by the American George Eastman and sold with his Kodak cameras. These were intended for taking a series of snapshots, of course, but they provided the material upon which a moving picture could be photographed.

The Lumière Brothers

Chronophotographers at once set to work producing motion pictures on continuous rolls of film, while Thomas Edison and his assistant, W. K. L. Dickson, devised the Kinetoscope, a sort of peepshow through which the first 'movies' were shown to the public. Meanwhile, the race was on to project the first moving images onto a screen large enough for an audience to view the action in a theatre. To the Lumière brothers of France must go the honour of showing the first movies to a paying public. This they did at the Grand Café, Boulevard des Capucines, Paris, on the 20th February 1896. This was the first cinema show and was quickly followed by many others in all parts of the world. The first films made for public showing were simple action shots of people and vehicles, newsreels of processions and wars, and short comedies. France again led by the production in 1901 of the first dramatic film, *The Story of a Crime*, which was followed by *The Great Train Robbery* in the United States in 1903 and *Rescued by Rover* in England in 1905. Meanwhile, the fantasy possibilities inherent in the technical process were being exploited in the trick films of Méliès, a French conjurer turned film-maker. Among his remarkable early productions are *Voyage to*

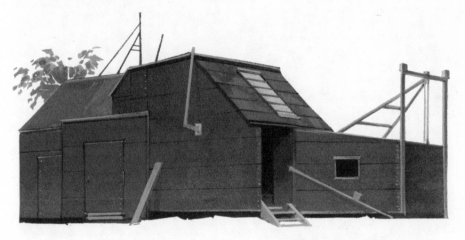

the Moon (1902), *Voyage Across the Impossible* (1904) and *The Conquest of the Pole* (1912).

It was in France, in 1896, that Charles Pathé founded the company which was, within ten years, to become the most important in the world. It manufactured its own equipment, produced films, owned and managed its own cinemas and distribution networks, and created subsidiary companies all over the world, notably in the United States, Britain and Russia. At first, films travelled about wherever a showing could be arranged, in music halls, fairgrounds, shops called penny gaffs and nickelodeons. By 1908, permanent film theatres were being built to give regular programmes. In America, Thomas Edison was unsuccessful in maintaining his monopoly in the new invention after the opening of his first kinetoscope parlour in New York, but in the process he built up a flourishing film production department. His rivals included the Biograph and Vitagraph companies, and some of the

great Hollywood names—Loew, Zukor, Selznick, Laemmle, Fox and Lasky—were coming into the business.

Hollywood Stars

The United States had the first film censorship, beginning in Chicago in 1907 and developing into the National Board of Censorship by 1909. That same year, the pioneer director D. W. Griffith engaged Mary Pickford to appear in *The Lonely Villa* and *The*

In 1894 Edison opened his Kinetoscope Parlour in New York City. The kinetoscope was a cabinet containing about 15 metres (50 feet) of film which revolved in spools. By looking through a peephole in the cabinet a person could watch the pictures move. The Kinetoscope Parlour had two rows of such peep-show machines. Edison made the films in his 'Black Maria' home-made studio (above).

Charlie Chaplin plays his famous character, the little tramp, in an early movie.

Violin Maker of Cremona, beginning a career that was to make her one of the first great international stars. Griffith supervised Mack Sennett's early films before the latter founded Keystone in 1912 and instituted the golden age of film comedy. Charlie Chaplin made his first film, *Making a Living*, for Keystone in 1914. Griffith meanwhile went on to direct his two great masterpieces, *Birth of a Nation* (1915) and *Intolerance* (1916). It was Griffith who invented or at least used to greatest effect the early camera techniques which were to become standard practice by all directors. Such were the 'dissolve' when the picture faded or merged into the next scene, the 'panning shot' with the camera turning to take in a large scene, the similar 'tracking shot' where the camera is moved along a track, even the 'dynamic frame' where the image on the screen changes in shape and position so that a particular part of the scene can be emphasised. The more recent introduction of camera dollies, handheld cameras, zoom lenses and many other improvements have given the cameraman great facilities, but few modern shooting techniques were not pioneered by Griffith with his cumbersome, hand-cranked cameras.

European Cinema

For a time, European cinema was

dominated by the French and the Danish. The latter concentrated on low-life and crime films, and launched the first European star in Asta Nielsen. The French producer, Léon Gaumont, gathered together a team of directors which included Louis Feuillade who created a 'life as it is' series and then went on to many crime series. Max Linder was the first great film comedian. Jasset's *Nick Carter* serial established the popularity of crime films which has never abated. The French film, *The Assassination of the Duc de Guise*, was the first attempt to produce an art film and to make the business respectable. The French actress Sarah Bernhardt appeared in such films as *Queen Elizabeth* (1912). It was a Frenchman, Louis Gasnier, who introduced Pearl White in the *Exploits of Elaine*, made for the American Pathé Company. Meanwhile, Italy was becoming internationally known for its spectacular films like Guazzoni's *Quo Vadis?* (1912) and Pastrone's *Cabiria* (1914). Their films made the actor Bartolomeo Pagano world famous and immortalised Bernhardt's great rival Eleonora Duse who appeared in *Cenere*

(1916). Before the 1917 Revolution, the Russian film industry was also making headway after its early domination by Pathé. Protazanov's *The Queen of Spades* (1916) and *Father Sergius* (1918) both starred Ivan Mosjoukine who later emigrated to Paris and joined the French films' avant garde movement. In Sweden, the great silent film era was founded by Charles Majnusson who, in 1909, became production manager for the Svenska Biografteatern, later the Svensk Filmindustri. With two actors, Victor Sjöström and Mauritz Stiller, he created an international reputation for Swedish films which were notable for their fine photography, outdoor locations exploiting the beautiful local scenery and a natural style of acting.

During the First World War, the European film industry faltered. American salesmanship put the American film companies centred on Hollywood into a dominant position. The remainder of the silent era was notable for its great stars, Chaplin, Fairbanks, Pickford, Valentino, Lillian Gish, Ramon Novarro and Gloria Swanson; for its serials, especially those featuring

Pearl White; for its westerns by Broncho Billy Anderson, Tom Mix and W. S. Hart; and above all for its slapstick comedies with Chaplin, Keaton, Laurel and Hardy, Harold Lloyd, Harold Langdon and a host of others. Great directors emerged—Cecil B. de Mille, Erich von Stroheim and Rex Ingram. Robert Flaherty brought the documentary film to a new height with his *Nanook of the North* (1922) about the Eskimos. Sjöström came to Hollywood from Sweden, and Lubitsch from Germany.

Elsewhere, the 1920s brought into prominence the German directors Fritz Lang (*Dr Mabuse*, 1922), Wiene (*The Cabinet of Dr Caligari*, 1919), Robison (*Warning Shadows*, 1922) and others, using a heavily dramatic style known as expressionism. In France, the avante garde produced such experimental films as Dulac's *The Seashell and the Clergyman* (1926), René Clair's *Entr'acte* (1924) and Buñuel's *L'Age d'Or* (1926), together with the films of Louis Delluc, the journalist who founded film criticism and the first French cine-clubs. Russia passed through a period of experiment and

Filming on location during the making of an historical 'epic'.

Jean Renoir, Jacques Feyder, Marcel Carné, the scriptwriter Jacques Prévert, and actors Jean-Louis Barrault, Michel Simon, Jean Gabin and the unforgettable Louis Jouvet who was also the leading stage star. Experiment was discouraged in Soviet Russia. Nevertheless, directors found a satisfying outlet in historical films, notably Petrov with *Peter the Great* (1937–39), Eisenstein with *Alexander Nevsky* (1938) and *Ivan the Terrible* (1944 and 1946), and Dovzhenko with *Shchors* (1939). In Italy, Cinecitta was built to rival Hollywood, with the directors Blasetti and Camerini, and actor Vittorio de Sica, but little of outstanding value was produced. Swedish film was kept alive almost alone by Gustav Molander (*En Natt*, 1931). During the decade, the Indian and Japanese film industries reached second and

Walt Disney's popular cartoon character Goofy.

great achievement with its directors such as Eisenstein (*The Battleship Potemkin* and *October*), Pudovkia (*Mother, The End of St Petersburg* and *Storm over Asia*), Kuleshov (*By the Law*), Dovzhenko (*Zvenigora* and *Earth*), Ermler (*Fragment of an Empire*) and others. Then, in 1927, Al Jolson sang and spoke in the *Jazz Singer* made by Warner Brothers. The 'talkies' had arrived, and with them a new era in films.

The Talkies

As was to be expected, the *Jazz Singer* began a whole series of musical films in the making of which Hollywood became unbeatable. In quick succession, the *Gold Diggers* series was followed by *Forty Second Street*, the Eddie Cantor films, Busby Berkeley's unique geometrical patterns of dancers, the Rogers-Astaire films and many others. Sound also made possible the sophisticated comedies of directors like Lubitsch and Capra with their stars, William Powell, Myrna Loy, Cary Grant, Jean Arthur

and Carole Lombard. The wise-cracking films of the Marx Brothers, W. C. Fields and Mae West were also popular. Great romantic stars appeared —Clark Gable, Greta Garbo, Charles Boyer, Robert Taylor, Marlene Dietrich, Bette Davis, Joan Crawford, Barbara Stanwyck, and so on. New techniques were devised for monster films, notably *King Kong* of 1933. Horror films began a lasting popularity with James Whale's *Frankenstein* of 1931. Walt Disney reached pre-eminence with the animated cartoon film, though many others were in the field, notably Max and Dave Fleischer with their Popeye series. Action films continued to be made, the prohibition era of America being reflected in the gangster film which still flourishes. At the end of the decade, John Ford directed his classic Western, *Stagecoach*; at the beginning of the new decade, the almost revolutionary *Citizen Kane* came from Orson Welles.

France in the thirties saw the rise to prominence of a number of great directors, including Jean Vigo, Clair,

The artist who draws figures for animated cartoons will often use a mirror to study facial expressions.

Stars of the '30s (from left to right)
Clark Gable, Carole Lombard, W. C. Fields,
Ronald Coleman and Louise Rainer.

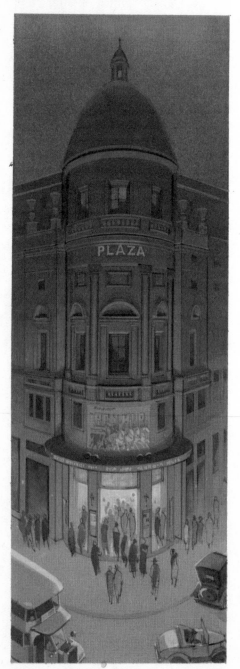

third positions in world output, although almost unnoticed in the West.

Another war depressed European film-making yet again. Britain's documentary movement, however, achieved perhaps its finest work. In France, directors Jean Gremillon, Henri-George Clouzot, Jacques Becker and Jean Cocteau were beginning to spread their wings. In Italy, Luchino Visconti made the first neo-realist film in *Ossessione* (1942). Sweden's revival began with Alf Sjöberg (*Road to Heaven*, 1942, and *Ordet*, 1943), and Ingmar Bergman's first film, *Crisis* (1945). Meanwhile, the National Film Board of Canada, which has done so much in experimental film-making, was founded, and Hollywood continued to turn out its professionally well-made films under the direction of such talents as Ford, Huston, Hitchcock, Minelli and many others.

The post-war period began on a note of optimism, with J. Arthur Rank in Britain making a determined effort to break into the American market, and with Italy's burst of neo-realistic films beginning with Rossellini's *Open City* and *Paisa*, de Sica's *Bicycle Thieves* (1948) and Zampa's *To Live in Peace* (1946). Jean Cocteau directed one of the most remarkable films ever made in *Orphée* (1949). Hollywood continued to feed the world's cinemas with magnificent musicals, often featuring the work of Gene Kelly, and other films for its vast stable of star names.

Modern Cinema

But the impact of television and the economics of film-making were to throw the whole industry into a state of uncertainty. Hollywood's first answer was a new style based on the Actor's Studio in New York, at first founded to revitalise the stage, and

giving the film world directors like Elia Kazan and actors like Marlon Brando and James Dean. Many low-budget pictures were very successful, and television provided cross-fertilisation with such films as *Marty* and *Twelve Angry Men*. Hollywood's next weapon against the small screen was the super-blockbuster production using one or other of the new optical processes, Cinerama, Cinemascope, Vistavision, Superscope, Todd-AO or Three-D, that could be shown only in theatres. Nothing prevailed for long, and nothing stopped the final dismantling of the mammoth studios. Some survived as television production companies, but the movies were forced to move out on location, making films with international capital throughout the countries of the world.

Perhaps the environment of Hollywood was bound to deal the death blow to the big studio production programmes. Tied distribution networks were no longer enough to guarantee a profit. Films had to become international to find an adequate audience. The rediscovery of Japanese films, to an important extent, and Indian films, to a lesser extent, was a revelation because they were concerned with the fundamentals of the human condition, and because they made their points without the often spurious gloss of the Hollywood article. Post-war travel opportunities have also made people more aware of the world as a whole. Higher standards of living, at least in the West and Japan, have lessened the demand for pure escapism. Change and uncertainty in the film industries of the world have been painful experiences. But now it is television, once the great enemy, that has re-aroused interest in films, and it is television which has become something of a dinosaur, afraid to move

Japan is now a leading world film producer and has adopted western methods of publicity.

out of its comfortable swamps and lumber off in a new direction. It is a poor comment on the vitality of television when old films and sports events, neither deriving from television itself, attract the widest audiences.

Meanwhile, the television era has broken the monopoly of the big cinema chains and allowed the independent producer into the industry. The vast picture palaces of the thirties have given way to the cinema complex, perhaps with two or three auditoria, restaurants, bars and even sauna baths, giving a choice of entertainment within one building. Cinema clubs and art houses have mushroomed all over the world. France has exploded into the *nouvelle vague* (new wave) with directors like Chabrol, Rohmer, Truffaut, Rivette and Godard. Alain Resnais has experimented with time and memory using the novelists of the *nouveau roman* (new novel) as his scriptwriters. Jacques Demy has created a kind of screen opera in films like *Les Parapluies de Cherbourg* (1964). Italy has produced a new school of directors represented by Fellini, Antonioni and Pasolini. Sweden has exploited the towering talent of Bergman with his team of excellent actors and actresses now emerging on the international scene. The United States has discovered new directorial talent in Stanley Kubrick, John Frankenheimer and Sam Pekinpah, and others continue to appear. Britain's John Boorman, Ken Russell and many others are making international reputations.

New Techniques

While television provides old films with bigger audiences than ever, the production of new films is as much a vital industry as it ever was. All the time, new techniques are being developed. Though a brief survey of the history of film must necessarily concentrate on the names of outstanding players and directors, many other skills are employed. Chief technicians include the lighting cameraman, the recorder or sound engineer, the art director and the editor, all with their many assistants. Amid the long lists of credits, their names are often unnoticed, but without their skills, the director would not be able to realise his vision. Film-making is a team effort where the work of individuals often overlaps. It is at once a business, an industry and an art. Usually, a producer handles the business aspects,

and the director is responsible for final artistic achievement with a team of technicians providing the manufactured parts.

To what extent a film is a work of art depends perhaps on your point of view. As a series of shadows on a roll of film, it is man-made pictorial art, just as much as is a painted canvas. As a story told in images and dialogue, it is a work of literature that must first be written down in the form of a script. It uses the arts of music, dance and theatre. Perhaps it is not so much an art in itself as a gathering together of all the other arts to make, with the aid of technology, a new artistic whole. At its best, it has its mystical qualities and is capable of uplifting the spirit. It is artificial as are all the arts and, like them, it is both an entertainment and a refreshment for the mind.

Stars of modern cinema (from left to right) Richard Burton, Barbra Streisand, James Stewart, Natalie Wood, and Richard Wagner.

Radio and Television

Marconi demonstrates his work to representatives of the Italian government.

Broadcasting is not in itself an art, but a technological means of communicating the arts to anyone with a suitable receiving apparatus. As such, it is comparable to the invention of printing, which is used to disseminate the ideas of the creative artist through the written word and the pictorial image. Like printing, broadcasting has its limitations. Printing can exactly reproduce the words of the writer, and broadcasting can almost exactly reproduce the spoken word. With the other arts, both processes are inexact. With music, printing can reproduce the notation but not the performance. The extent to which broadcasting can reproduce performance depends upon the quality of the equipment used, the skill of the technician using it and the quality of the receiving equipment within its particular acoustic environment. With the pictorial arts, printing can approximate to the form and colour of the original, but cannot reproduce the texture. Broadcasting is most successful in the reproduction of form, less so with colour, and entirely unable to reproduce texture. The art of broadcasting can thus be said to lie in the skill with which the broadcaster overcomes his limitations and the extent to which the listener or viewer makes allowances for them. Successful communication depends upon this co-operation between broadcaster and audience. In this sense, technology has provided both the means of and an obstacle to communication. Nevertheless, like printing, broadcasting provides an immensely useful means of communicating ideas between artist and public. As such, it is the scientist's continual endeavour to remove the technical obstacles that still come between the two.

Marconi

In 1864, the British scientist Clerk Maxwell first predicted the possibility of generating waves into space by means of an oscillatory electric circuit. In his *Theory of Electricity and Magnetism* published in 1873, he identified the natural phenomenon of electromagnetic and light waves travelling through empty space. In 1888, Heinrich Hertz generated a radio wave by means of a coil and spark gap which produced a spark across an independent gap some distance away. Eventually, Guglielmo Marconi, an Italian inventor working in Britain, established radio communication between France and England in 1899, and from Poldhu in Cornwall to St John's, Newfoundland, a distance of more than 2,000 miles, in 1901. Thereafter, developments followed rapidly in the improvement of transmitting and receiving equipment. The invention of the thermionic valve in 1904 provided a useful means of amplifying signals, of generating and detecting oscillations, and of rectifying an alternating current to a direct current, the variations of which provide the link between microphone and loudspeaker. The valve has more recently been replaced by the transistor which has led to considerable miniaturisation of both transmitters and receivers.

From the artistic point of view, sound broadcasting has done much for music and literature. Its one unique contribution to the arts, however, has been the radio play. This differs from all other forms of drama in that it must, of necessity, be concieved from the outset in terms of sound. This does not mean that plays written for the stage cannot be broadcast by radio, but they would almost certainly require some adaptation so that their visual aspect can be put over to the listener in sound only.

Radio Plays

The original script for a radio play must set the scene by other means than the raising of a curtain upon a stage setting. A narration can be used, of course, but that detracts somewhat from the realism of the situation. It is thus that the art of the sound-effects engineer has arisen, since many settings have their own peculiar background of sound. A garden can be indicated by birdsong, a farm by domestic animal noises, an office by the clicking of typewriters and the ringing of telephones and so on. Similarly, certain actions can be created in sound only. For instance, footsteps indicate not only that characters are moving, either slowly or at a running pace, but also the surface they are moving across, the uncarpeted boards of a hospital corridor, the gravel of a drive, even the underbrush of a forest. The sound of a shot, a grunt and the dull thud of a falling body can give a 'picture' to the listener perhaps more effectively than a narrator's description of what is happening.

Once the script has been conceived in sound terms, the casting of the play is the next important step. Generally speaking, men's voices differ from each other more than women's voices do. If a play contains scenes with several women present, then actresses must be chosen whose voices are in some way distinctive. Sometimes, this can be achieved by the use of different dialects. Often, it has to be done by establishing several different levels of pitch. The listener must always be aware who is speaking by recognising the voice, and the different voices for the different characters must be established in the listener's mind as early as possible. This has resulted in certain actors and actresses specialising in radio drama. They have learned not only to establish character through the voice alone, but also to express emotion by the same limited means. Almost unconsciously, the listener creates a mental picture of each

Transistor radios provide portable entertainment.

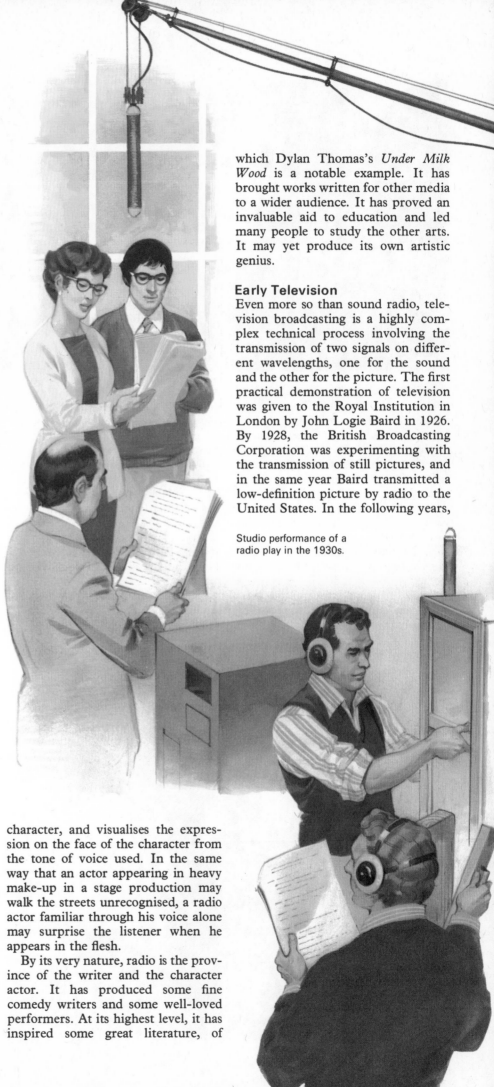

Studio performance of a radio play in the 1930s.

which Dylan Thomas's *Under Milk Wood* is a notable example. It has brought works written for other media to a wider audience. It has proved an invaluable aid to education and led many people to study the other arts. It may yet produce its own artistic genius.

Early Television
Even more so than sound radio, television broadcasting is a highly complex technical process involving the transmission of two signals on different wavelengths, one for the sound and the other for the picture. The first practical demonstration of television was given to the Royal Institution in London by John Logie Baird in 1926. By 1928, the British Broadcasting Corporation was experimenting with the transmission of still pictures, and in the same year Baird transmitted a low-definition picture by radio to the United States. In the following years,

character, and visualises the expression on the face of the character from the tone of voice used. In the same way that an actor appearing in heavy make-up in a stage production may walk the streets unrecognised, a radio actor familiar through his voice alone may surprise the listener when he appears in the flesh.

By its very nature, radio is the province of the writer and the character actor. It has produced some fine comedy writers and some well-loved performers. At its highest level, it has inspired some great literature, of

Baird and the BBC combined their efforts into a low-definition, experimental service on a 30-line system which was later abandoned. Finally, on the 2nd November 1936, the BBC began the world's first public television service from the Alexandra Palace, London. The outbreak of the Second World War put an end to the service in Britain, and the initiative in the production of a comprehensive public service temporarily passed to the United States. Since the war and including the introduction of various systems of colour transmission, television has become the greatest world-wide growth area of the entertainment industry. It has everywhere spawned mammoth production companies even larger than the great film studios of the past.

Television companies are concerned with a wider range of activities than any previous public entertainment and information service. In addition to news coverage, there is a regular output of drama, light entertainment, sport and outside broadcasts, documentaries and current affairs, religion and music programmes. Linkages have been built up around the world by means of satellites. The first live television communication between Europe and America using a satellite came with the launching of Telstar from Cape Kennedy in 1962. Since then, a number of Telstar and Relay orbiting satellites have been launched. By 1964, there was a direct live link between Japan and Europe. The latest development has been in the launching of synchronous satellites which travel at the same speed and in the same direction as the earth's rotation, thus remaining 'parked' in space above a fixed point on the earth's surface. In 1965, the Early Bird synchronous satellite was thus parked over the Atlantic Ocean at a height of 35,888 kilometres (22,300 miles) above the surface. Early Bird can relay events as they happen from Europe to America and vice versa without interruption.

Studio Production

From the performer to the viewer, television sound and picture pass through a complex process beginning on the studio floor. There, a whole series of settings, for a drama production, for instance, are positioned in such a way as to provide access to the cameras and a convenient flow of movement for the performers from one to the other. Overhead battens carry lighting and sound equipment, and also projection equipment for special background effects. Cameras are carried on highly mobile hydraulic dollies or on less mobile but smaller hydraulic pedestals. Apart from cameramen and performers, personnel on the studio floor include a studio director, a property man and their assistants. They are in communication

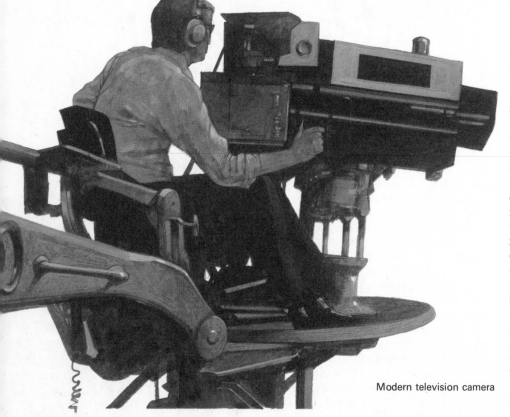
Modern television camera

with the control rooms through personal microphones and earphones, and have monitor screens scattered about the sets to watch the output picture. Output from studio sound equipment is fed into a sound control room with consoles controlled by a sound engineer. Output from the cameras is fed into a lighting and vision control room, with an engineer for each seated at his individual console. Controlling the output from both of these is the production control room where a row of monitor screens is watched by the director and his assistants. It is they who select the picture from any one of the cameras for final transmission into the central control room. Of course,

erty department, an engineering department, production offices, a script department, as well as all the ancillary services such as canteens, rest rooms and VIP reception rooms, telephone exchanges and a transport section responsible for outside broadcast vehicles. Within these an army of technicians with a wider variety of skills is employed to back up those comparatively few people who actually appear on your screens.

The Influence of Television
Like radio, television is not an art in

a performance for the cameras and, indeed, create events only after the cameras have arrived or repeat them when they do.

In the success of television with its millions of viewers lies perhaps the danger of becoming trivial. In attempting to please a wide public, television may shoulder aside minority interests and real artistic achievement. It does indeed inhibit the artist whose work is not always a comfortable thing to admit into the living room. However, television has already displayed its ability to interest more people in the other arts. Compared with them, it is a young and lusty infant with a lot to learn, but with all its life before it.

Portable television enables two activities to be enjoyed at the same time.

the production has been rehearsed and the shooting pattern predetermined to a certain extent, but it is in the production control room that the exact timing of the switch from one camera to another is finally arranged.

In the central control room, the final sound and picture combination is either put onto video tape for later editing and transmission or passed live to the transmitter. It is here, too, that pre-filmed outdoor sequences can be inserted into the flow of action. The final programme is passed to a series of relay stations linked by directional aerials, and so to the final transmitting aerial from which the signals are picked up by the viewer's aerial and carried to the receiving set.

In addition to a complex of studios and rehearsal rooms, a modern television centre has dressing-rooms for the performers, a make-up department, a costume and laundry department, a scene-building bay and prop-

itself, though employing specialised skills from all the other arts. Most of these skills were first developed in the live theatre and adapted for the peculiar demands of television. Because of the volume of its output, much of the television production is a hurried art and ephemeral in its impact on the public. The criticism has been made, with considerable justification, that the variety of television diffuses both quality and significance of programmes. With fact and fiction following each other so closely and using broadly the same techniques, the viewer is inclined to confuse the two in his mind. Indeed, since the actor is trained to be more credible than a member of the general public, fictional drama can often seem more real than actual events. Real events themselves may be falsified by the very presence of the television cameras. Demonstrators, sportsmen, politicians and many other makers of history tend to put on

Four major subjects for television presentation are sport, drama, education and news.

Language and Literature

Without the invention of language it is very doubtful whether man could have been capable of the complicated thoughts that have occupied him for centuries. We think words, and words are ideas. We actually think in a language, as anyone who has learned another language will know. In order to *speak* a language well, we have to *think* it.

Language also makes each of us part of an individual nation. Although an American speaks a national variety of English, American English is typically American, just as the dialects of the same language help to identify people within the British Isles.

Language is so important that political arguments continue to take place about it, and even wars have been fought in its cause. At the United Nations, each of the important members jealously guards the rights of his own language, and a complicated system of translation exists, so that anyone can pick up a pair of earphones to hear the language of his choice.

Some people have believed that language not only unites nations, but has helped keep others apart. One such man was Ludovic Zamenhof (1859–1917), a Polish oculist, who lived in the town of Bialystok, then part of the Tsarist Empire.

Zamenhof was Jewish, and therefore spoke and understood not only Hebrew, but also the dialect of German called Yiddish, spoken by Jews in Eastern Europe. He was also an educated man, and knew German, because a large German colony existed in his town. He spoke Russian, because that was the language of the ruling nation, and Polish, because that was the language of the country in which he lived.

A mild and peaceful man, Zamenhof thought that the constant quarrelling that went on between people was due mainly to the fact that the various minority groups could not understand each other's language. How wonderful, he thought, if everyone could learn just *one* language; not instead of their own, native tongue, but in addition to it.

An International Language

Zamenhof was thinking of the international language. Such languages had existed before, Latin, for example, had been the language of educated people until the Middle Ages, no matter where they came from. Invented languages were not new, either, for a German priest named Johann Martin

The mechanics of the seemingly simple operation of speaking are in fact quite complicated, employing a number of vital organs in the head and chest. The final quality of the sound uttered is shaped by the tongue and lips.

Schleyer had invented one called Volapük in 1880, apart from other rather strange earlier attempts.

Some people have said, and still say, that one cannot just *invent* a language; it needs to evolve gradually as a living thing among the people who speak it. Ludovic Zamenhof agreed with this, but pointed out that an auxiliary language would not belong to any one people, but to the whole world. So, in 1887, he introduced his own artificial language called Esperanto.

It was very much easier to learn than anything that had gone before and included all the national tongues. There are still large numbers of people who speak and use it, although not enough to make it the success that its followers would like.

There are other people who think that we should adopt one of the national tongues, like English, for international use. In fact, English is the most widely-spoken language in the whole world, excluding Chinese, which is really not one language, but many. The adoption of English would give the speakers of that language a great advantage over everyone else, since they would have to learn no other. For this reason, there are many other contenders for the job of supplying an international language to serve the world.

Language, that is the actual sounds we speak, came before writing. Early man had no writing at all, and there are still some primitive races who have never developed any system of writing of their own.

Systems of writing differ almost as much as the languages themselves, but with the rapid progress of means of communication, there is more and more pressure for a standard of writing to be used everywhere.

Latin Characters

The Japanese, although using a syllabary quite different from anything found in Europe, can quite easily write their language in Latin characters and do so whenever it becomes necessary. The Chinese are working on a similar idea, although it will probably take some time before agreement is reached.

Almost every Russian or Greek is familiar with the Latin characters, and in a country such as Yugoslavia, inscriptions are normally found in two alphabets. There seems to be little doubt that if one alphabet is to be adopted universally, it will be the Latin one, despite its imperfections.

This does not mean that the other alphabets will die out. Latin or Sanskrit are no longer everyday languages, but there are many people who have gone to the trouble of learning both, as well as ancient Greek, Coptic or medieval French. In the same way, we shall always be ready to learn the other alphabets, if only to be able to

18th-century scrapbook pictures.

a provision in his will for the setting up of a competition to invent a new alphabet. After the prize was awarded, some of Shaw's works were printed in the winning alphabet.

Yet none of these projects has been adopted, for it seems that we are even more conservative about our letters than our language. We like the familiar shapes which exist, no matter how imperfect are the sounds represented by the letters.

Language and Writing

Without language and without a writing system, there would be no literature. Unlettered nations can pass on folk-tales by word of mouth, but much will be lost, and much can be altered in the telling. The original form of the story cannot be retained by memory alone; this can only be done when the ideas are written down. To do that, we need an alphabet or some similar system, to make the ideas permanent.

Of course, in this modern age, there are such things as tape-recordings, gramophone records or motion-picture films which can carry a message vividly and accurately. But it is unlikely that any such system will take the place of the written word.

Literacy, or the ability to read and write, is important to modern man but primitive races have existed for centuries without these talents. The figures on the right set out a record of the work done by a labourer in the 19th century with the final image of the hanged man signifying 'account settled'. Such simple sign language can be as effective as any book in the literate man's library.

read the old books written in them. It is certain to be a very long time before the Russians, Bulgarians, Greeks, Israelis and Indians give up using their individual alphabets, and it would be a great pity if they did. It adds to the variety of life when we see books or newspapers written in alphabets, or even languages other than our own.

Just as men have thought of introducing new, artificial languages, so have others conceived the idea of a new, phonetic alphabet which would really express the sounds properly. Isaac Pitman, inventor of the shorthand system, thought up one such idea, and so did the English poet, Robert Bridges. George Bernard Shaw made

127

The Origin of Language

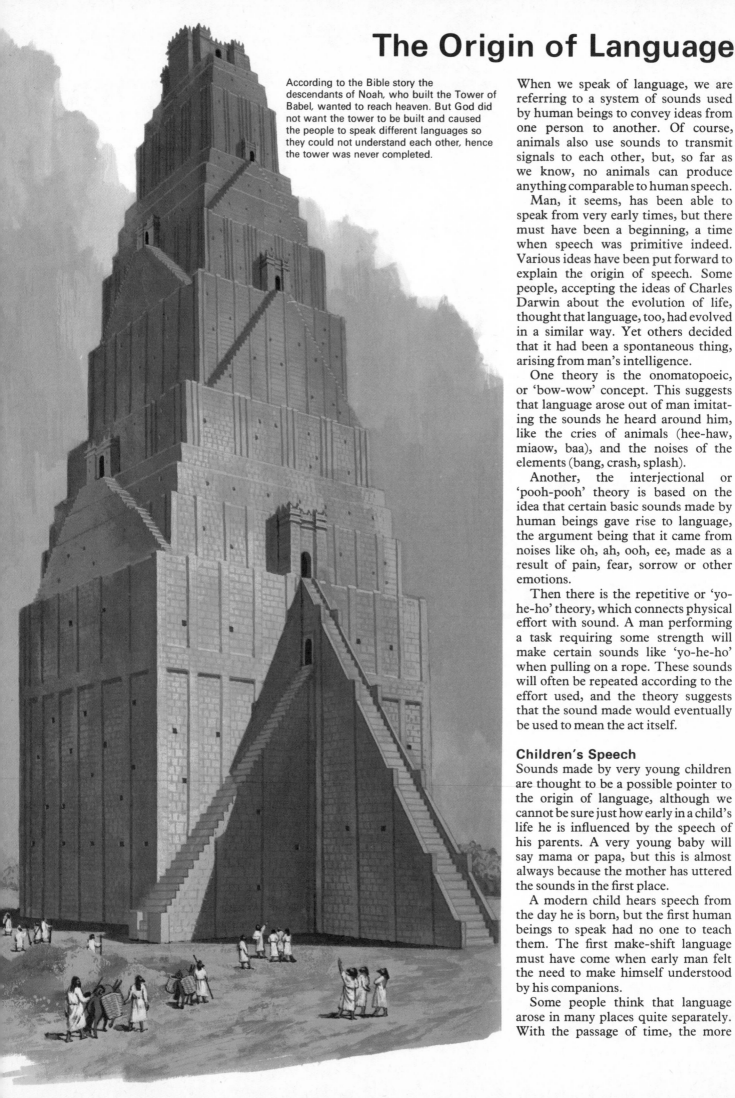

According to the Bible story the descendants of Noah, who built the Tower of Babel, wanted to reach heaven. But God did not want the tower to be built and caused the people to speak different languages so they could not understand each other, hence the tower was never completed.

When we speak of language, we are referring to a system of sounds used by human beings to convey ideas from one person to another. Of course, animals also use sounds to transmit signals to each other, but, so far as we know, no animals can produce anything comparable to human speech.

Man, it seems, has been able to speak from very early times, but there must have been a beginning, a time when speech was primitive indeed. Various ideas have been put forward to explain the origin of speech. Some people, accepting the ideas of Charles Darwin about the evolution of life, thought that language, too, had evolved in a similar way. Yet others decided that it had been a spontaneous thing, arising from man's intelligence.

One theory is the onomatopoeic, or 'bow-wow' concept. This suggests that language arose out of man imitating the sounds he heard around him, like the cries of animals (hee-haw, miaow, baa), and the noises of the elements (bang, crash, splash).

Another, the interjectional or 'pooh-pooh' theory is based on the idea that certain basic sounds made by human beings gave rise to language, the argument being that it came from noises like oh, ah, ooh, ee, made as a result of pain, fear, sorrow or other emotions.

Then there is the repetitive or 'yo-he-ho' theory, which connects physical effort with sound. A man performing a task requiring some strength will make certain sounds like 'yo-he-ho' when pulling on a rope. These sounds will often be repeated according to the effort used, and the theory suggests that the sound made would eventually be used to mean the act itself.

Children's Speech

Sounds made by very young children are thought to be a possible pointer to the origin of language, although we cannot be sure just how early in a child's life he is influenced by the speech of his parents. A very young baby will say mama or papa, but this is almost always because the mother has uttered the sounds in the first place.

A modern child hears speech from the day he is born, but the first human beings to speak had no one to teach them. The first make-shift language must have come when early man felt the need to make himself understood by his companions.

Some people think that language arose in many places quite separately. With the passage of time, the more dominant tongues ousted the lesser ones. Another theory has it that there was but one human speech, which gradually became divided into the thousands of tongues spoken today.

Finally, there is the religious doctrine which maintains that speech was bestowed ready-made on man by God; and that this speech split into diverse tongues during the building of the Tower of Babel. It is a matter of religious faith whether or not one accepts the idea of God-given speech.

Language Families

Languages have been classified by language scholars, or philologists, into ten main families, so grouped because the languages in each are related to each other like members of a family. The first of these is the great Indo-European family which includes such languages as English, Russian, Greek and Sanskrit.

Second is the Finno-Ugrian family to which Hungarian and Finnish belong. Thirdly, there is the Semitic

Indo-European	Dravidian	Korean/Japanese
Uralic/Altaic	Semitic	Polynesian/Malay
Tibetan/Burman	Bushman/Hottentot	Unclassified
Chinese	Bantu	

Map showing some of the world's main language groups.

Some of the words of foreign origin common in the English language.

Wigwam MAST chess rodeo SHERRY sherry Cigar duck magazine Sonnet Khaki check

family, including Hebrew and Arabic, and fourthly, the Hamitic family, containing the Berber language spoken by people in parts of North Africa.

The fifth family is the Indo-Chinese, including Chinese and Burmese, the sixth is Malayo-Polynesian, which includes Malay and Maori, the seventh, Turco-Tartar contains Turkish, the

The sound of the voice can be recorded in the form of a print as a means of identification since no two voices are identical.

eighth is Dravidian, including languages spoken by peoples of southern India, and the ninth is the Bantu family, which includes the tongues spoken by the Negro people of Africa.

Strictly speaking, there is no tenth family, but there are some hundred or so other languages taken together which do not fall into any group or family at all, such as Japanese, Basque, and the Indian tongues of America.

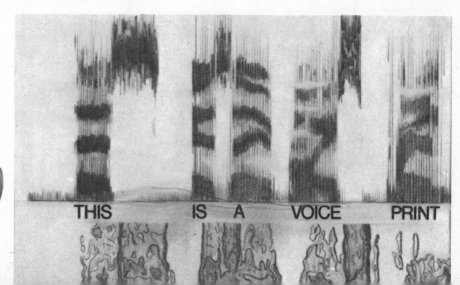

THIS IS A VOICE PRINT

Indo-European Languages

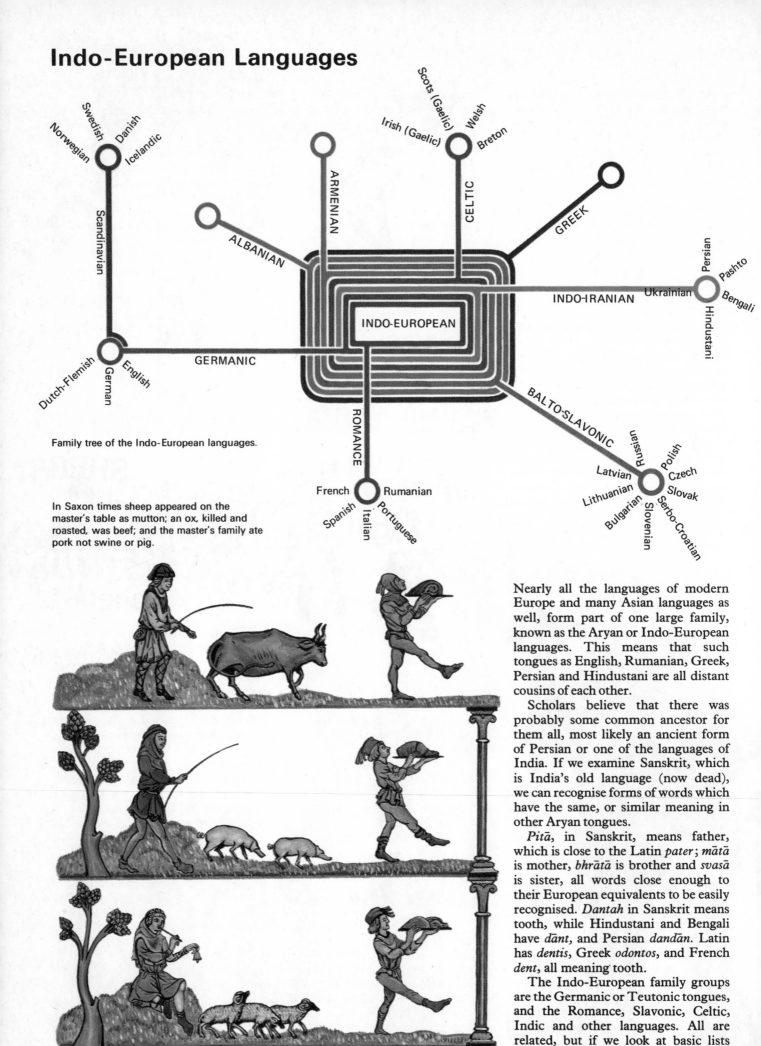

Family tree of the Indo-European languages.

In Saxon times sheep appeared on the master's table as mutton; an ox, killed and roasted, was beef; and the master's family ate pork not swine or pig.

Nearly all the languages of modern Europe and many Asian languages as well, form part of one large family, known as the Aryan or Indo-European languages. This means that such tongues as English, Rumanian, Greek, Persian and Hindustani are all distant cousins of each other.

Scholars believe that there was probably some common ancestor for them all, most likely an ancient form of Persian or one of the languages of India. If we examine Sanskrit, which is India's old language (now dead), we can recognise forms of words which have the same, or similar meaning in other Aryan tongues.

Pitā, in Sanskrit, means father, which is close to the Latin *pater*; *mātā* is mother, *bhrātā* is brother and *svasā* is sister, all words close enough to their European equivalents to be easily recognised. *Dantah* in Sanskrit means tooth, while Hindustani and Bengali have *dānt*, and Persian *dandān*. Latin has *dentis*, Greek *odontos*, and French *dent*, all meaning tooth.

The Indo-European family groups are the Germanic or Teutonic tongues, and the Romance, Slavonic, Celtic, Indic and other languages. All are related, but if we look at basic lists of words in any of these Aryan languages, it sometimes seems that words from one group are not really like those of another.

For instance, the word fish appears in German as *Fisch*, in Swedish as *fisk*, and Dutch as *vis*, all somewhat similar in sound. But Latin has *piscis*, French *poisson*, Spanish *pez*, and Italian *pesce*, which although similar to each other, are not like those in the first, or Teutonic group.

Letter Changes

Early in the nineteenth century, a German scholar named Grimm realised that there were certain regular changes or sound-shifts in the words which appeared in the Teutonic languages, compared with their opposite numbers in the Latin. One of these shifts, Grimm found, resulted in the Latin *p* changing to the Teutonic *f*, so that the Latin *piscis*, with the initial *p* changed to *f* is not so far from the Germanic fish. In this way, Latin *pater* became father, *fader* and *Vater* in English, Swedish and German, while Latin *pedis* became foot, *fot* and *Fuss*.

Of all the Teutonic languages—indeed of all known tongues—English

With the coming of the Normans, a variety of French became the official language of England, Anglo-Saxon being relegated to the status of a peasant dialect. With the passage of time, Norman-French and English became fused together, so that by the time Chaucer was writing, the language used was a mixture of a Romance language (French) and Teutonic (English). In addition, many words of Latin came into use through the Church, and also because Latin was used in early times by philosophers and learned men of various kinds.

We can understand what this means if we examine the words kingly, royal and regal. All have *similar* meanings, but there is a shade of difference between them. Kingly is Anglo-Saxon, royal is Norman-French (from *roy*, modern French *roi*) and regal is directly from Latin *regalis*.

Anglo-Saxon was the language of the servants, while Norman-French was spoken by the nobility, which explains why English still has special

The body of this fish is made up of eight words each meaning fish in different languages: *Fisch* (German), *fisk* (Swedish), *vis* (Dutch), *piscis* (Latin), *poisson* (French), *pez* (Spanish), *pesce* (Italian), fish (English).

is the most widespread, being spoken by about 300,000,000 people, as well as being used as a second language by millions more. English derived from the dialects brought to the British Isles by the Germanic Angles, Saxons and Jutes, and by later Scandinavian peoples, such as the Danes.

words for various meats. The peasants tended the animals, and used the old names for them: a sheep (Anglo-Saxon) appeared on the master's table as mutton (*mouton*), an ox, killed and roasted, was beef (*boeuf*), and the master's family ate pork (*porc*) not swine, or pig.

Borrowed Words

As a result of its mixed origin, English is able very easily to absorb words from other languages. Some quite common English words borrowed from other tongues are whisky, from Gaelic, arithmetic from Greek, curriculum from Latin, cannibal from Spanish, balcony from Italian, ticket from French, jute from an Indian language, dungarees from Hindi, monsoon from Arabic, kangaroo from aboriginal Australian, and tea from Chinese.

From Britain's former Empire came words like the Australian billabong and corroboree, the South African springbok and chimpanzee, and the Indian pyjamas, khaki and tattoo.

Many American words have passed into standard English, such as trademark, best seller, prairie, as well as the earlier reliable, influential, talented and lengthy. Surprisingly enough, these words originated in the United States, although most people would regard them as truly English expressions. Words like fall for autumn, gotten, deck for a pack of cards, sick for ill, and to loan instead of to lend are not really Americanisms at all, but old English words and expressions which have fallen from use in Britain, but which have been retained in America.

English, together with Dutch, Flemish and Frisian, is a member of the Low German branch of Teutonic. Dutch and Flemish are very similar, while in South Africa, the people of Dutch descent speak Afrikaans, which is a simplified version of Dutch. About 13,000,000 speak Dutch, while Frisian is spoken only by about 300,000 people in the islands off the coast of Holland and Denmark.

The German Language

High German, or the German language proper, is spoken, not only in Germany itself, but in Switzerland (where a local variety is called *Schwyzertutsch*), Austria and the fringes of the countries bordering Germany, a total of about 100,000,000 people. However, in the country areas of North Germany, people speak a dialect called *Plattdeutsch*, which is closer to Dutch.

The order of words in a German sentence is important, and is different from English. For instance, one says in English, 'the cat has not drunk the milk', but in German the sentence would read *Die Katze hat die Milch nicht getrunken,* or 'the cat has the milk not drunk'. In German, nouns are always written with a capital letter.

131

International road signs give instructions and warnings which do not depend on individual languages.

The Romance Group

The languages of the Romance group are derived from Vulgar Latin, that is, the everyday language spoken by the people of the Roman Empire. This was often different from the literary language, as it contained slang words and popular expressions.

One of the most important Romance languages is French, spoken by about 85,000,000 people in France, Belgium, Switzerland, Canada and French overseas territories. It has also been used as an international language in diplomacy and politics, and was spoken by members of the Tsarist and other European courts in preference to their own language.

French developed from one or two language varieties known by the words used for the word yes. In the north, this was *oïl* (modern *oui*) and in the south, it was *oc*. The north became known as Languedoil and the south, Languedoc (*langue d'oïl* and *langue d'oc*). Modern French developed from Languedoil, while Languedoc became the present-day Provençal language. It is related to the Catalan tongue of Spain, and closer to Latin than modern French.

Of all the Romance languages, French is the least phonetic. The written language has many silent letters, and some letters, combined together, are pronounced quite differently. The last three letters of

speaker), *Sauerstoff* (acid-substance) and *Zweirad* (two-wheel).

Closely allied to German is Yiddish, originally spoken by the Jews of Germany, but now used by their descendants in other countries. Based on the dialect once used in Franconia (an area of medieval Germany), Yiddish has a large mixture of Hebrew, as well as some English, French and Polish. It is written in Hebrew characters.

Teutonic Languages

What is called the Northern branch of the Teutonic languages are all grouped together under the title of Scandinavian. These languages are

Another form of communication which standardises information without reference to language is the use of ideographic symbols on a car dashboard.

Swedish, Danish, Norwegian, Icelandic and Faeroese. Swedish and Danish are close enough together to be understood by speakers of either. About 8,000,000 people speak Swedish in Sweden and in parts of Finland, and Danish is spoken by about 5,000,000.

Norwegian, spoken by about 3,500,000 people, is also understood by speakers of the other two languages, and new spelling reforms have meant that when written it is even closer. The grammar of all three is very similar, and simpler than German. The order of words in a sentence is much more similar to that of English.

Icelandic and Faeroese are akin to each other, and are modern versions of the old Norse language which was used in writing the Norse sagas. About 190,000 people speak Icelandic, and about 26,000 Faeroese.

words like *donnaient* and *avaient* are not pronounced at all, while such words as *écritoire* and *abbatoir* are pronounced 'ekritwar' and 'abatwar'.

So proud are the French of their language that they have set up the Académie Française simply to make sure that French is maintained in a pure form. Despite this, a large number of English (and American) terms have crept in, known in France rather disparagingly as 'franglais'. Words commonly used are *club*, *jockey*, *football*, *sport bifteck* (beef-steak), *rosbif* (roastbeef) and *tramway*.

Some French words borrowed from English were originally borrowed by the English language from the French. English ticket was taken from *étiquette*,

Another habit in German is to string a number of words together to form one long one. This produces some rather alarming-looking combinations. For instance, *Sicherheitsrasiermesser* means safety-razor and *Dampfschiffahrtsgesellschaftdirektors-stellvertretersgemahlin*, means steam navigation company manager's deputy's wife. This is something of a joke-word, of course, but the Germans are quite fond of long ones, and even have a jocular name for them: *Schlangenwörter*, snake words.

Unlike most other modern European languages, German prefers not to form new words from Greek and Latin. In English, during the last hundred years or so, the words television, telephone, oxygen and bicycle have been coined. German, however, uses its own rootwords to form *Fernsehen* (*fern* = far, *sehen* = seeing), *Fernsprecher* (far-

façon became English fashion, and *entrevue* turned into interview. All these words have appeared in French with their English spelling and meaning.

Yet in the past, French was itself formed from the popular jargon of the Roman Empire, including many slang words used by Roman soldiers and others. The Latin word for head is *caput*, but French has *tête*, from the old French *teste*, and this in turn comes from the Latin *testa*, a pot, which was a slang word for *head*. *Loquor* was the Latin word for to speak, but in early times, the church was talking of *parables*, or Christ's word, which gave rise to the French *parler*, to speak.

The Spread of Spanish

As we saw earlier, Catalan and Provençal are two closely linked languages of Spain and France. Provençal is spoken by about 9,500,000 people in southern France, and Catalan by about 5,000,000 in Spain, Andorra, the Balearic Islands and south-west France.

Spanish proper, another important Romance language, is not only the language of Spain, but also of nearly all the countries of South and Central America and many in the West Indies. It is also a major language of the Philippine Republic and of the Spanish colonies. In all, there are about

Bank notes and coins display the great variety of letter forms of different languages, while the well-known trade mark (below) becomes a form of international language.

115,000,000 Spanish speakers in the world. It is probably the easiest to learn of all the Romance languages because of its regular grammar and spelling. The Moorish invasions of Spain in the eighth century brought many Arabic words into the language.

Some Spanish words taken from the Arabic, and which have since spread to other languages are *algebra*, *alcohol* and *albaricoque* (apricot). The place-name Gibraltar is Arabic-Spanish,

meaning the 'mount of Tariq' (*gabal* = mount in Arabic), named from the Moorish general Tariq who landed there in A.D. 711.

Portuguese and the Galician dialect of western Spain are very close to Spanish, particularly in the written language. Since Portuguese is pro-

nounced very differently from Spanish, it is not easy for a speaker of one tongue to understand someone speaking the other.

A manual alphabet (shown above is the sign for the letter R) for the deaf and dumb was first devised in the 18th century. The deaf are also often skilled in lip reading.

133

	one	two	three	four	five	six	seven	eight	nine	ten	hundred
ENGLISH	one	two	three	four	five	six	seven	eight	nine	ten	hundred
ANGLO-SAXON	an	twégen	Þri	feower	fíf	siex	seofon	eahta	nigon	tien	hundredu
DUTCH	een	twee	drie	vier	vijf	zes	zeven	acht	negen	tien	honderd
AFRIKAANS	een	twee	drie	vier	vyf	ses	sewe	agt	nege	tien	honderd
FRISIAN	än	tâw	tri	fjâwer	fiw	säks	söwen	acht	njugen	tjin	hunnert
GERMAN	ein	zwei	drei	vier	fünf	sechs	sieben	acht	neun	zehn	hundert
DANISH	en	to	tre	fire	fem	seks	syv	otte	ni	ti	hundrede
NORWEGIAN	en	to	tre	fire	fem	seks	sju	åtte	ni	ti	hundre
SWEDISH	en	två	tre	fyra	fem	sex	sju	åtta	nio	tio	hundra
ICELANDIC	einn	tveir	Þrir	fjórir	fimm	sex	sjö	átta	níu	tíu	hundrað
LATIN	unus	duo	tres	quattuor	quinque	sex	septem	octo	novem	decem	centum
ITALIAN	uno	due	tre	quattro	cinque	sei	sette	otto	nove	dieci	cento
FRENCH	un	deux	trois	quatre	cinq	six	sept	huit	neuf	dix	cent
SPANISH	uno	dos	tres	cuatro	cinco	seis	siete	ocho	nueve	diez	ciento
PORTUGUESE	uma	dous	três	quatro	cinco	seis	sete	oito	nove	dez	cem
PROVENÇAL	un	doui	tre	catre	sinc	sièi	sèt	vuèce	nòou	dès	sèn
CATALAN	un	dos	tres	quatre	cinc	sis	set	vuit	nou	deu	cent
RUMANIAN	unu	doi	trei	patru	cinci	sase	sapte	opt	nouă	zece	sută
ROMANSCH	un	dói	tre	quatri	cinc	sîs	sièt	vòt	nûf	dîs	cent
GREEK	énas	dúo	treis	tessereis	pénte	éxi	eptá	októ	enniá	déka	ekatò
RUSSIAN	odin	dva	tri	čjetyrje	pjat'	šjest'	sjem'	vosjem'	djevjat'	djesjat'	sto
POLISH	jeden	dwa	trzy	cztery	pięć	sześć	siedem	osiem	dziewięć	dziesięć	sto
CZECH	jedan	dva	tři	čtyři	pět	šest	sedm	osm	devět	deset	sto
WELSH	un	dau	tri	pedwar	pump	chwech	saith	wyth	naw	deg	cant
BRETON	un	daou	tri	péder	pemp	c'houéc'h	seic'h	eiz	nao	dég	kant
IRISH	aon	dó	trí	ceathair	cúig	sé	seacht	ocht	naoi	deich	céad
MANX	un	da	trù	kaire	queig	shey	shiaght	hoght	nuy	jeih	ciad
GAELIC	aon	da	tri	ceithir	coig	se	seachd	ochd	naoi	deich	ciad
HUNGARIAN	egy	kettö	hărom	négy	öt	hat	hét	nyolc	kilenc	tiz	száz
FINNISH	yksi	kaksi	kolme	neljä	viisi	kuusi	seitsemän	kahdeksan	yhdeksan	kymmenen	sata
TURKISH	bir	iki	üç	dört	beş	altı	yedi	sekiz	dokuz	on	yüz
BASQUE	bat	bi	hirur	laur	bortz	sei	zazpi	zortzi	bederatzi	hamar	ehun
HEBREW	ekhad	shnajim	shloshah	arba'ah	khamishah	shishah	shiv'ah	shmonah	tish'ah	'asarah	me'ah
ARABIC	wahid	'itnen	talata	'arba'a	khamsa	sitta	saba'a	tamanya	tis'a	'ashara	miyya
CHINESE	i	erh	san	szu	wu	liu	chi	pa	chiu	shi	pai
JAPANESE	ichi	ni	san	shi	go	roku	schichi	hachi	ku	ju	hyaku

The numbers one to ten and one hundred in 36 different languages reveal both the differences between language groups and their similarities.

Spoken by about 9,000,000 people in the home country and colonies and by about 45,000,000 in Brazil, Portuguese is one of the major European languages. More nasal than Spanish, it contains fewer Moorish words, while some quite ordinary things have totally different names in each language. Street in Spanish is *calle*, but *rua* in Portuguese, hat is *sombrero* in Spanish, *chapéu* in Portuguese, and window is *ventana* in Spanish and *janela* in Portuguese.

The last of the important Romance languages is Italian, which, because it is spoken in the original country of the Romans, remains closest to Latin. As with most languages, there are a number of dialects, but the standard Italian is Tuscan, as spoken by the educated people of Florence. Italian speakers number about 65,000,000 mostly in Italy itself and Switzerland.

Just how close Italian has remained to Latin can be seen when we compare some words: *credo* is I believe in both languages; *vendo* is I sell; *primo* is Latin for first, *prima* Italian, while *quasi* means as if in both.

Rumanian has somehow survived as a Romance island in a sea of Slavonic tongues. Rumania was the old Roman province of Dacia, but the language, despite the passage of time and the influence of the surrounding languages, is still properly a Romance one. We can see this by comparing the opening words of the Lord's Prayer in Latin and Rumanian. Latin: *Pater noster qui es in celis, sanctificetur nomen tuum*; Rumanian: *Tatal nostru care in ceruri, sinteasca-se numele tau.*

The last remaining Romance language is Romansch, which is divided into three dialects. Romansch proper is spoken mainly in Switzerland, but a far greater number of people speak a similar tongue in northern Italy. In all, there are about 450,000 speakers of the language which has similarities to both French and Italian.

Slavonic Languages

The third big group of Indo-European languages is the Slavonic, which includes Russian, Ukrainian, Slovene, Serbo-Croatian, Bulgarian, Polish, Czech and Slovak. Each of these languages is much closer to the others of the group than are the languages in each of the Teutonic and Romance groups. A speaker of Polish can understand a Czech with much less difficulty than an Englishman can understand a Dutchman, or an Italian make sense of the Portuguese language.

Russian, with 125,000,000 speakers, Ukrainian, spoken by about 37,000,000 and Bulgarian, with about 8,000,000 speakers, are written in the Russian, or Cyrillic alphabet. Serb and Croat are virtually one language, except that Serbian is written in the Cyrillic alphabet and Croatian in the Roman. Together, Serbo-Croatians number about 17,000,000.

The other Slavonic tongues are written in the Roman alphabet. These are Polish, spoken by about 35,000,000 people, Slovenian (the language of about 1,500,000 people in Yugoslavia), Czech, with about 10,000,000 speakers, and Slovak, with about 4,000,000. The Slavonic tongues have kept a whole armoury of archaic grammatical forms long since abandoned by the Romance and Teutonic groups, which makes them fairly difficult languages to learn.

Two languages which are distantly related to the Slavonic are Lithuanian and Latvian, the first spoken by about 3,000,000 people, and the second by about 2,000,000. Still within the Indo-European family, but quite separate from the others are Greek and Albanian, which although spoken by people in neighbouring states, are quite different from each other.

Greek, spoken by about 11,000,000 people is surprisingly close to the classical Greek of ancient times. It still uses its own alphabet, very much as it was over 3,000 years ago. Albanian, spoken by about 2,000,000 people, is something of a language 'loner', for, although an Indo-European tongue, it does not fit into any language group, although it has borrowed extensively from others.

The Celtic group of languages includes Irish, Gaelic, Welsh, Breton, Manx and Cornish. Although an official language of the Irish Republic, the Irish tongue is spoken only by about 10,000 people. Gaelic, spoken in Scotland, and Manx, are closely related to Irish, while Welsh is akin to Cornish and Breton. About 700,000 people speak Welsh, and a similar number know Breton. Although attempts to revive the Cornish language are being made, the last native speaker of the language died in 1777.

Indic Languages

The other Indo-European tongues are found outside Europe—in Asia. These include the Indic languages of Armenian and Persian. Among the Indic tongues are Sanskrit, the 'Latin' of India, which was used even before India possessed an alphabet, Romany

The inscription on this coin is an example of the flowing calligraphy of the Arabs.

(the language of the gypsies), Hindustani, Urdu, Bengali and Sinhalese.

Today, the most widely spoken language is Hindi, which falls into two main groups, Eastern and Western. Western Hindi has given rise to Hindustani, now used as a common tongue throughout India. A variety of this is called Urdu, which is written in Arabic letters rather than in the Indian alphabet.

Bengali, spoken by 65,000,000 people in Bangladesh and other areas of India and Pakistan, is the next most important language of the subcontinent. Others are Bihari, with 35,000,000 speakers, Marathi, with 20,000,000, Punjabi, with 25,000,000, Rajasthani, with 18,000,000, Gujerati, with 16,000,000 and Sinhalese, spoken by about 4,000,000 people in Ceylon (Sri Lanka).

The Indo-Chinese Family

Chinese, Thai, Tibetan and Burmese are related languages spoken mainly in South-east Asia and in parts of the East Indies. Each is similarly constructed, but uses different root-words. The largest of them is Chinese itself, spoken by about 750,000,000 people, more than any other *single* language in the world. In fact, Chinese is really a number of dialects which are virtually languages in themselves, and speakers of one dialect cannot understand those speaking another.

The main Chinese dialects are: Northern Chinese, which includes Mandarin and Pekingese; Cantonese; Wu; Min; Hakka and Minchia. After the First World War, the Pekingese dialect was adopted by the government as the national language, and, since the tongue is spoken by about

Credivuelo

Iberia planado je iompostioma pago
Vojaĝu rapide... pagante malrapide!

This airline poster looks familiar enough, except for the language in which it is printed. This is Esperanto, an international language invented by Ludovic Zamenhof in 1887.

meaning, 'I agree'; a hesitantly and drawled 'yes', meaning 'perhaps', or else we can say 'yes?' as a question, all different meanings depending on the tone of voice. Chinese is able to do this with all its words. As an instance, the word *daï* in Chinese can mean 23 different things depending upon how it is pronounced. The word *fu* pronounced in a level tone means husband, in a rising tone, it means fortune, in a low rising tone, it is government office, and in a falling tone, it means rich.

The Placing of Words
Two Chinese words placed next to each other can also mean something quite different when spoken together.

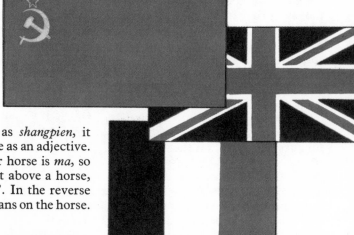

two-thirds of the people, Pekingese is still so regarded.

In Chinese, the same word can be used as a verb, noun, adjective or adverb. We can do something similar in English. For instance, take the word house. This can have the meaning of a dwelling as a noun; to accommodate as a verb (e.g. to house a family) or it can be an adjective, as in house agent. The word keeps the same form in every case.

The addition of another word in Chinese can confirm the meaning of the first. For example, the word *shang* in Chinese means above. As a noun, *shang* can mean the person above, or in other words, 'the ruler'. If another

word is added, such as *shangpien*, it can mean simply above as an adjective. The Chinese word for horse is *ma*, so *shang-ma* means to get above a horse, i.e. 'to mount a horse'. In the reverse position, *ma-shang* means on the horse.

Use of Tones
Chinese and related languages also use tones to distinguish between words. In a sense, these languages have to be sung. There are only 450 distinct sounds in Chinese, but by making them with different tones, the language can produce about 40,000 words.

We do something similar in English, when, for instance, we use the word yes in various tones. We can say 'yes',

Similarly in English, cup and board as separate words mean something quite different from cupboard, while short and hand when placed together mean something totally different from the individual words. In Chinese, the word *tung-hsi* means thing, but the two component words have entirely different meanings: *tung* is east, and *hsi* is west.

Unlike western languages, Chinese rarely borrows from other tongues, nor has it given many words to Europe. An example is tea, but there is also the Anglo-Indian soldier word *char*. Both words mean the same thing, but come from two Chinese dialects. Other words, commonly thought to be Chinese, are from other languages completely. Mandarin and pagoda are Portuguese, while junk, a Chinese sailing ship, comes from Malay.

The Chinese word *fu*, pronounced in level tone means husband; in a rising tone, a fortune; in a low rising tone, government office; and in a falling tone, rich.

Other Language Families

The Japanese language seems to be related to no other in the world, although there are some scholars who think that, because of its construction, Korean may have a distant connection. Japanese has about 100,000,000 speakers, and Korean about 38,000,000.

Japanese is quite different from Chinese, although it has borrowed a large number of words from that language, as well as from others, including the European tongues which have come into contact with it. The Japanese have one sound for the Latin L and R, which, to European ears sounds more like an R. So when the Japanese borrowed the American word gasoline, they pronounced it *gasorin*. English has given the Japanese language the words *beikon, hamu, botan, kara* and *hoteru* (bacon, ham, button, collar and hotel).

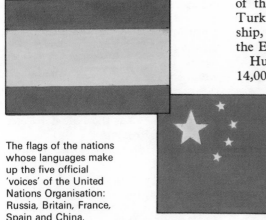

The flags of the nations whose languages make up the five official 'voices' of the United Nations Organisation: Russia, Britain, France, Spain and China.

An agglutinating language, Japanese uses root-words to which a number of affixes can be added. 'Agglutinating' simply means 'sticking together'.

For example, the word for dog is *inu*, which can mean either a male or female dog. By adding the prefix *o*, we have the word *o-inu*, which means a male dog, and by adding the prefix *me*, we have the word *me-inu*, which means female dog, or bitch. *Go* means language, while *nihon* is Japanese. *Nihon-go* is Japanese language, and *ei-go* is English language.

Pronunciation

Although not related to Japanese or Korean in any way, the European languages, Finnish (with its relatives Estonian and Lappish), Hungarian and Turkish are also agglutinating languages. Turkish is part of a separate family, but Finnish and Hungarian (or Magyar) together are called Finno-Ugrian.

Some idea of the way Hungarian is formed can be seen in this example:

house is *ház*; *a ház* means the house; *a házak*, the houses, *a házaknak*, to the houses; *a házakban*, in the houses; and *a házakból*, from the houses. One peculiarity of Hungarian is that certain letters are pronounced differently from most other European languages. *Sz* = English s; while Hungarian *s* = English sh. This means that Budapest is pronounced *Budapesht* and Liszt is pronounced *List*.

Finnish follows a similar plan to Hungarian. *Talo* is the Finnish word for house, so that *talossamme* means in my house, *talossanne*, in your house and *talossansa* in their house.

Turkish also does something like this. The Turkish word for father is *baba*, which becomes *babam* for my father; *babası* for his father, and *babamız* for our father. Fathers is *bablar*, so *bablarım* is my fathers, and so on. Notice that the letter *i* in each of these words has no dot, since in Turkish, this has the short *i* sound in ship, whereas the dotted *i* sounds like the English one in machine.

Hungarian is spoken by about 14,000,000 people, Finnish by about 4,000,000, Estonian by about 1,000,000 and Turkish by 26,000,000 people.

The Semitic Family

Other languages outside the Indo-European family include the Semitic family, which covers Arabic, Ethiopian Hebrew and Maltese, while the related Hamitic family covers the ancient Egyptian language (now extinct), modern Coptic, Somali, and the Berber language. Arabic is the most important of these, spoken by about 75,000,000 people, while Hebrew is used as a religious language by the Jews. It is also the national language of Israel, and probably has well over 1,000,000 speakers.

Mongolian, which is related to Turkish and the Tartar language, has about 3,500,000 speakers, while Tartar has about 5,000,000.

The languages of the East Indies and the South Seas are called the Malayo-Polynesian family, and include Malay, Fijian, Tahitian and Maori. The largest group is Malay, with about 65,000,000 speakers. In southern India, the Tamil, Telugu and Canarese languages form a family totalling about 100,000,000 speakers. Lastly we have the Bantu family of Africa, which includes the Swahili tongue.

The language curiosity of Europe is Basque, which is spoken by about 700,000 people on either side of the western Pyrenees. Most Basques live in Spain, the remainder in France, but their language has no known connection or relationship with any other tongue. It has certainly nothing in common with either French or Spanish.

Writing and Alphabets

Of all the hundreds of alphabets used in the world today, the most widespread is the Latin or Roman alphabet, the type normally employed for the writing of English, French, Dutch and many other modern languages. The Roman alphabet of early times varied slightly at different periods of its history, but finally settled down to the following letters:

A B C D E F G H I K L M N O P Q R S T V X Y Z

Of these, G, K, Y and Z were later additions, since Latin used C for both the sounds C and G. This last letter was formed by adding a cross-stroke to the letter C. K, Y and Z were imported from the Greek alphabet, although the Romans had an earlier Z which was dropped because it was rarely used. The modern letters J, U and W were formed from the letters I and V during the Middle Ages.

The original 21 letters, however, were not invented by the Romans themselves. They were taken from the alphabet used by the Etruscans, a somewhat mysterious people who lived in Italy before the days of the Roman Empire. They lived in a country called Etruria (modern Tuscany), and borrowed their letters from the Greeks, as we can still see if we study ancient Etruscan stone tablets. An Etruscan ivory tablet about 2,700 years old, is on view in a Florence museum, and this shows the complete alphabet of 26 letters as used in those days. Unfortunately, we are quite unable to read any Etruscan inscriptions.

The Greek Alphabet

The classical Greek alphabet is well known, and is used even today for writing modern Greek, although a few of the sounds have changed slightly. Our word alphabet comes from the names of the first two letters of the Greek system: *alpha*, A, and *beta*, B.

The Greek alphabet was probably first used in the ninth or tenth century B.C., having been adapted from that used by the Phoenicians, a Semitic race of seamen who traded throughout the countries of the Mediterranean and even beyond. They picked up their letters from the alphabet used by the Canaanites who lived in Palestine. This script was an off-shoot of the north Semitic alphabet, from which the Hebrew script is also derived. The other branch, or south Semitic alphabet gave rise to somewhat different systems, and one of the few examples of this still in existence is the Amharic script used in Ethiopia.

Semitic alphabets dating back to at least 1,500 years before the birth of Christ have been found, and many scholars think the alphabet was invented somewhere in the area of Palestine. At one time, it was thought that the alphabet was adapted from the hieroglyphic writing used by the ancient Egyptians, but now it seems more likely that, while Egyptian writing

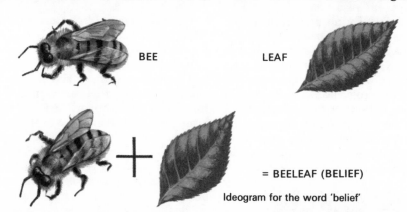

BEE

must have had an influence on the letters, it was not necessarily the original source.

The earliest known Semitic alphabet, at least 3,500 years old, was discovered only in 1929 at a place called Ras Shamrah, in Syria. Hundreds of clay tablets inscribed with cuneiform, or wedge-shaped, characters were found. These were later deciphered and found to be inscriptions written in a script containing 32 letters, since named the Ugaritic alphabet. Cuneiform writing is produced by impressing wedge-shaped pieces of wood or similar material into soft clay.

The Ugaritic alphabet should not be confused with other cuneiform writing which was used by a people called the Sumerians in Mesopotamia, since this was quite different from the Syrian examples.

The area of Palestine and Syria in early times was the meeting-place of nations, so that it is not an unlikely place for the alphabet to have been invented.

Egyptian Hieroglyphics

Egyptian writing was the other important script used in the ancient world. Until the the late eighteenth

LEAF

= BEELEAF (BELIEF)

Ideogram for the word 'belief'

century, no one knew the meaning of the thousands of inscriptions found on Egyptian tombs, mummy cases and innumerable papyrus scrolls. But in 1799 an officer of the French army discovered an interesting-looking inscribed stone near the Nile delta at a place called Rosetta.

Scholars examined the Rosetta stone, as it came to be called, and found that it was inscribed in three ways: in the Egyptian writing called hieroglyphics, in a cursive, or script version called Demotic, and in Greek. The three inscriptions obviously said the same thing in different ways. Greek was a known language, so the Rosetta stone provided the first key to Egyptian writing.

Egyptian was an ideographic system, which used ideograms, or small pictures to represent the meaning of words.

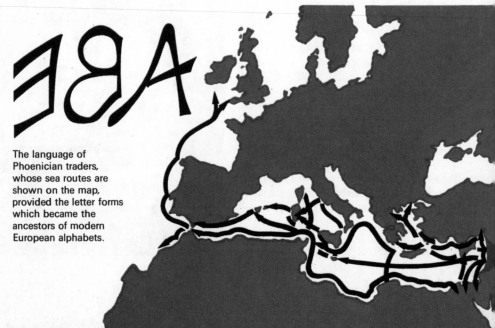

The language of Phoenician traders, whose sea routes are shown on the map, provided the letter forms which became the ancestors of modern European alphabets.

Thus a simple circle might mean the sun, but this symbol, used in certain other ways, could also be made to convey the idea of light, or day. Later, the actual sounds of these symbols were used phonetically. A parallel example, using the English language, would be like using an ideogram to mean bee, and another to mean leaf. Placed together, the sounds of the words could be used to express belief. A later development of the Egyptian symbols was their use as an alphabet, where each character meant a simple

'Th tm hs cm,' th Wlrs sd,
'T tlk f mn thngs:
'F shs—nd shps—nd slng wx—
'F cbbgs—nd kngs.'

The Hebrew and related alphabets gave each letter a name, each with a meaning ℵ *aleph*, an ox; ℶ *beth*, a house, ℷ *gimel*, a camel. When the Greeks took over the letters, they also adopted the names in slightly changed form: A *alpha*, B *beta*, Γ *gamma*, although these words mean nothing in Greek except as names for the letters.

The Aramaic alphabet gave rise to

several other scripts, among them, the Armenian, which is still used in that country. There are 38 letters, including 16 which have been added to represent special Armenian sounds. Neighbouring Georgia has an alphabet which comes in two quite different forms. The oldest, or church script, resembles the Armenian, since both alphabets are believed to have been invented in the fifth century by St Mesropius, who based them on his knowledge of Aramaic.

The second Georgian script is supposed to have been invented by King Parnavaz, and is called *Mhedruli* or 'soldier's hand', and is used for ordinary writing. Modern Georgian has an alphabet of 39 letters, written from left to right, as in Armenian.

Nearly all Semitic scripts, on the other hand, are written from right to

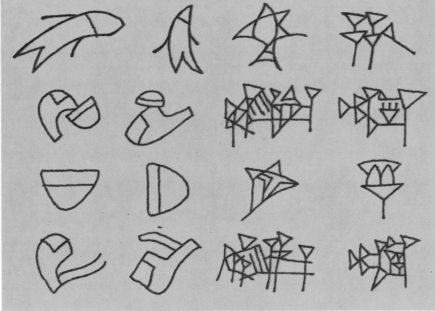

sound, just as in the Roman alphabet.

Development of the Alphabet

The Semitic alphabets, Egyptian, Phoenician, Hebrew, Aramaic (in which parts of the Bible were written) and their relatives, are written without vowels, although nowadays vowels are sometimes indicated by adding small marks or accents above or below the letters. It may seem strange to people familiar only with European languages that one can write something down without using vowels. But it is quite possible to read the following English lines from which the vowels have been omitted:

These cuneiform symbols show the development from picture signs to Assyrian script. The images (top to bottom) mean fish, to eat, food, and to drink.

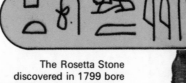

The Rosetta Stone discovered in 1799 bore inscriptions in hieroglyphic, Demotic and Greek. The cartouche, which appeared on the stone, stands for Ptolemy.

left, including modern Hebrew. When the Greeks adopted the alphabet, they also wrote it in the same way, although they added some extra letters to represent sounds not present in the Semitic alphabets. First they converted some letters into the vowels A *alpha*, E *epsilon*, I *iota*, O *omikron*, and Y *upsilon*. Next they added some new symbols Φ phi, Ψ psi, X chi, and Ξ xi (equivalent to F, PS, CH [as in Scottish loch] and X). With one or two other alterations, the classical Greek alphabet came into being.

Boustrophedon

Sometimes Greek was written from left to right, and sometimes *both* ways! When this was done, it was called boustrophedon (meaning 'as the ox ploughs', since the writing ran backwards and forwards). There was no punctuation, nor spaces between words. It was rather as if English was written like this:

ASENTENCEWRITTENI
ΥBOUSTROPHEDONWO
ULDLOOKLIKETHISRUN
THϽIЯOTTꟻƎ⅃ПHИ

Later still, the Greek alphabet settled down to being written from left to right, which, of course, is much easier for right-handed people. The alphabet was adopted officially by the government of Athens in 403 B.C. and later in the rest of the country.

The Greek alphabet was also adopted by the Copts, a people of Egypt whose language is directly descended from that of ancient Egypt. The Coptic alphabet is similar to normal Greek, but several extra letters were taken from the Egyptian Demotic script to express special sounds.

Pens and Papyrus

Early writing tended to be square and angular, largely because it was used at a time when the common way of writing was with a pointed stylus on waxed tablets. The Greeks wrote in this way, but the Romans learned to write their alphabet from an early date, using more flexible pens on parchment or papyrus, thus giving rise to much more rounded letters. The Hebrews too developed their alphabet into shapes which changed with the use of pens.

When the Romans carved their letters on stone, the carvers finished off the strokes with a swept line cut across the end, a practice which is still retained in modern letters, where these finishing lines are called serifs.

For some time, all writing in the

Examples of Cretan pictographic symbols (*c.* 1800 B.C.) found engraved on tablets on baked clay.

Medieval illuminated manuscripts showing decorated initials and capital and lower case letters.

Roman alphabet consisted entirely of capital letters, but the work of skilled scribes led to variations. In addition to the beautifully proportioned square capitals, elegantly shaped book capitals came into being, as well as some rather less formal shapes called rustic capitals.

Scribes began to produce pages in books where the initial letters were large and decorated, while the bulk of the text was smaller, with less complicated letters developed from the rustic capitals. These smaller letters, called minuscules, were the forerunners of our small letters or lower-case, as the printer calls them.

With the spread of the alphabet across western Europe, the letters began to take on local variations. Scribes, using quill pens, produced letters with thick downstrokes, and these, in some countries developed into the Gothic black letter style, which was, and sometimes is still, used in Germany and the neighbouring countries. The style died out in

England quite early, but some newspapers still use it for their titles, where it is known as Old English.

Cyrillic Letters

One group of people in Europe were without a means of writing until the ninth century, and it was the spread of Christianity which brought them their letters. These people were the Slavs, and their alphabet was invented especially to bring the scriptures to them by St Cyril, after whom it is named the Cyrillic alphabet. 'St Cyril' was really two people, Constantine and Methodius, and the alphabet contained 43 letters. Most of these were similar to those in the Greek system, but with some extra letters adapted from the Hebrew.

Today, the Cyrillic alphabet is used, with slight variations, by the Russians, Ukrainians, Bulgarians and Serbs. It is also used throughout the Soviet Union for writing other languages, many of which are quite different from Russian or any other Slavonic tongue.

The same inventors also produced another alphabet called the Glagolitic, a rather strange collection of symbols which is still used by a number of people living along the northern coast of Dalmatia. It is difficult to understand why such an alphabet was

Storage jar from Knossos, on Crete, decorated with the double axe symbol.

thought necessary, since all the sounds can be found in the regular Cyrillic alphabet.

The Cyrillic, sometimes called the Russian alphabet, has been reformed at different times, especially by Peter the Great of Russia, and more recently, after the Russian Revolution in 1917. Some unnecessary letters have been dropped, so that the present Russian alphabet contains 33 letters. The alphabets used in the Ukraine, Bulgaria and Yugoslavia are slightly different.

Several other alphabets have been used in Europe. From about the first century, a system of angular symbols called runes came into use among the Germanic tribes, and inscriptions can still be found in Scandinavia, Germany and England. The most recent runes known date from about the twelfth century A.D. Two runic symbols, representing the soft and hard 'th' sounds, are still used in the Icelandic language.

The Ogham alphabet was once used by the Celtic people in the British Isles. Probably invented about the fourth century, Oghams were a kind of secret writing, being based on varying numbers of strokes cut along a baseline.

Linear A and B

Early alphabets surrounded in some mystery have been found on the island of Crete, and were used by the Minoan civilisation which began there some 5,000 years ago. During the early period, a form of pictographic writing developed. This later gave way to a simpler script arranged in lines, and was called by its discoverer, Sir Arthur Evans, Linear A. Evans later discovered yet another script, containing about half the characters from Linear A, but with other quite different symbols. He named this script Linear B.

Neither of the Cretan scripts could be read until 1952, when Michael Ventris, a scholar who had been working on them for some years, announced that he had deciphered the second set of characters, or Linear B. Linear A was still a secret, but Linear B, Ventris discovered, was in Greek.

Alphabets Across the World

After the Roman alphabet, the most widely used script is the Arabic, which is found, not only in the Islamic countries of northern Africa and Arabia, but in Iran, India, Pakistan and the East Indies. It has been used

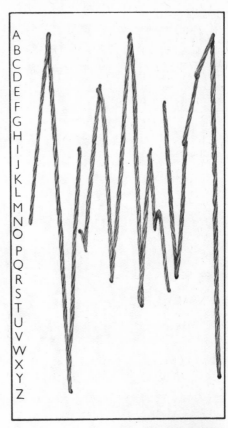

During the Second World War an embroidery code was devised using a zig-zag pattern which pointed to successive letters of the alphabet where the lines ended.

A system of secret signs has been used by tramps for many years. The signs, some of which are shown on the right, tell other travellers on the road what sort of reception they can expect from a particular house.

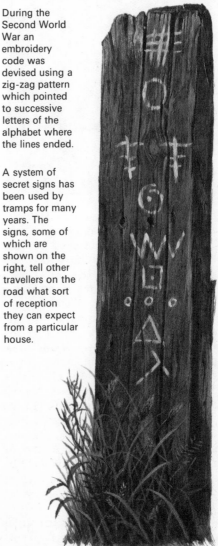

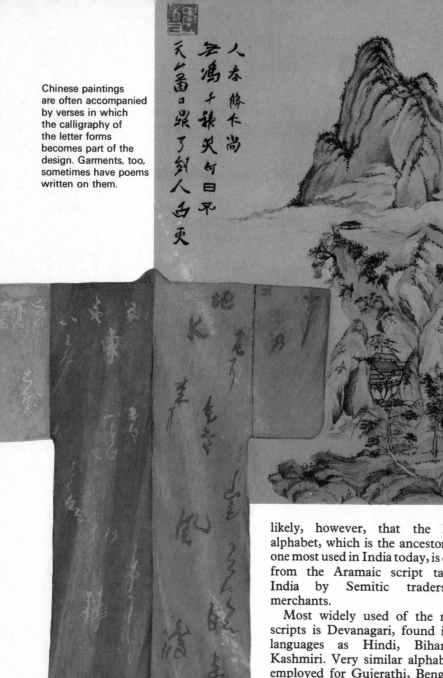

for such varied tongues as Hebrew, Swahili, Spanish and some of the Balkan Slavonic languages. Until the Roman alphabet was introduced by Kemal Ataturk in 1918, the Turkish language was also written in the Arabic script.

Its exact origin is somewhat obscure, although it is thought to be derived from an early Semitic script. The oldest example of Arabic writing dates only from A.D. 512. As with other Semitic alphabets, Arabic is written from right to left. It contains 28 consonants, sharing with other Semitic alphabets the lack of vowels, although these can be indicated by accents or marks alongside the consonants. The names of some of the letters, such as the first one in the system, *alif*, are similar to Hebrew.

Very little is known about the origin of the Indian alphabets. It seems likely, however, that the Brahmi alphabet, which is the ancestor of the one most used in India today, is derived from the Aramaic script taken to India by Semitic traders and merchants.

Most widely used of the modern scripts is Devanagari, found in such languages as Hindi, Bihari and Kashmiri. Very similar alphabets are employed for Gujerathi, Bengali and Punjabi. All are written from left to right, as with European scripts.

The Devanagari alphabet contains 34 consonants, 14 vowels and diphthongs, and 19 signs used for certain combinations. Also derived from the Brahmi script are the Sinhalese, Canarese, Telugu and Malayalan alphabets, but the characters in these have changed considerably over the years. Tamil, a related script, was the first Indian alphabet ever to be printed, some 400 years ago.

Other alphabets used in Asia include Burmese, whose letters have a curious form consisting of circles and part-circles, Thai, which originated in India, and the Korean alphabet, which has been in use since the fifteenth century.

Chinese Writing

Chinese writing is at least 5,000 years old, if not older. We know very little about its beginnings, except that the earliest examples show that the characters started as picture-writing, and that it almost certainly originated in China itself.

Until the third century B.C., Chinese was written with a stylus, and the characters still retained the picture-forms from which they had sprung. About 2,300 years ago, however, the Chinese writing-brush was invented, and this resulted in many changes, and the script took on the appearance it has today.

Chinese is written down the page from top to bottom, and starting on the right-hand side. This means that books are made with the title-page at what a western reader would think of as the end of the book. The sounds of Chinese speech are not represented in the written language, which means that any Chinese, no matter what his dialect, is able to read the same Chinese script.

This happens to a much lesser degree in other countries. In Europe, certain symbols are used which are not alphabetic or phonetic. Our figures 1, 2, 3, 4 and so on are immediately recognised by French, English, Russian or Greek readers, but each gives the figures a different name. The symbol & means and in English, *et* in French and *og* in Danish. International road signs, now standard in Europe, convey an immediate meaning to the traveller, but each one 'reads' them in his own language.

Chinese characters no longer look like pictures, since writing quickly with a brush has long since produced mere arrangements of brush-strokes:

Braille is a code of small raised dots representing letters and speech sounds that enable blind persons to read by touch.

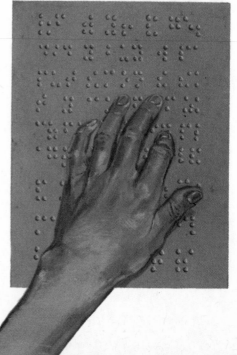

sounds. As time went on, the Japanese began to use the characters as syllables only, giving them short sounds.

Japanese Syllabaries

About a thousand years ago, Japanese writing was more or less standardised, but there were still many complications Today, the Japanese use two syllabaries called *kata kana* and *hira gana*. The problem for the reader remains, as the Japanese sometimes use the Chinese sounds for the characters and sometimes give them Japanese sounds. What usually happens is that the Chinese character is followed by *hira gana* characters to indicate the Japanese pronunciation.

It would be much simpler for everyone if the Japanese stopped using the Chinese characters altogether, and wrote their language only in one of the syllabaries. But tradition dies hard, and it has never been done. It is perfectly possible to write Japanese in the Roman alphabet, for in 1937 the government officially adopted such a system, called *kunrei-siki*.

Here is the word AUSTRALIA as written in the Japanese *kata kana* syllabary:

オーストラリア

The Japanese language cannot express consonants falling together like the STR in this word, and uses syllables with vowels attached to them. Also, the L sound is shown as R.

but originally, the Chinese sign for a tree was a picture of a tree. The script goes much further than this. The word for bright is expressed by a combination of the characters for moon and sun, while the character for woman, twice repeated, means quarrel. But the sounds for all these words would vary, according to the part of China in which the reader lived.

Today, written Chinese uses about 8,000 characters, of which only about 1,000 are used for popular books, magazines and newspapers. A Chinese learning to read has to know these characters by heart, so that mastering the written language takes some time. Several attempts have been made to produce a Roman script for the language, but none has yet been really satisfactory. The present Chinese government has introduced a new system which it hopes will be better suited to the language than those of the past.

Although totally different from Chinese, the Japanese written language uses characters borrowed from China. At first, the Japanese simply used the Chinese characters as they stood, pronouncing them either as the Chinese did, or else giving them new Japanese

Food can labels display an interesting variety of scripts and letter forms.

Literature

Literature can mean either anything written or printed, or it can describe writing which is of exceptional merit or beauty. The literature of a nation does not always produce great writers, but once a system of writing exists, then literature, whatever its standard, begins.

Even the songs and ballads of strolling minstrels can be regarded as a kind of literature, but in their original form they are impermanent, and to become true literature they need to be written down. Some of the world's most famous literature started through being told by word of mouth, for story-telling has always been a favourite way of entertaining friends and one of the most popular pastimes ever conceived by man. There are fables and legends in every land, and the famous *One Thousand and One Nights*, usually better known as *The Arabian Nights*, is simply a collection of old stories told in the market place, and later written down.

Religion and Mythology
Much early literature is based on religion or mythology, or perhaps tells some sort of history. But the popular fiction enjoyed everywhere today is of comparatively recent origin. Tales were told in ancient times, but only the worthy ideas were ever considered fit to be written down.

So we find a similar pattern repeating itself, the old folk-tales and fables existing for years before anything was written. In northern Europe, there were the Nordic legends of Scandinavia, and in the south the tales of gods and goddesses in Greece, Rome, Egypt and the other lands of the ancient world.

Literature could only spread with advance of learning, and to achieve that, technical skill was needed. The invention of printing was the one single event after the invention of writing that brought the world's learning to the man in the street.

Ancient and Eastern Literature

Most of the early books of the East were of a sacred nature, usually arising from, or connected with, religion. Oldest of the Indian literary collections are the Vedas of the Brahmans, the highcaste people who follow the Hindu religion. We shall not discuss the religion here, except with reference to the writings which form part of it.

The word *Veda* means knowledge, and the collection of writings are in the form of poems or hymns, divided into four groups. The oldest of these groups is called the *Rigveda*, written, like the others, in Sanskrit. Part of this collection is called *Atharvaveda*, made up of poems, charms, incantations and spells. Another of the *Rigveda* collections, called *Samaveda*, consists of songs, while the *Yajurveda* is a book describing religious rites.

The second group of writings is called *Brahmanas*, which are commentaries on the Brahman ritual and worship; the third are the *Aranyakas*, or meditations, and fourth, the *Upanishads*, or system of Hindu philosophy. The *Vedangas* are a kind of supplement to the other books and deal with varied subjects, such as astronomy, origins of words, grammar and pronunciation.

Epic Poems
Other works written in Sanskrit include two great epic poems: the *Ramayana* and the *Mahabharata*. Both are very long indeed, the *Mahabharata* containing over 200,000 verses. It

Bahram Gur killing a lion in China, an episode from *Shah Namah*, the Persian epic poem by Firdausi.

The Indian god Khrishna with Radha, from an 18th-century painting.

tells of the rivalry between the *Kurus* (or evil spirits) and the *Pandus* (or good spirits). The evil spirits win the first battles, but the Pandus triumph in the end.

The *Ramayana* is only about a quarter of the length of the *Mahabharata*, yet it is still 48,000 verses long. It is the older of the two epic poems, and tells the story of an Indian king and his four sons. The main character is Prince Ram Chandra who travels about southern India. His wife, Sita, is captured by Ravana, the giant of Ceylon, but with the help of Ravana's brother and others, Rama is able to conquer Ceylon and rescue his wife.

Apart from Hindu works, there are many Buddhist literary collections written in the Sanskrit language.

Buddha wrote nothing himself, but as with the Christian New Testament, the teachings of the Master were written down afterwards by his followers. The Buddhist sacred writings are divided into three parts called the *Tripitaka* or 'three baskets'. First are the *Sutras* or 'discourses', second are the *Vinayas* or 'disciplines', and third are the *Abidhammas* or 'metaphysics'.

Great poets of Buddhist literature include Asvaghosha, who lived in the first century A.D. His best works are *Nanda the Handsome*, telling of the conversion of Buddha's half-brother Nanda to the faith, and a *Life of Buddha*, which is a favourite among all peoples of that religion.

Kalidasa, who lived about the fifth century A.D., is generally regarded as the greatest of all Hindu dramatists and poets. The work for which he is particularly remembered is *Sakuntala*, a drama telling the story of the daughter of a wise man called Viswamita and a water-nymph named Menaka. Sakuntala, their daughter, is courted by a great king, who marries her, and they become founders of the great race of *Bharatas*.

Urdu and Hindi

Later writings in India have been written in the Hindustani language, either in the form of Urdu, used by the Islamic peoples, or Hindi, used by the Hindus. Hindustani literature

Scene from a Kabuki play. The Japanese theatre has produced some outstanding dramatists, particularly those who wrote for the Kabuki, or popular drama.

Confucius is the Latin name for the Chinese philosopher, K'ung Fu-tse. In early life he was a politician and teacher, but is revered in China as the authority on moral behaviour.

begins with the writings of Chand Bardai, dating from the thirteenth century, although the language did not generally become a literary one until 300 years later. Urdu writing was greatly influenced by Persian poetry which had been established much earlier.

Among the great Persian epic poets was Abul Qasim Mansur, usually known as Firdausi. His greatest work is *Shah Namah*, the story of a blacksmith who marches against a cruel king. Another of his poems is *Yusuf and Zuleikha*, an Islamic version of the Biblical story of Potiphar's wife and Joseph.

The Persian poet best known in the West is Omar Khayyam, who lived in the twelfth century. His fame in his own country was based not on his poetry (of which he wrote little), but on his work as an astronomer and mathematician. His *Ruba'iyat* was translated in the nineteenth century by the English poet Edward Fitzgerald, whose romantic free style no doubt helped to make the poem popular.

The founder of the Mogul Empire in India was the Emperor Babur, whose full name was Fehir-ed-din-Mohammed. Babur was also an Islamic

poet and writer, although he wrote in a kind of Turkish. His greatest work was his celebrated autobiography, *Babur-nama*.

In recent times, a name which stands out in Indian literature is that of Rabindranath Tagore, a poet, playwright and novelist. He lived from 1861 to 1941, and, although greatly influenced by western literature, wrote almost all his work in the Bengali language. His poem *Gitanjali* won him the Nobel Prize in 1913.

Chinese Literature

The earliest Chinese literature still in existence dates back about 3,000 years. From the time of the Han Dynasty, starting about 200 years before Christ to some 200 years after, many classical Chinese works were produced. Later these were collected together and studied by the Chinese philosopher K'ung Fu-tse, or Confucius, as he is known in the West. Confucius lived from 551–479 B.C.

Although much of this literature has been called 'Confucian classics', it is very unlikely that Confucius himself was the author. This classical material includes the *I Ching*, or Book of Changes, a mystic work which

China's most famous poet, Li Po, recites his work before the sixth T'ang emperor. Li Po was fond of the good life and it is said he met his death by drowning, from leaning too far over the edge of a boat one night in a drunken effort to embrace the reflection of the moon.

contains details of fortune-telling and politics, the *Shih-Ching*, containing more than 300 folk-songs, hymns and poems; and the *Shih Shu*, which explains the doctrines put forward by Confucius.

One of the followers of these doctrines was the Chinese sage Meng-tse, or Mencius, who lived from about 372–289 B.C. His *Book of Mencius* was written to explain the ideas and way of life of Confucius.

Most of the great poetry of China was written during the T'ang Dynasty, (A.D.618–906). During this time lived such great poets as Wang Wei (who was also a painter), Li Po, who wrote romantic verse, Po Chu-I, who was a master of the ballad and folk-poem, and Tu Fu, whose work was of a more serious nature. Most Chinese poems are quite short and make their impact by their mood, rather than by telling a story.

Well before such concepts had made their appearance in Europe, the Chinese had developed many dictionaries and encyclopedias. One Chinese dictionary, still in use, was produced over 250 years ago. An encyclopedia produced during the Ming Dynasty (1368–1664) appeared in as many as 24,000 volumes, all written by hand.

Many books of a popular type appeared, including novels such as *San Kuo*, a tale of war and chivalry, written during the thirteenth century. *Pilgrimage to the West*, written in the fifteenth century, tells of a journey to India, containing something of the flavour of *Gulliver's Travels*, while *The Water Margin* is a book which collects folk-tales together.

The Dream of the Red Chamber by Ts'ao Chan, written in the eighteenth century, is considered to be the greatest of all Chinese novels. This tells the story of a large family from the time of its highest success to the years of its decline. It covers some 2,500 pages and introduces more than 400 characters.

Japanese Literature

Until the third century there was no written language in Japan, and for some time, classical Chinese was in use. Indeed one of the early Japanese poets, Kino Tsurayuki, writing in the tenth century, felt it necessary to apologise for publishing his verse in Japanese.

Shortly afterwards, some talented novelists appeared on the scene, one of the best being a woman, Murasaki Shikibu, who wrote what is considered to be the greatest Japanese novel, *The Tale of Genji*, in 54 sections. Other women writers of the period were Sei Shonagon, who wrote the *Pillow Book*, and Izumi Shikibu, a poet who specialised in romantic love poems.

By the nineteenth century, there were romantic novelists such as Kyokutei Bakin, who produced over 300 works, his stories being based mainly on the folklore of China and Japan, while another woman novelist was Ichiyo Higuchi, who wrote more realistic tales.

Modern Japanese novelists have often adopted a western style, and one of the best twentieth century Japanese novelists is Shiga Naoya.

The Japanese theatre has produced some outstanding dramatists, particularly for the *Kabuki*, or popular drama, and for the *Nō* (or classical) and *Jōruri* (puppet) plays. An outstanding writer of *Jōruri* plays was Chikamatsu Monzaemon (1653–1725), sometimes called the 'Japanese Shakespeare'. Kabuki plays are really a more popular form of the *Nō* classical type, although much freer, with a less formal text which encourages the actors to improvise.

The Koran

Among Islamic peoples, the *Koran* ranks as the most important work, since it is a belief of the followers of Islam that the sacred book was dictated by God to Mohammed during the life of the prophet. Mohammed died in A.D. 632, but according to tradition he had written down most of the *Koran* on papyrus, palm-leaves, bone, stones, and strips of leather. All this material was collected and arranged by the prophet's secretary, Zaid ibn Thabit, by order of the Caliph Abu Bekr.

The *Koran* is written in Arabic, and

Some of the most beautiful examples of the bookbinder's art are to be found enclosing the pages of the Bible.

is divided into 114 chapters or *Suras*, arranged according to their length. The longest chapters appear first.

Although usually regarded as the best-known collection of Arabic writings, the famous *Thousand and One Nights* is only partially Arabic in origin. It is actually based on an old Persian book called the *Thousand Stories*, which spread through the Arab world and was translated into Arabic during the tenth century.

The Persian book itself most likely derived its stories from India, but with the arrival of the work among Arabic peoples, particularly the Mamelukes of Egypt, many references to local people and customs were incorporated. The *Thousand and One Nights*, although popular, was not considered to have any high literary value by the Arabs, who were introduced to the stories mainly by word of mouth from story-tellers in the bazaars and coffee-houses.

By the fifteenth century, written collections of the *Nights* had been made, and some included extra stories from other sources. The work was first translated into a western language by Antoine Galland, a French oriental scholar, at the beginning of the eighteenth century. Other translations quickly followed, and the book has since become one of the most popular collections of stories in the world.

The Bible

Of much earlier date than the *Koran* of the Arabs is the Bible of which the Old Testament, together with the Talmud, forms the basis for the beliefs of the Jewish people. Although the date of the writings themselves is much older, the various books of the Old Testament are said to have been collected together by the Jewish scribe Ezra about 2,500 years ago.

The Old Testament used by the Jews has been adopted by the Christians, although a few books, accepted by Roman Catholics and others, are omitted by some Protestant groups. These books, called the *Apocrypha*, appeared in some Jewish versions, but not in others.

The earliest existing example of the Hebrew Bible is a manuscript dating from A.D. 1010. This is because the Jews regarded the scrolls as sacred, and tended to destroy them when they became worn and tattered. There are, however, some fragments of the scriptures which are much older.

The New Testament, of course, is of later date. What is believed to be the oldest copy of both the Old and New Testament in Greek is preserved at the Vatican, having been written in

One of the most popular stories in the *Thousand and One Nights* concerns Ali Baba and the forty thieves, who hid in oil jars when they tried to recover their stolen treasure.

the fourth or fifth century. Next in age is the *Codex Alexandrinus*, of the fifth century, and now in the British Museum in London. Parts of the *Codex Sinaiticus*, dating from the fourth century, are held in different parts of Europe, but most of its ancient leaves are also in the British Museum.

Epic of Gilgamesh

A Semitic work of importance is the *Epic of Gilgamesh*, a poetic legend of Babylonia, containing about 3,000 lines written on twelve tablets. A Gilgamesh did rule Sumeria about 4,500 years ago, but the hero of this

The Old Testament tells the story of the fall of Jericho when it was captured by the Israelites. The walls of the city are said to have fallen down to the blast of trumpets.

pessimistic poem was involved in purely legendary activities. Only about half the work still exists, but the epic tells how Gilgamesh wandered forth, meeting the half-man, half-bull Enkidu in his search for immortality.

Homeric Poems

In Europe, the Greeks possessed an early literature dating back to 800–500 B.C., consisting of what are called the Homeric poems, written in the Ionic dialect. The author is unknown. Among the great epics of Greece are the *Iliad* and the *Odyssey*, the first telling of the siege of Troy, and the second, of the adventures of Odysseus. Although Homer is traditionally regarded as the author of both, there are many scholars who doubt this, and some who believe that each of the epics was the work of a different author.

The *elegy* was another form used by Greek poets, mainly to comment on topics of the day. The earliest poet to write in this way was Callinus (*c*. 650 B.C.), followed by Tyrtaeus, Solon, Theognis, and the poet—philosopher Xenophanes. Lyric poetry, that is, verse written to be sung to the accompaniment of the lyre, was greatly developed by Alcaeus, the poetess Sappho, and the satirist Anacreon.

These songs were also used in the theatre, where, with the addition of dancing, a new dramatic form began. Athens was the home of drama, where plays, often performed in sets of three, or trilogies, were dedicated to the wine god Dionysus. Greek tragedy was more than entertainment, since it had a deep religious meaning. Three of the world's greatest tragic dramatists flourished in ancient Greece; Aeschylus (525–416 B.C.), Sophocles (*c*. 496–405 B.C.) and Euripides (480–406 B.C.) Such was the power of their work that their tragedies remain with us as living examples of great literature.

The festivals of Dionysus were also the occasion for comedies, among the best of which were written by Aristophanes, (*c*. 448–388 B.C.), a great wit and master of satire.

Greek Historians

Greek writers on historical subjects were foremost among the prose writers in early times. Herodotus, born in *c*. 485 B.C., was the author of a history of the wars between Persia and the Greek states, his narrative including many quaint observations made on his personal journeys. Thucydides, born in *c*. 460 B.C., wrote an account of the Peloponnesian War. Xenophon, born in *c*. 435 B.C., produced a wonderful account of the march of ten thousand Greek warriors through Asia, a biography of Cyrus, the founder of the Persian Empire, and a collection of the sayings of Socrates, who wrote nothing himself.

As a master of philosophy, Socrates (469–399 B.C.) was equalled only by his pupil, Plato (427–347 B.C.) who based his ideas on those of his master. These concepts have influenced western thinking ever since.

Greek literature was not only written, but spoken, for some of the best expression of Greek ideas came through oratory, when men of such fine intellect as Demosthenes (384–322 B.C.)

Gilgamesh

and Aeschines (389–314 B.C.) addressed their fellows in city squares and market-places.

Greek thought and writing had a great influence in Rome. The earliest Latin literature really began with plays by Livius Andronicus (284–204 B.C.) adapted from Greek originals. He was a Greek slave captured while a child during the Roman wars against King Pyrrhus of Epirus. Apart from his Greek adaptations, he was also an actor and playwright, producing both comedies and tragedies.

So great was Greek influence that the first history of Rome was written in Greek by Fabius Pictor (*c*. 200 B.C.) while the historian Cato (234–149 B.C.) followed the Greek tradition in airing his views by oratory.

Latin Literature

The golden age of Latin literature came during the reigns of Sulla and Augustus (78 B.C. to A.D. 14). Drama became less important, its place being taken by prose writing, epic and lyric poems, and historical works whose quality was sometimes often better than the Greek which had influenced them. The scholarly Varro (116–27 B.C.), Rome's greatest orator, was supreme master of the Latin tongue. Like other Roman speakers, he also published his speeches which dealt with themes like friendship, old age, and oratory itself. Another orator of distinction was Julius Caesar, (100–44 B.C.) whose fame was not confined to matters of state and the battlefield. He was author of commentaries on the Gallic and Civil wars, and of a book dealing with the formation of words.

Sallust (86–34 B.C.) is known mainly for his *History of Rome*, and for the development of short historical studies. Cornelius Nepos (99–25 B.C.), a friend of Cicero, was also an historian and a poet; but the greatest historical work

One of the most popular fables attributed to Aesop, who lived probably in the 6th century B.C., concerns the race between the tortoise and the hare.

Among the many adventures which befall Odysseus and his companions on their way home from the war with Troy, none is more terrible than their encounter with the fearsome one-eyed Cyclops, the giant Polyphemus.

of this time was another *History of Rome*, the life-long occupation of Titus Livius, or Livy (59 B.C.–A.D. 17). Livy's *History*, begun when he was aged thirty, filled 142 volumes, of which 35 have survived.

Among the leading Roman poets was Lucretius (99–55 B.C.) whose great work, *De Rerum Natura*, was written in an attempt to free men from superstition. The greatest of all Roman poets, Virgil, was born in the year 70 B.C., the son of a farmer.

The Aeneid

The first known work by Virgil is collected under the title *Eclogues*, or Pastoral Poems, which tell of the loves and quarrels of herdsmen. His *Georgics* are concerned with the countryside and farming, with birds, animals and plants. But Virgil's greatest work of all

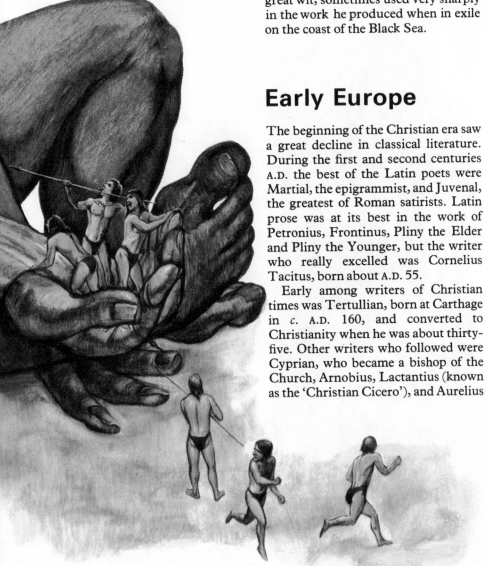

tells of the wanderings and adventures of Aeneas the Trojan, the legendary founder of the Roman nation, after the siege of Troy. Entitled the *Aeneid*, the poem was completed in twelve books, which were published after the poet's death in 19 B.C.

Ranking next to Virgil is Horace (65–8 B.C.) whose finest work is found in his *Odes*, which tell of the expansion and conquests of Rome. Horace's earliest works include the *Satires*, followed by the *Epodes*, the *Odes* and the *Epistles*. Other poets of note were Tribullus, (c. 54–19 B.C.) and Propertius (c. 48–c. 15 B.C.), both masters of the elegy.

Ovid (43 B.C.–A.D. 17) is noted for his love poems, some of which are full of advice to those in love. But his best-known work consists of fifteen books of *Metamorphoses*, which include passages of great beauty and of such power that they influenced European literature for centuries afterwards. Ovid had great wit, sometimes used very sharply in the work he produced when in exile on the coast of the Black Sea.

Early Europe

The beginning of the Christian era saw a great decline in classical literature. During the first and second centuries A.D. the best of the Latin poets were Martial, the epigrammist, and Juvenal, the greatest of Roman satirists. Latin prose was at its best in the work of Petronius, Frontinus, Pliny the Elder and Pliny the Younger, but the writer who really excelled was Cornelius Tacitus, born about A.D. 55.

Early among writers of Christian times was Tertullian, born at Carthage in c. A.D. 160, and converted to Christianity when he was about thirty-five. Other writers who followed were Cyprian, who became a bishop of the Church, Arnobius, Lactantius (known as the 'Christian Cicero'), and Aurelius

Augustinus, who became St Augustine.

Augustine became a Christian only later in life, and he tells of his life and conversion in the famous *Confessions*, written in thirteen books between A.D. 397–401. Other writers of the time included St Hilary, St Jerome, and St Ambrose. These early Latin and Greek writings of the Christian era are called patristic literature.

Greek writing was also greatly influenced by the Church, but many writers, such as Methodius and Athanasius were able to produce work which could appeal to both believers and non-believers, despite the fact that both were Christian bishops.

Byzantine literature, also written in Greek, dates from A.D. 330 and was largely of a religious nature. Chief among its writers were St Basil, St Gregory of Nazianzus, St Gregory of Nyssa, and St John Chrysostom.

With the break-up of the Roman Empire and the spread of Christianity throughout Europe. Latin literature was carried into the new barbarian kingdoms. Far from dying out, Latin became the literary language of the West, and continued so into medieval times. In fact, until about the tenth century, a form of Vulgar Latin was the ordinary speech of the people, after which it began to break up into various national languages.

In the British Isles, important Latin literature was appearing from the pens of such writers as St Columba, St Gildas, St Aldhelm and the Venerable Bede (c. 673–735), whose great masterpiece was his *Historia Ecclesiastica Gentis Anglorum* (An Ecclesiastical History of the English People), which remains the chief source of early English history.

Beowulf

Yet alongside the Latin literature, writings in local languages were beginning to appear. *Beowulf*, a poem of over 3,000 lines, is the only surviving Anglo-Saxon work, and indeed, the greatest. Dating from the tenth century, it tells of the deeds of the Nordic hero Beowulf, who frees the court of King Hrothgar the Dane from the terror of Grendel, the monster in human form. Although pagan in content, *Beowulf* shows signs of Christian influence.

Cynewulf was an Anglo-Saxon poet who lived during the eighth century, but little of his work has survived. Four poems exist, *Elene*, *Juliana*, *The Ascension*, and *Fates of the Apostles*.

The largest chained library in the world is probably that at Hereford Cathedral in England. Books were so valuable in the days when they were handwritten and in the early days of printing, that only by securely fastening them to a bookcase could they be saved from theft and damage. Hereford has about 1,500 books, a number of them printed before the year 1500.

Most notable of Gaelic literature in early times is the *Eulogy of St Columba*, written by Dallan Forgaill, the chief Irish poet of about the sixth century, and the much later *Book of Ballymote*, written by the friars of a Franciscan order in about the fourteenth century.

Edda, a collection of early Icelandic poetry, dates from between the ninth and thirteenth centuries. The first part is given over to mythology, telling of Norse gods, while the second consists of poems of heroes like Wayland the Smith, Attila the Hun, Hamdir, and others.

Scaldic poetry also comes from Iceland, telling stories of kings and chieftains. It is so named from the *scalds* who composed and recited the lines, which were not written down until the twelfth and thirteenth centuries, having been passed down by word of mouth only.

German Literature

All that survives of the old German pagan literature is a fragment of heroic legend in verse called *Hildebrandslied*, dating from the ninth century. In early times, war-songs and beast-epics like *Reynard the Fox* had been popular among the Germanic peoples, but most died out with the coming of Christianity under Karl the

Great, better known as Charlemagne.

Charlemagne himself actually began a collection of old German poems, and started to compile a German grammar. During his reign, Latin was adopted as the language of literature, but a few pieces in German have survived, one of which was the *Heliand* (meaning 'healer' or 'saviour'), a collection of Christian writings written in Low German by a ninth-century poet.

The Minnesänger

Except for Einhard, who wrote a biography of Charlemagne, there were no German writers of note before the thirteenth century, when the *Minnesänger* poets appeared. From about 1200 to 1300, these knights travelled the land singing their songs of love, chivalry and romance. The *Minnesänger* (love-singers) were led by such poets as Walter von der Vogelweide, and so great was their importance that they were joined by the emperor himself, Henry VI.

In the centuries of the Dark Ages, when art and literature are believed almost to have died, books were still copied with loving care by monks in special rooms in the monasteries called scriptoriums.

Some of the old pagan and heroic poems were revived and gathered together into one book, called the *Heldenbuch*, or 'Book of Heroes', while another collection, containing tales of Prince Siegfried and the Scandinavian race of dwarfs called Nibelungs, has the title *Nibelungenlied*.

Reynard the Fox was also revived in the twelfth century, transformed into a long satire in verse. With the coming of the Hohenstaufen rulers in the twelfth and thirteenth centuries, more importance was given to native German literature, and by the fourteenth century, *Minnesänger* poetry had died out.

A German middle class had arisen,

and with them came a new literature of stories, fables and satirical writing. Comic drama began to develop, and during the fifteenth century, the groups called *Meistersänger* came into being. Unlike the earlier aristocratic *Minnesänger*, these were poets of the people, mainly workmen who sang the praises of their crafts. Most famous of the *Meistersänger* was Hans Sachs (1494–1576), the son of a tailor who settled in Nuremberg as a master cobbler. His life was immortalised in Wagner's opera *Die Meistersinger von Nürnberg*.

The Revival of Learning
During the fifteenth century, under the Revival of Learning, Greek and Latin classics were studied, and popular satires against the Church and ruling classes appeared. Among these works were *Ship of Fools* by Sebastian Brandt, which appeared in 1494, and the sermons by the witty but quarrelsome monk, Thomas Murner. During the fifteenth and sixteenth centuries some of the famous German popular tales first appeared, among them *Tyll Eulenspiegel*, *Dr Faust*, and *Amadis of Gaul*.

An important landmark in German literature came with the Reformation, and in particular, the writings of Martin Luther (1483–1546). His use of German was largely responsible for the standardisation of the Bible between 1522 and 1534 and some hymns which remain in world-wide use to this day.

After the Thirty Years War, when German literature had declined, a new standard in poetry was introduced by Martin Opitz (1597–1639). He attracted many followers, who tended later to imitate the style of French writers of the period. By the eighteenth century, German writing was being influenced by English literature.

Daniel Defoe's *Robinson Crusoe*, which appeared in England in 1719, was very favourably received in the German-speaking countries, giving rise to dozens of imitations. There were German Crusoes, Austrian Crusoes and even Swiss Crusoes, best-known among whom remain the members of the *Swiss Family Robinson*.

In the second half of the eighteenth century, men like the poet Friedrich Klopstock taught Germans about love of the German fatherland with his verses of the glorious past, while Christoph Wieland's style was much lighter and full of gaiety. After about

The Nordic sagas of Scandinavian countries were not written works of literature, but living stories declaimed before an audience, often during the course of some feast or celebration.

1770, German literature entered its richest period, and writers adopted a more national style.

Goethe and Schiller
Gotthold Lessing (1729–81) created the style of modern German drama. German writing took the form of a reaction against the old classical writing, followed by a freer and more varied literature, seen at its best in the works of Johann Wolfgang von Goethe (1749–1832) and Friedrich Schiller (1759–1805). Goethe stands out as Germany's great man of letters; a poet, dramatist, and novelist. His finest drama acclaimed by all nations, is *Faust*, while *Wilhelm Meister* is one of his best-known novels. *Hermann*

and Dorothea is a narrative poem telling of a farmer's son who falls in love with a refugee from the French Revolution.

Schiller, a close friend of Goethe's, was also a poet and dramatist, best-known for his lyrical and philosophical poems. His plays include *Wilhelm Tell*, written in 1804 *Die Jungfrau von Orleans* (1801) about Joan of Arc, and his finest work, *Wallenstein*. This is an historic drama in three parts, which tells of the deeds of Count Albrecht von Wallenstein, who was commander of the German forces during the Thirty Years War.

Second only to Goethe and Schiller was Heinrich Heine (1797–1856), composer of witty and romantic poems, many of which were gathered together

The Ride of the Valkyries from the German epic *Nibelungelied*, which features Brunnhilde and Siegfried.
This saga was used by the composer Wagner as the story for his opera cycle *The Ring of the Nibelung*.

in his *Das Buch der Lieder* (Book of Songs). The brothers Schlegel (August Wilhelm and Friedrich) were popular poets, the first being well known for his translations into German of the plays of Shakespeare.

The Grimm Brothers

The Grimm Brothers (Jacob and Wilhelm) were concerned with much scholarly work on the study of language itself, together with studies into the origins of legends and myths. They are famed, however, for their collections of fairy-tales, first published between 1812–15 as *Kinder-und Hausmärchen*.

Two outstanding nineteenth-century dramatists were Franz Grillparzer, an Austrian, and Friedrich Hebbel, who made his reputation with his play *Judith* in 1841. Grillparzer, who is Austria's greatest dramatist, had a series of successes, among them being his plays forming *Das Goldene Wies* (Golden Fleece) trilogy, but he fell foul of the censor with another drama in 1826.

Modern Writers

Three of the greatest figures of modern German literature were Stefan George (1868–1933), Rainer Maria Rilke (1875–1926) and Hugo von Hofmannstahl (1874–1929). George, a poet and language student, was greatly influenced by his travels in France and Spain. Although admired in Nazi Germany, he refused all honours by the state, and left the country.

Both Rilke and von Hofmannstahl were Austrians, the first being one of the greatest of all lyrical poets in German literature. The second was a poet, dramatist, essayist and brilliant classical scholar. Among other works, he wrote the words for Richard Strauss's opera, *Der Rosenkavalier*. Another great Austrian writer was Franz Kafka (1883–1924). It is only in recent years that the true genius of this man has been appreciated. Interested in philosophy and religion, his novels include *The Trial*, *The Castle*, and *America*.

After the Nazis came to power, the work of Jewish writers like Kafka, Jakob Wassermann, Lion Feuchtwanger, Stefan Zweig, Bruno Frank and Emil Ludwig was ignored or banned, but the end of the Second World War saw a great revival of interest in their writings. Thomas Mann (1875–1955), one of Germany's greatest novelists, although not Jewish, refused to work under the Nazi regime, and went into voluntary exile. Another writer who adopted a similar attitude was the Marxist poet and playwright Bertolt Brecht (1898–1956), who was violently anti-Nazi.

The stranglehold of the régime tended to hold back the advance of German literature. Great strides have, however, been made since 1945, with the appreciation of writers such as the poets Gottfried Benn (1886–1956) and Rudolf Schröder (1878–1962), and more recently, the novelists Ernst Jünger and Hans Werner Richter. Erich Kastner is a satirist, but is also well known as an author of novels for children.

French Literature

The literature in early Gaul was little more than an imitation of the classical writing of Rome itself, but this Latin literature disappeared with the coming of the barbarians. By the eleventh century, two separate schools of poetry arose in northern and southern France.

South of the River Loire, groups of lyrical poets called troubadours sprang up, and they introduced a new kind of poetry into Europe. Chief among them were Bernart de Ventadour, Guirant de Bornelh, Pierre Vidal, Bertrand de Born, and many other men of noble birth. The first troubadour known was William IX, Count of Poitiers (1071–1127), but even kings could be counted among their numbers, including England's Richard I.

Troubadours and Trouvères

The troubadours were, in fact, minstrels who wrote and sang in the Provençal language, their songs mainly concerned with 'courtly love' and chivalry, sometimes passionate, sometimes romantic. Alongside this love poetry, there was often a simple, homely literature consisting of ballads, songs and prose stories. The only surviving specimen of these is a charming story called *Aucassin et*

Johann Wolfgang von Goethe.

During the 15th century the groups called *Meistersänger* came into being. Most famous of these was Hans Sachs, whose life formed the basis for Wagner's opera *The Mastersingers of Nuremberg*. In this scene the young knight Walther since his prize song.

Nicolette, a tale of a Saracen youth who falls in love with the Christian girl Nicolette.

In the north of France, the narrative poets were called *trouvères*, and it was these more realistic artists who were the true fathers of French literature. Before the end of the fourteenth century, the northern French dialect gained strength and overtook the *Langue d'Oc* or Provençal tongue, which resulted in the troubadours giving way to the trouvères.

Although less charming than the poems of the Provençal writers, the work of the trouvères was more Gallic in spirit, reflecting the national sentiments in stories of war and adventure. The very earliest example of a northern French epic is the eleventh-century *Chanson de Roland*, which tells of the death of Roland and other knights, and of the vengeance of Charlemagne.

Beginning at about the end of the twelfth century, came writings of chivalry and romance featuring Arthur and his knights, mostly from sources in Brittany. Then followed classical stories, taken from Greek history and legend, and in the thirteenth century short stories in verse called *Fabliaux* appeared. These varied from serious to downright comic, and are still found in French folk-lore.

Humour was also shown in mock-heroic poems, especially the parodies of famous stories like *Reynard the Fox*. Most famous of the northern French *trouveres* or *chansonniers* (song-writers) was Rutebeuf (*c.* 1250–85) who wrote about 56 pieces, including plays, songs, *fabliaux* and poetry.

Roman de la Rose, a poem of over 20,000 lines, was typical of the literature of the thirteenth century. Begun by Guillaume de Lorris about 1235, it was completed by Jean Clopinel de Meung about 1280. It is an allegorical story of love, hatred, pity, envy, happiness, fear and youth, and had a great influence over later work.

Jean Froissart

French literature almost died out during the Hundred Years War (1338–1453), the only writers of note being Jean Froissart, the chronicler (*c.* 1333–*c.* 1405), and the poets Alain Chartier (1385–*c.* 1435) and Eustache Deschamps, known as 'Morel' (*c.* 1345–*c.* 1406).

In the fifteenth century, French poetry was mainly concerned with ideas taken from earlier *chansons*, praising the spring, sun, grass and the singing of birds. Verses tended to be repetitious and without much original thought, although some names are remembered. Among them are the outstanding poets of the century—Charles d'Orleans (1391–1465), who sometimes wrote in English, Mellin de Saint-Gelais (1491–1558), famed for his wit, and François Villon (born 1431). Sentenced after killing a priest, Villon fled and wandered through the country, and his work shows his understanding of the suffering of ordinary people. Villon, who is regarded as one of the greatest of French poets, probably died about 1480.

Last of the poets of the Middle Ages was Clément Marot (1496–1544), for in the early years of the sixteenth century, the Renaissance or Revival of Learning began to have its effect on French literature. It reached its height during the middle of the century, but the work of François Rabelais (*c.* 1494–1553) made a great impact during the earlier years. A scholar, physician, satirist and wit, Rabelais, greatest of French humorists, is best-known for his satirical books *Gargantua* and *Pantragruel* which burlesqued religion and politics.

The leader of the new movement in literature was Pierre de Ronsard (1524–85), who founded the *Pleiade* poetic school. His verse was light and full of grace, yet after his time, French poetry fell into a decline.

Jacques Amyot (1513–93) was the translator of Plutarch's works into French, Pierre de Brantôme (*c.* 1530–1614) an entertaining writer of memoirs, and Michael Montaigne (1533–92) the scholarly essayist, was brought up to speak Latin as his mother tongue, which undoubtedly affected his later work.

Although French literature at the beginning of the seventeenth century was trifling and affected in content, it became much more polished in style. François de Malherbe (1555–1628)

The first meeting between the princess and the frog from the Grimm Brothers' tale *The Frog Prince*.

was a careful and witty writer, but Pierre Corneille (1606–84) was the first great French dramatist. René Descartes (1596–1650) and Blaise Pascal (1623–62) rank among the most important of European thinkers, both being men of science and literature.

Molière

During the reign of Louis XIV, French literature flourished once more, when such poets as Molière, Racine, Boileau and La Fontaine came to prominence. Molière (1622–73), whose real name was Jean Baptiste Poquelin, was not only a poet but the greatest of all French playwrights, frequently acting in his own plays.

His best known works include *The School for Husbands* and *The School for Wives*, *Tartuffe*, *Le Misanthrope*, *Don Juan*, *Le Bourgeois Gentilhomme*, and *Le Malade Imaginaire*. Nicolas Boileau (1636–1711) criticised the literary and social ideas of the time, Jean Racine (1639–99) was a dramatist who had a simple effective style, his masterpiece probably being *Phèdre*, while Jean de la Fontaine (1621–95) was famed for his skill as a story-teller. His most famous work is the well-known *Fables*, which are stories in the style of Aesop.

Leading prose writers of the late seventeenth and early eighteenth century include the philosopher Nicolas Malebranche (1638–1715), the historian Jacques Bossuet (1627–1704), the theologian François Fenelon (1651–1715), and the very popular François de la Rochefoucauld (1613–80), best-known for his *Maxims* and *Memories*. Marie de Sévigné (1626–94) is remarkable for her letters, mostly writ-

Bertold Brecht

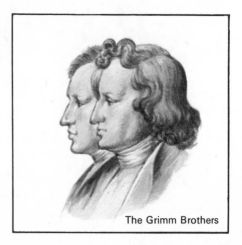

The Grimm Brothers

The 11th-century *Chanson de Roland* tells of the death of Roland and other knights during the time of Charlemagne.

outstanding playwright and poet of the period, while the best-known poets include Théophile Gautier (1811–72), Charles Baudelaire (1821–67), Sully Prudhomme (1839–1908) and Paul Verlaine (1844–96).

The two novelists named Alexandre Dumas were father and son. The elder (1802–70) was author of such classics as *The Three Musketeers*, *The Count of Monte Cristo*, and *The Black Tulip*, while the younger (1824–95) wrote *La Dame aux Camélias* (Camille) when he was only twenty four years old.

George Sand (1804–76), a woman, whose real name was Armandine Aurore Lucie Dupin, was famous for her 'problem' novels and for her love affairs with famous men, while Prosper Mérimée (1803–70) was the author of the novel *Carmen*. Stendhal was the pseudonym of Henri Beyle (1783–1842), author of psychological novels, while Honoré de Balzac (1799–1850) is regarded as the greatest of French novelists, his best-known work being *La Comédie Humaine*, which took him twenty years to write.

Imaginative Novels

Gustave Flaubert (1821–80) was the author of *Madame Bovary*, while Emile Zola (1840–1902) was leader of the Naturalist school of writers. Jules Verne (1828–1905) was the author of a long list of imaginative novels anticipating scientific progress, and these have remained very popular all over the world.

Pierre Loti was the pseudonym of Louis Viaud (1850–1923), whose exotic novels told of lands abroad, while

ten to her children. Clear and fluent in style, they are valuable for their descriptions of French social life.

During the eighteenth century, the great names of Voltaire, Diderot and Rousseau dominated the French literary scene, together with the poet André Chénier (1762–94) and the dramatist Pierre Beaumarchais (1732–99). The latter's plays *The Barber of Seville* and the *Marriage of Figaro* were the basis of the famous operas by Rossini and Mozart.

Voltaire

François Marie Arouet, better known as Voltaire (1694–1778) opposed certain aspects of religion, and was against intolerance and superstition. A poet, dramatist and historian, he was very critical of the work of Shakespeare, the most famous of his own works being the brilliant ironical novel *Candide*.

Denis Diderot (1713–84) is famous for his *Encyclopédie*, which occupied him for twenty years, while Jean Jacques Rousseau (1712–78) was the father of the Romantic school of writers, his autobiography *Confessions* being the greatest of its kind.

Novelists of the eighteenth century include Alain le Sage (1668–1747), Pierre Marivaux (1688–1763) and Antoine Prévost (1697–1763), author of *Manon Lescaut*, a love romance.

The French Romantic movement took place in the early half of the nineteenth century, the first among the writers being François Chateaubriand (1768–1848) and Alphonse de Lamartine (1790–1869). Foremost among the Romanticists was Victor Hugo (1802–85) whose novels *Notre Dame de Paris*, *Les Misérables*, and *Toilers of the Sea* are famed internationally.

Alfred de Musset (1810–57) was an

Troubadours were originally minstrels who wrote and sang in the Provençal language. Their songs were mainly concerned with love and chivalry but they also sang the popular ballads and stories of the day.

among other more recent French writers are Anatole France (Jacques Anatole Thibault, 1844–1924), the Belgian novelist Maurice Maeterlinck, (1862–1949), Colette (Sidonie Gabrielle Colette 1873–1954), André Maurois (1885–1967) the Swiss novelist Charles Ramuz (1878–1947) and the young novelist Françoise Sagan.

André Gide (1869–1951), an outstanding novelist and dramatist of the early part of the present century,

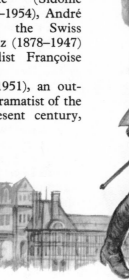

wrote of the conflict within men's minds, while Marcel Proust (1871–1922) ranks among the really great novelists with his huge À la Récherche du Temps Perdu. François Mauriac (1885–1970) is a playwright, poet and novelist of distinction whose writing introduces problems of Catholic conscience.

Albert Camus (1913–59) was a novelist interested in social reform. A friend of the brilliant Jean-Paul Sartre he was opposed to much of the latter's ideas. Sartre's works are often witty, but a mood of pessimism is usually present. André Malraux is a leading political figure, and his novels deal with contemporary political problems.

Italian Literature

Italian literature begins in the twelfth century, earlier writing having been in Latin, rather than in one of the country's dialects, from which modern Italian has been derived. The earliest known Italian poet of note was a Sicilian named Cielo d'Alcamo, who is believed to be the author of a verse-dialogue between two lovers, written between 1231 and 1250.

Following this, the most important writers were Brunetto Latini (c. 1210–c. 1295), who wrote partly in the French language, Guido Guinicelli (1235–76), known only for a few surviving beautiful poems, and Guittone d'Arezzo (1225–95), who

The three musketeers in the novel by Dumas the Elder swear eternal allegiance.

Jules Verne wrote imaginative novels which anticipated many of the realities of the modern scientific world. This scene is from his *Journey to the Centre of the Earth*.

wrote poems much in the style of the French troubadours.

None reached the excellence of Guido Cavalcanti (c. 1230–1300), whose 50 or more love-poems were unequalled in their time except by those of his friend and admirer, Dante Alighieri (1265–1321), greatest of all Italian poets.

Dante Alighieri

Dante (a shortened form of Durante) who was born in Florence, is widely considered to be the greatest poet the world has ever known. His finest achievement, *The Divine Comedy*, begun in about 1308, was only completed just before the poet's death. It contains no less than 100 cantos or divisions, telling of the poet's journey through Hell, Purgatory and Heaven. The whole poem is written in *terza rima*, a special style invented by Dante, in which three verses are so arranged that the middle line of each rhymes with the first and third of the succeeding.

The Tuscan dialect used by Dante later became accepted as the literary language for the whole of Italy. Two of the poet's greatest friends were Giovanni Boccaccio (1313–75) and Francesco Petrarca (1304–74), better known as Petrarch. Boccaccio was also a poet of some standing, but his best-known work is a collection of stories called the *Decameron*. Some of his poems were adapted by the English poet Chaucer in the *Canterbury Tales*. Petrarch, a poet and scholar, wrote some poems in Latin, while his other work in Italian was in the medieval style symbolising courtly love.

From 1400 to 1500, when the Italian Renaissance reached its full bloom, a host of brilliant, scholarly writers made their appearance. Leading poets included Angelo Poliziano (1454–94), a Greek and Latin scholar, Luigi Pulci (1432–84), who had a genius for comic verse and Matteo Maria Boiardo (1434–94), famous for his epic poem, *Orlando Innamorato* (Roland in Love).

Niccolo Machiavelli (1469–1527) was one of the few really outstanding figures of the Italian Renaissance. A prominent political figure of the day, his most famous literary work is *Il Principe* (The Prince), which seeks to explain how rulers may resort to any treachery to uphold their authority. But a better-written book is his *Discourses on the First Ten Books of Livy*, a commentary on Livy's work as an historian.

In Victor Hugo's *Notre Dame de Paris* the hunchback Quasimodo rescues Esmeralda and seeks sanctuary in the cathedral.

The Age of Poets
The second greatest period in Italian literature was from 1500 to 1600, which may be considered as the Age of Poets, producing such genius as that of Ludovico Ariosto (1474–1533), and of Torquato Tasso (1544–95) himself the son of a poet. Ariosto's masterpiece is *Orlando Furioso* (Mad Roland), a continuation of the poem by Boiardo, while Tasso's authorship of *Jerusalem Delivered* brought him great acclaim until insanity overtook him.

Other poets of the time were Giangiorgio Trissino (1478–1550), Pietro Bembo (1470–1547), champion of Italian against Latin as a literary language, Pietro Aretino (1492–1557), a satirical and comic poet, and Giambattista Guarini (1538–1612), who achieved fame with his *Faithful Shepherd*, a tragi-comedy.

Seventeenth-century Italy produced little poetry of any quality, possible exceptions being some of the work of Francesco Redi (1626–97) and the burlesques of Alessandro

Tassoni (1565–1635). An example of some of the more criticised poetry of the time can be seen in the *Adone* of Giambattista Marini (1569–1625).

The *History of the Council of Trent* by Paolo Sarpi (1552–1623) was an important prose work of the period, but during the eighteenth century, Italian literary genius was apparent mainly through the works of dramatists like Carlo Goldoni (1707–93) and Vittorio Alfieri (1749–1803). Goldoni's early plays were unsuccessful tragedies, but he eventually turned to comedy, rapidly becoming Italy's greatest comic playwright, with over 120 successes to his name.

Alfieri, on the other hand, succeeded with his tragedies, many of which contained brilliant political satire. Pietro Metastasio (1698–1782) was a poet and master of the melodrama, writing a number of dramas adapted to a musical setting with many graceful lyrics. Carlo Gozzi (1720–1806) retained an older Italian style of farcical comedy in his plays, undeterred by the more modern and stylish work of Goldoni.

The best-known Italian poets of the late eighteenth and early nineteenth century were Giacomo Leopardi (1798–1837) and Giuseppe Giusti (1809–50). A new school of writing began to make itself apparent at this time, the leader being Alessandro Manzoni (1785–1873), a poet and historical novelist, who combined

religion and patriotism in his work. His novel *The Betrothed*, set in Italy during the Spanish occupation, is one of the best in Italian literature. Two other successful historical novelists were Domenico Guerazzi (1804–73) and Massimo d'Azeglio (1798–1866).

Giosuè Carducci (1835–1907), still regarded as the national poet of modern Italy, was influenced by a classical education. He looked to early times for inspiration, although with the formation of the united Italian kingdom, many other writers were chiefly concerned with the great political events of the time.

Gabriele d'Annunzio

Gabriele d'Annunzio (1863–1938) could be regarded as the first of the modern writers, although his earlier poems were influenced by those of Carducci. He was, however, also a dramatist and novelist, his most successful novel being *The Triumph of Death*. His best work appeared at about the turn of the century, including the play *Francesca da Rimini*, but as a result of a fine war record he remained a national hero until his death.

A popular children's author of the late nineteenth century was the very prolific Carlo Collodi (1826–90), author of *Pinocchio*, a story which first appeared in a children's magazine.

Luigi Pirandello (1867–1936), both novelist and playwright, was the author of about 300 short stories, 6 novels and over 50 plays, one of which, *Come tu mi vuoi*, was made into a film in 1931 entitled *As You Desire Me*, with Greta Garbo in the leading role.

Benedetto Croce (1866–1952) has been a leading Italian literary figure, mainly as a critic and historian. Italian

Boccaccio's *Decameron* contains a series of stories told by a group of young people who leave the city of Florence to stay in the country during the time of the plague in the 14th century.

political affairs loomed large in the late 1920s, but unlike d'Annunzio and Pirandello, Croce was always an opponent of Mussolini's fascist régime, and retired from public life during the 1930s.

Alberto Moravia is the pen-name of Alberto Pincherle whose first novel, *The Time of Indifference*, was a story of middle-class Rome, a thinly disguised criticism of the earlier years of Mussolini's rule. His later novels, realistic in tone, include *The Wheel of Fortune*, and *The Woman of Rome*.

Spanish Literature

The literary language of modern Spain is Castilian, which is based on the dialect of old Castile, itself derived from a variety of Vulgar Latin. It was a written language by at least the tenth century, although the earliest known example of it dates from about 1140. This is the well-known epic called *Poema del Cid Campeador*, which tells of the chivalrous deeds of Rodrigo, or Ruy Diaz de Bivar, who probably lived about 1040–99. Also known as El Campeador, or El Cid, he is the Spanish national hero, a defender of Christianity against the Moors.

A few anonymous poems exist from a slightly earlier date, but the first Spanish poet known by name was a priest, Gonzalo de Berceo (c. 1180–c. 1246), author of about 13,000 lines of religious blank verse. Alfonso X (the Learned), king of Castile (1221–84) was a writer of both prose and verse, while his nephew, Don Juan Manuel (1282–1349) was an important short-story writer. Juan Ruiz, archpriest of Hita (who died about 1350), founder of a style of burlesque writing, was Spain's greatest medieval poet.

Moorish Ballads

Even older than these works by known authors were the ballads or *romanceros*, of which *El Cid*, mentioned earlier, is one. The origin of these popular verses is not certain, some scholars believing them to be purely from Spanish sources, while others think that they may have been introduced by the Arabs. They are often referred to as 'Moorish ballads'.

Ballads led on to rhymed chronicles, one of the foremost writers of these being Pedro Lopez de Ayala (1332–1407), poet and translator. He was also the author of a fine prose work concerning the history of Pedro I, Enrique II, Juan I, and Enrique II of Castile. In the fourteenth and fifteenth centuries, Spanish literature came under Italian and Provençal influence, when romantic tales of chivalry, similar to those of the troubadours in France, spread across the country. Typical of these is *Amadis de Gaul*, a novel of knightly prowess, somewhat similar to the stories of Arthur and the Knights of the Round Table. The author is unknown, but the work appeared in 1508. The stories of chivalry were very popular, but were much criticised by such men as the scholar Juan Luis Vives (1492–1540). *Don Quixote de la Mancha*, the novel by Miguel de Cervantes Saavedra (1547–1616), satirises these books of chivalry, and tells the story of a simple-minded country gentleman who, having spent his time reading them, sets himself up as a knight and goes forth to put the world to rights. Apart from its rôle as critic of the earlier romantic stories, *Don Quixote* remains as one of the world's greatest novels on the idealism of man.

The Novel and Drama

The seventeenth century was one of Spain's best literary periods, when poetry, the novel and drama flourished. Noteworthy novelists included Mateo Alemán (1547–c. 1614), whose best work is his novel *Guzmán de Alfarache* telling of a young man forced to live the life of a rogue. Such stories, which were very popular in Spain, dealt with the lives of rogues and thieves, and are called picaresque. Another of the type is *La Historia de la Vida del Buscon* by Rancisco de Quevedo (1580–1645).

Greatest of the dramatists was Lope de Vega (1562–1635) an outstanding poet, and said to have been the author of 1,800 plays. Only 500 still exist, however, and some of these may not be authentic. His best plays are of an historical type, with peasants overthrowing their wicked landlords, a typical example being *Peribañez*. Other playwrights were Tirso de Molina (pen-name of Gabriel Téllez, c. 1571–1648), and Pedro Calderon de la Barca (1600–81), who stylised the form of the comedy used by Lope de Vega.

Many poets were mystic and religious writers, particularly St Teresa of Avila (1515–82), whose simple prose was influenced only by her reading of the Bible and other devotional works. She founded a convent at Avila, and her Way of Perfection was a guide to her nuns. Her friend and adviser, St John of the Cross (1542–91), was a poet of some standing, while others of note were Fray Luis de Leon (1527–91), Luis de Gongora (1561–1627) and the non-religious poet Fernando de Herrera (1534–97), a great man of letters.

Dante's *Divine Comedy* describes the poet's journey through Hell, Purgatory and Heaven. He enters Hell with Virgil and sees on its gate, 'All hope abandon, ye who enter here!'

Alberto Moravia

(1833–91). The latter's greatest strength was in his short novels, and his story *The Three-Cornered Hat* is the basis for the famous Russian ballet on Spanish themes.

José Maria de Pereda (1833–1906) was firmly in accord with realism. Although a great descriptive writer, his novels are weak in plot, while the work of his friend, Benito Pérez Galdós (1843–1920) shows a deep understanding of human nature. A prolific writer, Pérez Galdós produced 80 novels, 24 plays and a number of other books. His great series of historical novels called *Episodios Nacionales* occupies 46 volumes.

Emilia Parso Bazan (1852–1912) combined both realism and romanticism in her novels, and Vicente Blasco Ibañez (1867–1928), a journalist and politician as well as a novelist, was often criticised for the 'popular' appeal of his books, although he died a millionaire.

More recently, the chief Spanish writers have been the dramatist Jacinto Benavente (1866–1954) winner of the 1922 Nobel Prize for Literature and the South American poet Rubén Dario (1867–1916), founder of the 'modernist' movement of Latin

French influence was noticeable in later Spanish literature, which went into a decline for almost three-quarters of a century. Imitators of French styles included Ignacio de Luzan (1702–54), Valesques de Valdeflores (1722–72), and Leandro de Moratin (1760–1828). But the novelist José de Isla (1703–81) revived the Spanish picaresque novel, and made an excellent translation of Lesage's *Gil Blas*.

With the dawn of the nineteenth century romanticism and realism began to influence Spanish literature. First among the successful leaders of the Romantic movement was the Duque de Rivas (1791–1865) with his play *Don Alvaro*, later used by Verdi for his opera *La Forza del Destino*.

Playwrights and Poets
José Zorrilla (1817–93) was another dramatist and poet of the Romantic movement, who achieved a phenomenal success with his *Don Juan Tenorio*, which remains the most popular of all Spanish plays. José de Espronceda (1808–42) and Manuel Quintana (1772–1857) were romantic poets, the last-named even finding inspiration in such an unlikely subject as the printing press.

Although a dramatist and novelist, Mariano José de Larra (1809–37) was more successful as a satirist, under the pseudonym Figaro. Of mixed German, Irish and Spanish descent was Cecilia Böhl de Faber (1796–1877) an exponent of the romantic style, and although not a great writer herself, she was responsible for a new school of writing, in which she was surpassed by her followers.

More realistic novels appeared towards the end of the century with the appearance of work by Juan Valera (1824–1905) and the journalist-turned-novelist Pedro Antonio de Alarcón

Cervantes's gentle knight Don Quixote tilts at windmills, imagining himself in battle.

America which seeks to exalt art and musicality in verse. The spirit of the movement was captured and reformed by the Spanish poets Juan Ramón Jimenez (1881–1958) and Manuel Machado (1874–1947).

Catalan Literature

Catalan literature saw a revival in the middle of the nineteenth century, and the language continues to be used by a number of prominent writers.

Joan (the Catalan form of Juan) Maragall (1860–1911) was a prominent poet, with Carlos Riba Bracons (1893–1959) and Josep Maria de Sagarra (1894–1961) representing the present century.

Scandinavian Literature

No real Danish literature existed before the beginning of the fourteenth century. In fact, the early language of Scandinavia was common to Denmark, Norway and Sweden, the basis of modern Danish being that used in the translation of the Bible made in 1550 by Christien Pedersen. Denmark's greatest literary treasure of its early period are the many ballads, of which over 500 exist, and these were first published in 1591.

During the Renaissance, some Danish poets of note were Anders Arrebo (1587–1637), and Thomas Kingo (1634–1703) best known for his hymns. Anders Bording (1619–77), also a poet, was founder of Denmark's first newspaper. In the eighteenth century, the gifted and versatile

Ludwig Holberg (1684–1754) was the most prominent literary figure. Although born in Norway, he is often referred to as the 'father of Danish literature', since he set Danish writing on a path comparable with other European literatures. Later in the century came the works of Johannes Ewald (1743–81), considered by many as the greatest lyrical poet of Denmark.

Early in the nineteenth century, Johan Heiberg (1791–1831) was a prominent dramatist and poet, but more influential was Adam Oehlenschläger (1779–1850). Other writers include Nicolai Grundtvig (1783–1851), the poet, and the internationally famed Hans Christian Andersen (1805–75), author of fairytales.

A modern writer with a hint of Andersen's brand of humour is the dramatist Kjeld Abell (1901–61). Other writers of the present century include Martin Andersen Nexø (1869–1954), novelist, Johannes Jensen (1873–1950), poet, novelist and essayist and the great patriot and dramatist Kaj Harald Munk. A clergyman, Munk was born in 1898 and died at the hands of the Nazis in 1944.

Norwegian Literature

From 1380, the literary language of Norway was Danish, and the country was not separated from Denmark until 1814. In the early nineteenth century Norwegian literary figures of note were Henrik Wergeland (1808–45), the poet and playwright, and his great literary rival, the poet Johan Welhaven (1807–73). Peter Asbjørnsen (1812–85) and Jørgen Moe (1813–82) produced a collection of traditional Norwegian tales from folklore. But the greatest

Contemporary woodcut of the Spanish playwright Lope de Vega.

names of the century were Henrik Ibsen (1828–1906), the playwright, Björnstjerne Björnson (1832–1910), Jonas Lie (1833–1908), and Alexander Kielland, (1849–1907), the last three all being playwrights and novelists.

Of a later date were the novelist Arne Garborg (1851–1924), playwright and essayist Gunnar Heiberg (1857–1929), and the greatest name in modern Norwegian literature, Knut Hamsun (1859–1952), novelist, playwright and poet. Second only to Hamsun is the name of Sigrid Undset (1882–1949), a novelist of a very high order, and winner of the Nobel prize in 1928.

Swedish Literature

Beginning with the translation of the Bible into Swedish in 1540 by Olaus Petri (1493–1552), the language began to assume a literary form later in the sixteenth century when the first poet appeared—Georg Stiernheilm (1598–1672). In the following century came the poet Gunno Dahlstierna (1661–1709) and in the eighteenth century Olof von Dalin (1708–63), historian, playwright and poet. The religious leader Emanuel Swedenborg (1688–1772) was a prominent writer of the time, but an important place is held by Carl Michael Bellman (1740–95), poet and writer of songs who is still popular today.

The Romantic movement made some impact on Swedish literature at the beginning of the nineteenth century, a leading writer being the dramatist Per Atterbom (1790–1855). A leading poet was Erik Johan Stagnelius (1793–1823), and a Finnish literary giant was Johan Runeberg (1804–77), a poet who wrote in Swedish.

Sweden's greatest genius of literature was August Strindberg (1849–

One of the great dramatic moments in Tolstoy's *War and Peace* is the disastrous retreat of Napoleon's army from Moscow.

1912), dramatist, novelist and poet, while the most widely known Swedish novelist was Selma Lagerlöf (1858–1940), Nobel prize-winner of 1909. Another winner of the Nobel prize was Verner von Heidestam, a poet who received his award in 1916. Of greater stature was Gustaf Fröding (1860–1911) now regarded as Sweden's best lyric poet.

Important novelists include Hjalmar Söderberg (1869–1941), Hjalmar Bergman (1883–1931) and Pär Lagerkvist, who are equally talented as dramatists.

Russian and Slav Literature

Popular story-poems, called *bilini*, are the earliest literature of any kind to have existed in Russia, but no written literature appeared in the language until about the eleventh century. A manuscript containing the Ostromir Gospels exists which was completed in the years 1056–7, but the first Russian printed book did not appear until 1564.

Some interesting accounts of life in the seventeenth century appear in some pamphlets written by Grigory Kotoshikhin (died 1667) and a Croat Jesuit priest called Yury Krizhanich who was exiled to Siberia.

Due to the great changes brought

The Finnish epic poem *Kalevala* contains many references to gods and spirits derived from the natural elements of air, fire and water.

about by the reforms of Peter the Great, Russian literature began to look to Western countries for inspiration. One of the first 'new-style' poets was Antioch Kantemir (1709–44), who imitated the French of Boileau. Mikhail Lomonosov (1711–65) was a scientist, poet, dramatist and language reformer, but his verse lacked life.

The playwright Alexander Summarokov (1718–77) was able to support himself by writing dramas and comedies in the French style, and another French imitator was the novelist Mikhail Kheraskov (1733–1807). Best among the writers of the time was Vasily Zhukovsky (1783–1852), who produced some superb translations of German and English poetry.

By far the greatest literary figure to appear on the Russian scene up to that time was Alexander Pushkin (1799–1837), whose narrative poem *Eugene Onegin* and drama *Boris Godunov* are masterpieces by any standards. Mikhail Lermontov (1814–41) was, in his short life, a poet second only to Pushkin.

The Russian Novel
Novels of everyday life now began to make their appearance, first among writers of these being a Ukrainian, Nikolai Gogol (1809–52). His best-known, and most successful work is *The Government Inspector*. Then followed Fedor Dostoyevsky (1821–81), a powerful writer and author of the great novels *Crime and Punishment*, *The Idiot*, and *The Brothers Karamazov*.

Outstanding among Russian playwrights who were both also novelists, are Ivan Turgenev (1818–83) and the versatile Anton Chekhov (1860–1901). They were, however, lesser writers than the great Leo Tolstoy (1828–1910), whose novels, including the magnificent *War and Peace* and *Anna Karenina*, are classics all over the world.

Greatest of the literary figures in the present century is Maxim Gorky (1868–1936), whose work covers the period both before and after the Russian Revolution of 1917. Among the leading writers of present-day Russia are Mikhail Sholokhov, author of *And Quiet Flows the Don*, Boris Pasternak (1890–1960) author of *Doctor Zhivago*, Yev Yevtushenko, and Alexander Solzhenitzyn author of *The Gulag Archipelago*.

Among other Slav countries, Poland has a rich literature. Mikolaj Rej (1505–69) is regarded as the 'father of Polish literature'. Boleslaw Prus (1847–1912) was a novelist somewhat along Dickensian lines, while Henryk Sienkiewicz (1846–1916) is internationally known as the author of *Quo Vadis*?

Czech literature was revived in the nineteenth century, and at least one writer, Karel Čapek (1890–1938), the dramatist, has achieved international fame. Another is the dramatist and novelist František Langer (1888–1965). The related Slovak language has its own literature, but few writers have become known outside the country.

Other Slav literatures exist in Bulgaria and in Yugoslavia, where the languages used are Croatian, Serbian, Slovenian and Bosnian.

Literature in other countries

Portuguese as a literary language dates back to about the thirteenth century. What had been a corrupt dialect was forged into a language through the efforts of the Portuguese king, Diniz (1261–1326). Poetry and drama were largely modernised by the poet Francisco Sá de Miranda (1481–1558).

The historical writings of Joao de Barros (1496–1570) inspired Luis Vaz de Camões (c. 1524–80) to write his great epic poem *Os Lusiadas* (The Lusiads), which tells of the discovery of the sea-route to India by Vasco da Gama.

Gil Vicente (1492–1557) was the founder of Portuguese drama, and he was followed by Antonio Ribeiro Chiado (died 1591) and Antonio Prestes (dates unknown).

Alexander Solzhenitsyn

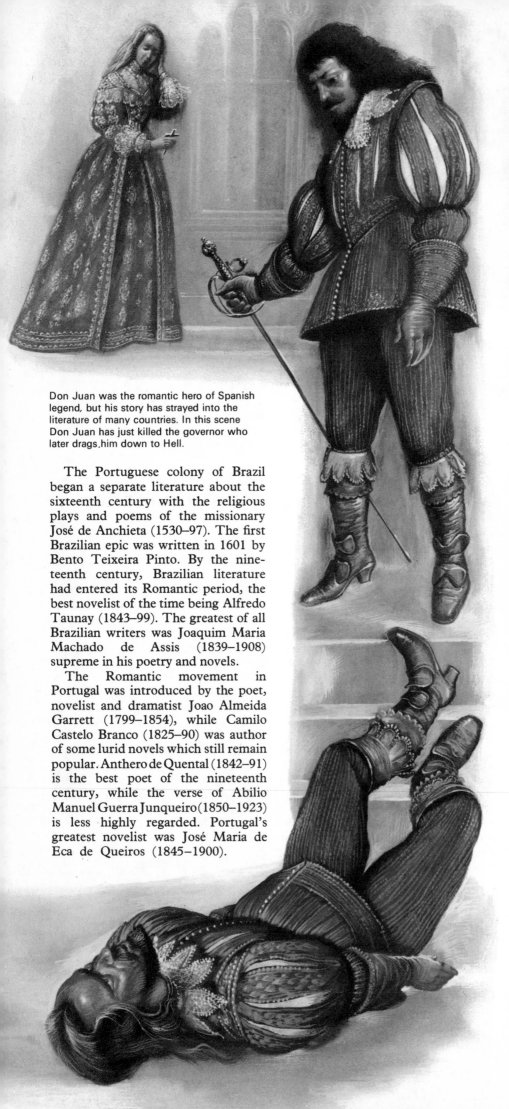

Don Juan was the romantic hero of Spanish legend, but his story has strayed into the literature of many countries. In this scene Don Juan has just killed the governor who later drags him down to Hell.

The Portuguese colony of Brazil began a separate literature about the sixteenth century with the religious plays and poems of the missionary José de Anchieta (1530–97). The first Brazilian epic was written in 1601 by Bento Teixeira Pinto. By the nineteenth century, Brazilian literature had entered its Romantic period, the best novelist of the time being Alfredo Taunay (1843–99). The greatest of all Brazilian writers was Joaquim Maria Machado de Assis (1839–1908) supreme in his poetry and novels.

The Romantic movement in Portugal was introduced by the poet, novelist and dramatist Joao Almeida Garrett (1799–1854), while Camilo Castelo Branco (1825–90) was author of some lurid novels which still remain popular. Anthero de Quental (1842–91) is the best poet of the nineteenth century, while the verse of Abilio Manuel Guerra Junqueiro (1850–1923) is less highly regarded. Portugal's greatest novelist was José Maria de Eca de Queiros (1845–1900).

Holland and Belgium

For the purposes of literature, the languages used in the Netherlands and Flanders can be regarded as the same. Desiderius Erasmus (1469–1536), the greatest Dutch writer of Renaissance times, used Latin, but the poet Jonker Jan van der Noodt (1539–95) and the author and dramatist Henric Laurens Spiegel (1549–1612) used Dutch. Samuel Coster (1579–1665) both surgeon and playwright, was famed for his farce, but the best writer of prose in the seventeenth century was Pieter Hooft, who was also one of the best poets. His poetry was at least equalled by Joost van den Vondel (1587–1635), whose dramatic works rank with the world's finest. The homely style of the poetry of Jacob Cats (1577–1660) led to his being called 'Father Cats'. Gerbrand Brederode (1585–1618) playwright and poet, succeeded with his comedies, and was also a fine lyrical poet, while Constantin Huygens (1596–1687) was learned enough to write poetry in Latin, French, Italian and his native Dutch.

Willem Bilderdijk (1756–1831) was a scholarly, talented man, a fine dramatist and poet, but the man who had greatest influence on Dutch prose style was Eduard Douwes Dekker (1820–87), who wrote under the name of Multatuli.

Hungary

Until the nineteenth century, the literary language of Hungary was Latin, and the oldest document in the Hungarian language was a piece called *The Funeral Oration* dating from about 1230. In 1844, Hungarian was officially taught and used in the schools, and leading literary figures of the period included the Kisfaludy brothers Sandor and Karoly (1772–1844 and 1788–1830) poets and dramatists. The greatest epic poet was Janos Arany (1817–82), while an outstanding dramatist and poet was Mihaly Vörösmarty (1800–55). Sandor Petöfi (1823–49) was the greatest lyric poet, while the most widely-read Hungarian is Mor Jokai (1825–1904). In the present century, Hungary's best-known dramatist has been Ferenc Molnar (1878–1952) who became an American citizen.

Early Finnish literature possesses a rich treasure in its collection of old folk songs and stories called *Kalevala*, the national epic poem, which occupies about 23,000 verses. This has had a great influence on later Finnish writing. Modern literature in the Finnish

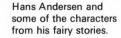

Hans Andersen and some of the characters from his fairy stories.

language became important in the middle nineteenth century, especially in the work of Alexis Kivi (1834–72), who was the first Finn to become a professional writer.

English Literature

The ancestors of modern English, which began in the later half of the fifteenth century, have been called Old English and Middle English. The first of these is usually known as Anglo-Saxon, which was spoken until about 1150.

After the Norman Conquest in 1066, peasants continued to use Old English, but alongside this, Norman-French was spoken by the ruling classes. Gradually, French words entered the English language, so that during the period from 1150 to about 1475, it was being shaped by a mingling of the older Anglo-Saxon tongue and the newer Norman-French.

The literature which arose during this period was beginning to take on the guise of Modern English. An important work to appear in Middle English was a long poem called *The Vision concerning Piers Plowman* believed to have been written by William Langland between about 1360 and 1399. Versions vary from 2,500 to 7,300 lines, the poem telling of the pious countryman Piers Plowman, who sees visions while asleep.

Wycliffe's Bible

Next came the English translation of the Bible by John Wycliffe (*c.* 1328–84), while *Sir Gawain and the Green Knight*, written by an unknown poet in the fourteenth century, is an interesting example of the north-west Midland dialect of English at that period. However, the really outstanding name is that of Geoffrey Chaucer, (*c.* 1345–1400) who can be regarded as the first poet to write in English. How different Chaucer's language was from modern English can be seen in the following extract from the poet's *Canterbury Tales*:

> *Whan that Aprill with his shoures soote*
> *The droghte of March hath perced to the roote*
> *And bathed euery veyne in swich licour*
> *Of which vertu engendred is the flour.*

Apart from the *Canterbury Tales*, Chaucer was also the author of *Troilus and Criseyde*, and the *Book of the Duchess*. Just how mixed the language had become by 1403 can be seen from this piece from a letter written to Henry IV by the dean of Windsor in which the writer has combined both French and English: *Jeo prie a la Benoit Trinite que vous ottroie bone vie ove tres sentier sauntee a tres longe durre, and sende yowe sone to ows in helth and prosperitee.*

Morte d'Arthur, the story of King Arthur and his Knights, was translated by Sir Thomas Malory from the French about 1470.

Modern English began to appear during the Renaissance, more or less coinciding with the setting up in England of a printing press in 1476 by William Caxton. As elsewhere in Europe, most of the literature up to that date had been written in Latin. Even *Utopia* by Sir Thomas More (1478–1535) was written in that language, but the author used English in other work, a good example being his *Dialogue of Comfort Against Tribulation*.

William Tyndale (*c.* 1494–1536) made a new translation of the Bible into English, and in 1539, a version of this was ordered to be used in the churches. Poets of the sixteenth century included John Skelton (*c.* 1460–

Chaucer reading his work at the court of the English king Edward III.

1529) and the Scottish poet-satirist Sir David Lindsay (*c.* 1486–1555). The fourteen-line poem, or sonnet, was introduced to England by the talented courtier Sir Thomas Wyatt (1503–42), translator of Petrarch, and Henry Howard, Earl of Surrey (1517–47), the first classical English poet. The work of both writers was published, together with that of other sixteenth century poets, by Richard Tottel in his *Miscellany*, in 1557.

Miracle and Mystery Plays

Since the thirteenth century, English drama had taken the form of the 'miracle' or 'mystery' play, the earliest of which was *The Harrowing of Hell*, a narrative poem of about 250 lines. Most were based on religious history or legends of saints, but later these plays gave way to 'moralities' which, instead of using personalities from the scriptures, introduced allegorical characters such as Vice or Virtue. Typical of such plays is *Everyman*.

Morality plays began to disappear after about 1550, and their place was taken by interludes, short dramatic pieces, often comedies or farces, which were performed in the halls of nobles or even at the royal court. It was only a short step to the drama of the theatre, and the first English comedy appeared in about 1550, performed probably by boys at Eton. The play, written by the headmaster, Nicholas Udall (1504–56), was *Ralph Roister Doister*.

Soon afterwards came *Gammer Gurton's Needle*, another comedy in verse, probably by William Stevenson (1546–75). A very early English tragedy was *Gordubuc*, by Thomas Norton (1532–83). Other dramatists were Thomas Sackville, Earl of Dorset (1530–77), John Lyly (1554–1606), George Peele (1546–96) and Robert Greene (1558–92).

Samuel Daniel (1562–1619) was another contemporary poet and dramatist, while Thomas Kyd (*c.* 1557–*c.* 1595) was the author of a play called *Hamlet*. This is now unfortunately lost, as it undoubtedly influenced the writing of the later play by William Shakespeare (1564–1616).

William Shakespeare

Shakespeare, England's greatest writer, can with justice be regarded as the world's most eminent dramatist. He lived at a time when the English Renaissance was in full flower, and was a contemporary of the playwrights Christopher Marlowe (1564–93), Thomas Dekker (1572–1632), Francis Beaumont (1584–1616), and John Fletcher (1579–1625).

William Shakespeare entered the theatre as an actor, and it was as a result of this experience that he wrote his first play, the second part of *Henry VI*, in 1590. A year later came the the third part of *Henry VI*, followed by the first part, and then *Richard III*.

His first comedy, *The Comedy of Errors* appeared in 1593, and after *Titus Andronicus* came *The Two Gentlemen of Verona*, *Love's Labour's Lost*, and *The Taming of the Shrew*. His most popular comedy is *A Midsummer Night's Dream*, (1596), but *Twelfth Night* and *As You Like It*, which were both written in about 1600, are usually considered better plays.

Although somewhat artificial in style, *Romeo and Juliet* has remained one of Shakespeare's most popular tragedies, but is surpassed in quality by *Hamlet*, *Othello*, *King Lear* and *Macbeth*. Among his histories, *Julius Caesar* stands out, followed by *Antony and Cleopatra*.

Shakespeare's Richard III

168

Shakespeare has not always been regarded so highly as he is today. During the seventeenth century, his work was considered to be inferior to that of Ben Jonson (1572–1637). Shakespeare, in fact, acted in some of Jonson's plays, including *Everyman in his Humour*, and Jonson himself was an admirer of Shakespeare's work.

Elizabethan Writers

Elizabethan England also saw the rise of other literary forms. The dramatist John Lyly wrote *Euphues*, a prose romance in two parts considered to be the first English novel, and this was followed by *The Arcadia*, by Sir Philip Sidney (1554–86). Thomas Nashe (1567–1601) published *Jack Wilton*, the first English picaresque novel, a story of high adventure, which appeared in 1594.

Among poets, Edmund Spenser (*c.* 1552–99) is outstanding in this period, with his *Shepheardes Calendar* and *The Faërie Queene*, his greatest work. Originally, this was to have occupied twelve books, but only six were completed. Michael Drayton (1563–1631) was best known for his historical verse, chief among which was the long poem *Polyolbion*.

Francis Bacon (1561–1626) was mainly a prose writer, often using Latin, but his *Advancement of Learning* is the most important of his works

in English. Robert Burton (1577–1640) is known for his great work *The Anatomy of Melancholy*, while other prose writers of the period were Sir Thomas Browne (1606–82), Jeremy Taylor (1613–67) and Izaak Walton (1593–1683), famous for his work on fishing, *The Compleat Angler*. He also wrote a biography of his friend, the poet John Donne (1572–1631), who was almost as well regarded as Ben Jonson. Other poets included William Drummond (1585–1649), Andrew Marvell (1621–78), and John Milton (1608–74).

Milton, whose work was largely influenced by his Puritan beliefs, is one of the great figures of English literature. According to some critics he ranks second only to Shakespeare. His most outstanding work is *Paradise Lost*, a poem in ten books, considered to be the greatest epic in any language. It tells of the fall of man, and of the conflict between Satan and the forces of good.

Among other poems by Milton are *Lycidas*, *Il Penseroso*, *Paradise Regained*, and *Samson Agonistes*.

In the later half of the seventeenth century, one of the greater poets was John Dryden (1631–1700), also a playwright. His best play, *All for Love*, a blank-verse drama about Antony and Cleopatra, followed a comedy, *Marriage-à-la-Mode*. As a reaction to the

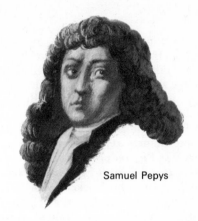
Samuel Pepys

austerity of the Puritan regime a number of lighter, and sometimes bawdy, comedies came to the theatre. These were called Restoration plays (named from the period of the Restoration of the monarchy in 1660).

The Restoration

First among the Restoration dramatists were Thomas Otway (1652–85), Sir George Etherege (*c.* 1634–91), William Wycherley (1640–1716), Thomas Shadwell (*c.* 1642–92), and Mrs Aphra Behn (1640–89). An improvement in standards came with the plays of William Congreve (1670–1729) including *The Way of the World*; Sir John Vanbrugh (1664–1726) who wrote *The Relapse*; and George Farquhar (1678–1707), author of *The Beaux' Stratagem*.

An interesting and important survey of the life and manners of the time

Admission of Sir Tristam to the fellowship of King Arthur's Round Table.

can be found in the diaries of John Evelyn (1620–1706) and Samuel Pepys (1633–1703). Pepys is particularly honest about himself and the life that went on around him. John Bunyan (1628–88) was a writer still influenced by Puritan ideas, and typical of his simple homely style is the allegorical story *The Pilgrim's Progress*.

The Essay Concerning Human Understanding, by John Locke (1623–1704) was one of the great works of philosophy to be written at the end of the seventeenth century.

Daniel Defoe (*c.* 1660–1731), Jonathan Swift (1667–1745) Joseph Addison (1672–1719) and Sir Richard Steele (1672–1729) began their writing at the end of the seventeenth century, but they were also the first of the literary figures of the eighteenth century.

By far the most famous work by Daniel Defoe is *Robinson Crusoe*. It was an immediate and remarkable success when it appeared in 1719, not

1748) published the famous 'O God, Our Help in Ages Past' and 'When I Survey the Wondrous Cross'. *Pamela*, the first English novel of the modern type, came from the pen of Samuel Richardson (1689–1761), and is written in the form of a series of letters. Later novelists of the century were Henry Fielding (1707–54), author of *Tom Jones*; Tobias Smollett (1721–71) who wrote *Roderick Random*, *Peregrine Pickle* and *Humphrey Clinker*; Laurence Sterne (1713–68) famed for his *Sentimental Journey* and *Tristram Shandy*; and Oliver Goldsmith (1730–74) poet, essayist and dramatist. His novels include *The Vicar of Wakefield*, while his most famous play is *She Stoops to Conquer*.

Samuel Johnson (1709–84) was a poet and critic, but his greatest work was the famous *Dictionary*. Although of great merit, it was not the first English dictionary, nor the most comprehensive, and many of his word derivations are faulty. It did however,

author of *Elegy Written in a Country Churchyard*, was foremost in his day. The poetry of William Cowper (1731–1800) was of a more simple style, while that of Robert Burns (1759–96) is usually in Scottish dialect. Burns, the national poet of Scotland, author of *Auld Lang Syne*, *Scots Wha Hae*, and *Comin' thro' the Rye*, not only wrote songs himself but was also responsible for conserving many old national ballands.

A poet who was also a fine artist and illustrator was William Blake (1757–1827), author of the famous *Tiger! Tiger! Burning Bright* and the hymn *Jerusalem*. Almost unknown in his lifetime, Blake is regarded very highly today.

The Lake Poets
Romantic poets included William

Abbotsford House in Scotland, the home of the novelist Sir Walter Scott, where he lived for over 20 years, devoting much of his time to rebuilding the house.

only in England, but also on the Continent, where it gave rise to many imitations. Of almost equal fame is *Gulliver's Travels*, by Jonathan Swift. Written as a satire on human behaviour the novel is also a fascinating story in its own right.

Addison and Steele were both political writers, who founded the *Tatler* as a periodical for publishing their essays. It was preceded by the *Spectator* which had a similar purpose. Among the poets at the beginning of the eighteenth century were Alexander Pope, (1688–1744) greatest of his time, John Gay (1685–1732) writer of the musical play, *The Beggar's Opera*, Matthew Prior (1664–1721), while James Thomson (1700–48) and Edward Young (1683–1765) were both masters of blank verse.

The English Novel
The hymn-writer Isaac Watts (1674–

serve to standardise English spelling, though according to some scholars, not always logically. Johnson, as a person, is best known to us through the writings of his biographer, James Boswell (1740–95).

A great political writer of the century was Edmund Burke (1729–97), while Horace Walpole (1717–97), printer, prose writer and novelist, also achieved fame as a letter-writer. Walpole's novel, *The Castle of Otranto* set the fashion in England for the 'Gothic' stories of horror and mystery. A later example was *Frankenstein*, by Mary Shelley (1797–1851).

The theatre had a number of successes, with comedies principally from the pen of Richard Brinsley Sheridan, (1751–1816) whose plays, *The Rivals*, *The School for Scandal*, and *The Critic*, are still performed. A charming lyrical poet was William Collins (1721–59), while Thomas Gray (1716–71)

Wordsworth (1770–1850), two of whose best-known poems are *Composed Upon Westminster Bridge* and *I Wandered Lonely as a Cloud*; and Samuel Taylor Coleridge (1772–1834), author of *The Rime of the Ancient Mariner*. The beginning of the nineteenth century saw other great English poets: John Keats (1795–1821), Percy Bysshe Shelley (1792–1822), Lord Byron (1788–1824) and Sir Walter Scott (1771–1832).

Scott was also a prolific historical novelist, and author of, among others, *Waverley*, *Ivanhoe* and *The Talisman*. Jane Austen's novels, including *Pride and Prejudice*, *Emma*, and *Sense and Sensibility* were more at home in the earlier century. Other novelists of the nineteenth century were Charlotte Brontë (1816–55) her sisters Emily (1818–48) and Anne (1820–49), George Eliot, pen-name of Mary Ann Cross or Evans (1819–80), Anthony Trollope

(1815–82), Charles Reade (1814–84), Charles Kingsley (1819–75), Wilkie Collins (1824–89), Elizabeth Gaskell (1810–65), Benjamin Disraeli (1804–81) and the great Charles Dickens (1812–70).

Dickens's characters are brilliant, if sometimes caricatured portrayals, and the novels themselves are also valuable as pictures of Victorian life. Nearly all were issued as serial parts, and some stories have suffered because Dickens felt it necessary to end each part with some sensational event to encourage readers to buy the next part.

Children's writers, of whom there were many, included the brilliant Lewis Carroll (Charles Lutwidge Dodgson, 1832–98), author of *Alice in Wonderland*, George Alfred Henty (1832–1902), Thomas Hughes (1822–96), author of *Tom Brown's Schooldays*, R. M. Ballantyne (1825–94), Edward Lear (1812–88) and Robert Louis Stevenson (1850–94), who wrote the famous *Treasure Island*.

American Writers
In the United States, the nineteenth century produced a great number of literary giants. First of the Americans to find acceptance outside his own country was Washington Irving (1783–1859). Irving was a prolific writer, an historian and author of short stories, including the very famous *Rip Van Winkle*.

A great historical novelist, James Fenimore Cooper (1789–1851) achieved his biggest success with stories based on American history. During

Alice at the trial of the Knave of Hearts from *Alice's Adventures in Wonderland*.

Charles Dickens with four of his best-loved characters.

The famous fence painting episode from Mark Twain's *The Adventures of Tom Sawyer*.

the first part of the nineteenth century, the important writers included Ralph Waldo Emerson (1803–82), essayist and poet; Henry Thoreau (1817–62), essayist, poet, and naturalist; Nathanial Hawthorne (1804–64), novelist and author of *The Scarlet Letter* and *The House of the Seven Gables*; Herman Melville (1819–91), novelist and poet and a great writer of short stories. *Moby Dick* and *Typee* are two of his fine novels.

Another writer with a seafaring background was Richard Henry Dana (1815–82), author of *Two Years before the Mast*. Oliver Wendell Holmes (1809–94) was an essayist, poet and novelist; James Russell Lowell (1819–91), an editor, essayist, and poet; while two of America's greatest poets were Henry Wadsworth Longfellow (1807–82), author of *The Song of Hiawatha*, and John Greenleaf Whittier (1807–92).

Whittier and Harriet Beecher Stowe (1811–96) both used their literary talents in writing to oppose slavery. Walt Whitman (1819–92) wrote *Drum Taps*, a collection of Civil War poems; and Emily Dickinson (1830–86) was not recognised as a poet until thirty years after her death.

The spread to the West introduced writers like Bret Harte (1836–1902) and Jack London (1876–1916) with early Western-style stories; Joel Chandler Harris (1848–1908) wrote 'Southern' stories, including the famous 'Uncle Remus' fables. Other writers included Louisa M. Alcott (1832–88), the novelist, and the humorist Mark Twain (pen-name of Samuel Langhorne Clemens, 1835–

1910), author of *The Adventures of Tom Sawyer*, and *The Adventures of Huckleberry Finn*, two of the world's great books.

The Nineteenth Century

The end of the nineteenth century in both America and Britain brought many names which were to last well into the twentieth century. Rudyard Kipling (1865–1936) was the novelist and poet who chose the British Empire for his themes; Stephen Crane (1871–1900), novelist and poet, succeeded with *The Red Badge of Courage*, about the American Civil War, Thomas Hardy (1840–1928) wrote on pastoral subjects. Outstanding poets included Alfred Tennyson (1809–92), Robert Browning (1812–89), and Elizabeth Barrett Browning (1806–61).

The leading dramatists were George Bernard Shaw (1856–1950), a witty writer and Socialist reformer; Henry Arthur Jones (1851–1929); Sir Arthur Pinero (1855–1934); and Oscar Wilde (1854–1900), whose scintillating comedies have lost none of their sparkle even today.

H. G. Wells (1866–1946) belongs to the twentieth century, especially when considering his remarkable prophetic science-fiction novels such as *The Time Machine*. Other great writers at the beginning of the century include John Galsworthy (1867–1933), Upton Sinclair (1878–1968), Joseph Conrad (1857–1924), and the short-story

Scene from *The Grapes of Wrath* by the American novelist, John Steinbeck.

writers O. Henry (pen-name of William Sidney Porter, 1862–1910), Ambrose Bierce (1842–1914), Richard Harding Davis (1864–1916), and Henry James (1843–1916) who achieved success not only in this field, but also as a novelist and dramatist.

More recently, the present century has produced some great poets. Among them are John Masefield (1878–1967), Walter de la Mare (1873–1956) Alfred Noyes (1880–1958), Rupert Brooke (1887–1915), Edmund Blunden, Ezra Pound (1885–1972), Carl Sandburg (1878–1967), W. H. Auden (1907–73), Stephen Spender, Louis MacNeice (1907–63), C. Day Lewis (1904–72), Dylan Thomas (1914–53) and John Betjeman.

Among dramatists of this century, Eugene O'Neill (1888–1953) ranks highest among Americans, followed by Maxwell Anderson (1888–1959), Elmer Rice (1892–1967), Clifford Odets (1906–63) Tennessee Williams and Arthur Miller. After Wilde and Shaw, British dramatists of note include Sir James Barrie (1860–1937), James Bridie, pseudonym of O. H. Mavor (1888–1951), Noël Coward (1899–1973), and Somerset Maugham (1874–1965) who reached equal fame as a novelist.

Other novelists include Arnold Bennett (1867–1931), W. H. Hudson (1841–1922), James Joyce (1882–1941), Aldous Huxley (1894–1963), D. H. Lawrence (1885–1930), Sir Arthur Conan Doyle (1859–1930), Sinclair Lewis (1885–1951), Willa Cather (1873–1947), Theodore Dreiser (1871–1945), Edith Wharton (1862–1937), Thornton Wilder, William Faulkner (1897–1962) and Ernest Hemingway (1898–1961).

The Printed Word

The earliest books were written on tablets of wood or strips of bark, although stone had been used earlier as a surface for writing. In Greece and Rome, the tablets of wood were covered with wax, and the writing impressed upon them with a stylus, or else tablets of soft metal served the same purpose. These tablets were bound together along one side with leather thongs or metal rings).

Since wood was used for this purpose, the Romans gave the name codex to such books, the word meaning originally tree-stump. The earliest existing copy of the New Testament, found near a monastery at Mount Sinai, Egypt, is known as the *Codex Sinaiticus*.

Clay Tablets

In Assyria and Babylonia, clay tablets were used for writing, the inscriptions being made with wedge-shaped pieces of wood upon the soft surface. After baking, the tablets were kept in storage on shelves, much as books are today. Although clumsy when compared with proper books, these clay tablets were long-lasting, some surviving until the present day.

The most useful writing material known in the ancient world was papyrus, made from a tall, reed-like plant. Strips of the pith were cut and laid side by side to form a continuous strip of paper-like material. Papyrus was used by the early civilised nations until about the fifth century A.D.

Another popular material was parchment made from the skins of young animals. This was more durable than papyrus, but much more expensive. An even finer type of parchment, called vellum, was also in use. The earliest books written on these materials took the form of a continuous strip, rolled from one cylinder (made of wood, metal, bone or some other suitable substance) to another. These scrolls were known to the Romans as *volumen* from which comes our word volume.

Because of the material used, the writings of Assyria and Babylonia have lasted to tell us their secrets, and as the ancient Egyptians preserved their papyri inside sealed tombs, many thousands of these also exist. In Greece and Rome, however, it is another story, for the earliest known Latin document still existing dates only from A.D. 55, and Greek manuscripts are no older than 160 B.C. Greece and Rome were the centres of wars and conflicts, so that important libraries and store-houses have been burned, destroyed, or otherwise lost for ever.

All the same, books were fairly commonplace in Rome, for we know that many booksellers existed, and that the first public library was set up there about 39 B.C. Only the wealthy could afford to buy books, and rich Romans would usually employ their own scribes to copy books from important libraries. The scribe, or *librarius*, was usually a slave, but highly prized for his writing skill.

The Art of Illumination

By the time of the Middle Ages, writing had reached a very high standard, most of the scribes being religious men, performing their life-long tasks inside monasteries. Time was of little importance to them, and members of religious orders spent many hours on writing and decorating one page alone. The art of illumination, as it was called, required a high degree of expertise, and we are fortunate that many of these wonderful books remain with us.

The early Irish monks were particularly talented, as we can see from the Book of Kells, now preserved in the Library of Trinity College, Dublin. It was not possible to make all books to such a standard, for, being handwritten, they were very expensive to buy.

Libraries made a practice of chaining books to the shelves so that they could not be removed from the building. This meant, of course, that books could only be consulted on the premises, and even then only by the few people able to read. It was not until printing was invented that more books could be made available, and until then, there was little point in learning to read. Illiteracy in those days extended even to the king and his court.

Although the Chinese seem to have invented printing from engraved

The art of illumination reached a high degree of skill during the Middle Ages.

wooden blocks, it seems unlikely that they passed their knowledge on to Europe. The European invention of printing was probably quite independent, although this too was from wooden blocks engraved with some design. In fact, the first items to be printed were most likely playing-cards.

Block-books, which were books whose pages were printed from single wood-cuts, contained only limited text, since every letter had to be cut by hand. It was the invention of movable type that really revolutionised book-production.

Early Printed Books

We can look to China once again for examples of early movable types. Here, 400 years before its invention in Europe, Chinese craftsmen were printing from individual characters cast in baked clay.

In Europe, there are a number of claimants to the title of 'inventor of printing from movable types', the two best-known being Johann Gutenberg of Mainz in Germany, and Laurens Janszoon Coster, of Haarlem, in Holland. Unfortunately, no books printed by Coster exist, although it is said that he first set up his press in Haarlem in about 1430.

Johann Gutenberg, born in Mainz about 1400, was the son of Friele Gensfleisch, but adopted as his surname the name of his mother's birthplace. He moved and settled in Strasbourg, where he set up a block-printing press, but returned to Mainz in 1444. His earliest printed work made from movable type was probably the 42-line Bible, made in 1452–55, and so called because the number of lines in a column totals 42.

This beautiful work, also known as the Mazarin Bible, is in Latin, and uses a type-face known as black letter, originally designed to imitate the handwriting then used in manuscript books. The Mazarin Bible is known to be printed on both vellum and paper. It seems that paper was invented around the same time as the invention of printing, but vellum was also used for a short time, even for printed books.

Gutenberg's books were of a remarkably high standard, but it was not long before imitators appeared elsewhere in Europe. Many of these learned their craft from men driven from their homes in Mainz by political upheavals. During the following two decades, printing presses were set up

Trade mark of the English printer, William Caxton.

Sketch by Dürer of a 16th-century printing press.

in Strasbourg, Cologne, Augsburg, Bamberg, Nuremberg, Speyer, Ulm, Lubeck and Breslau in Germany, Basel in Switzerland, Rome, Venice, Florence and Naples in Italy, Paris and Lyons in France, Bruges in Belgium, and in several cities in England.

Printing spread rapidly throughout Europe, and by the end of the century, there were more than 200 presses. These early printers were not only craftsmen, but also editors, publishers and booksellers.

The first printing press to be set up in England was that established by William Caxton at Westminster in 1476. He probably learned his craft in Cologne, and then moved to Bruges, where he set up his first press. His first book, printed in Bruges, was *The Recuyell of the Historyes of Troye*, completed in about 1475, followed by *The Game and Playe of the Chesse*. Caxton's first English printed book was *The Dictes or Sayengis of the Phylosophres*, which appeared in 1477.

By 1481, Caxton was publishing books with illustrations, his edition of the *Golden Legend* having 70 woodcuts.

Like his German colleagues, Caxton also employed the black letter type in his books, but before the end of the fifteenth century, what was known as the white letter was introduced. This was the forerunner of the Roman type we use today. It was first employed in Strasbourg about 1465, but was perfected by the French typographer Nicolas Jenson, who was working in Venice in Italy.

These Roman type-faces never became popular in Germany until quite recent times, but it was a style used and introduced in England by Richard Pynson in 1509. By 1518, he printed his first English book, entirely set up in Roman, or white letter type.

The Progress of Publishing

Very early printed books had no title-pages, but simply began on the first page with the subject of the book. Because of this, it is sometimes difficult to decide who printed and published the earliest volumes. A practice which developed among printers was to add a short note at the end of the book, which gave some information about its origin. This note, called the colophon, was usually printed in Latin, and what is probably the first printed colophon, when translated, reads: '*The present book of Psalms, adorned with the beauty of capitals, and sufficiently marked out with rubics, has been thus fashioned by an ingenious invention of printing and stamping, and to worship of God diligently brought to completion by Johann Fust, a citizen of Mainz, and Peter Schoffer of Gernsheim, in the year of our Lord, 1457, on the Vigil of the Feast of the Assumption*'.

The first English book with a title-page appeared about the year 1482, and by the early part of the sixteenth century, specially designed woodcuts were being used to decorate the title-pages.

Some examples of early title plages including (top) what is thought to be the earliest display title page from Venice (1476).

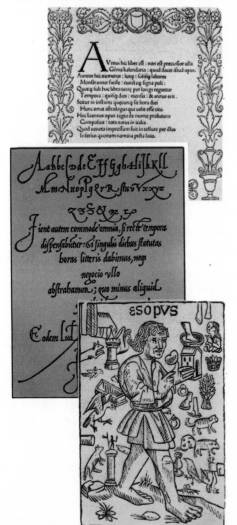

Aldus Manutius was responsible for some of the most beautiful type-faces ever invented.

One of the important developments in the art of the book was the design of new and better type-faces. The first printers in Italy were two Germans, Sweynheim and Pannartz, who had set up their press at Subiaco, near Rome in 1465. They tended to use the black letter type at first, but while in Italy, developed a type design which was more or less half-way between the heavy Gothic and the newer Roman faces. Jenson's white letter took the design a step nearer to the modern style.

Probably the most skilled of the Italian printers was Aldus Manutius, who was responsible for the design of some of the most beautiful type-faces ever invented. One of his new designs was based, it is said, on the handwriting of the writer Petrarch. Aldus Manutius called it Chancery, but it spread throughout the land, and was soon renamed Aldine in honour of the designer.

Aldine was the first *italic* type, so named by French printers who received it from Italy. The sloping type still has this name in France and the English-speaking countries, while elsewhere it is known as 'cursive'.

After Caxton's death in 1491, his assistant, Wynkyn de Worde became the proprietor of the printing press, and nine years later, moved to Fleet Street, where he set up in business at the sign of the 'Sun'. He also opened another shop in St Paul's Churchyard. Fleet Street, of course, has been associated with printing and publishing ever since, and until the Second World War the area around St Paul's was largely the home of book publishing houses.

Skilled Craftsmen
Printed books soon reached a high degree of excellence, the craftsmen taking great pride in their work. Yet after the middle of the sixteenth century, the urge for cheapness led to a sharp fall in quality, especially in England, and it was almost 200 years before standards recovered.

Some of the famous European printers of the sixteenth century were Johannes Froben of Basel in Switzerland who printed on vellum the Erasmus version of the Greek New Testament, Henri Estienne and Geoffroy Tory of Paris, and the famous Christopher Plantin of Antwerp in Belgium. Plantin, like his fellow-printers, was a designer of type-faces, but his printshop turned out a very large quantity of books. Most famous of his books was the *Polygot Bible*, published in 1569–73.

In England, some excellent work was produced by John Day in the middle of the century, and in the early years, the first Scottish printers, Walter Chepman and Andrew Myllar, were established in Edinburgh. The first book of note to be printed in Scotland was Chepman's *Breviary*, which appeared in 1509–10. Later in the century came Thomas Davidson and Robert Lekprevik, both of Edinburgh. Lekprevik was responsible for the first book ever to be printed in Gaelic.

The Dutch Elzevir family established their press in Leyden in the middle of the century. The family itself concentrated on publishing and selling, but Isaac Elzevir was the first member to become a printer himself, in 1617. Until that time books had tended to be very large and heavy, but the Elzevirs led the way with the first small-format books, and their products remain among the most prized and sought-after books in the world.

After the decline of standards in the sixteenth and seventeenth centuries, improvements in printing presses gradually led to better quality books, especially after the work of such men as William Caslon, the first English type-founder. He set up in business in London in 1720. Some years later he was followed in Birmingham by John Baskerville who became printer to the University of Cambridge. In Italy, Giambattista Bodoni was strongly influenced by Baskerville's work, as were François and Pierre Didot in Paris. All these men designed typefaces which still rank high in popularity. Samuel Richardson, the novelist, was also a printer and book-seller who started his business in 1706

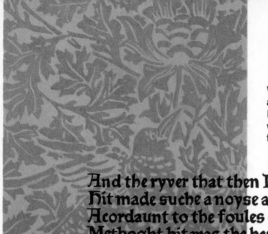

And the ryver that then I sat upon,
Hit made suche a noyse as hit ther ron,
Acordaunt to the foules ermonye,
Methoght hit was the beste melodye

in London, while the books produced by Thomas Bensley towards the end of the century were some of the finest ever made. Robert and Andrew Foulis of Glasgow were also responsible for some of the century's most attractive books.

Printing Presses

The inventions of the nineteenth century helped to speed up the printing of books, and also to make them cheaper and more attractive. The new presses were made from iron instead of wood, and type-faces were cut more accurately. Later on, steam-power was harnessed to the printing-press, helping to bring cheap books within the grasp of millions.

Throughout the centuries, all printing had been done by the letterpress method, that is, by taking impressions from the inked, upraised type or woodblocks. But in 1796 an Austrian actor named Aloysius Senefelder invented a new method of printing called lithography. Senefelder found that a certain kind of limestone was very sensitive to grease. By experimenting, he found that by applying grease to certain parts of the stone, he could make ink 'take' only on the non-greasy areas. An artist could then draw with greasy crayon upon the stone, and later, apply ink to the surface. Prints taken from it would then reproduce the artist's design.

Senefelder's idea was taken up by printers and improved, so that by later in the nineteenth century, lithography became a favourite method of reproducing drawings or making illustration plates for books. Book illustrations became more common and popular, and these were made, not only by lithography, but by means of wood, copper and steel engravings, executed by skilled craftsmen and artists.

The next step was to reproduce

William Morris

colour. At first, black and white drawings were coloured by hand, but this was never really satisfactory, and was not cheap. Crude colour blocks —one for each colour—were then made, for which the work had to be passed through the press as many times as there were colours.

Lithography

The invention of lithography enabled much better colour printing to be achieved. Artists drew each colour on separate stones, which were then placed in the printing press and coloured inks applied. One colour was superimposed on the next, until the final result was a picture in colours. The richness of the colour depended on the number of lithographic stones used. These coloured prints, or chromolithographs were very popular in the nineteenth century, and can be found in many old books.

Despite steam-operated presses, type still had to be set laboriously by hand, letter by letter. The first type-setting machine was invented in 1822 by Dr William Church, and this was followed by several other kinds throughout the century, the most successful being the Linotype of 1884.

With the spread of education, more and more people could read, and thousands of new books poured from the presses. The accent was on mass production, although a few skilled artist-craftsmen remained, outstanding among whom was William Morris and his Kelmscott Press. His magnificent books were among the finest ever made, and copies today fetch very high prices.

Illustrations in books of the nineteenth century were either lithographed or printed from engraved wood blocks. In wood-engravings, an artist's drawing was carefully traced onto a block of boxwood, and the engraver then proceeded to cut fine lines into the wood to produce a relief impression. This block was then placed in the printing press alongside the type matter, the whole locked together and printed in the usual manner.

The Half-tone Process

In 1878, an American photographer named Frederick Eugene Ives invented a method of printing photographs by what is called the 'half-tone' process. The photographic negative is printed through a screen made up of thousands of tiny dots. These have the effect of breaking up the picture into similar small dots of varying intensity.

Earlier, in Paris, a system had been invented of printing illustrations by etching the lines of an artist's pen-drawing onto a zinc plate. This produced a printing block with upraised lines which could be used alongside the type in the printing press.

Photographically produced blocks with the dotted screen surface (or 'half-tone') could be used in the same way. When inked, the blocks would print a reproduction of the original picture or photograph. Similar systems for producing illustrations are still in use. Etched plates with areas of black, or lines, such as in an artist's pen-drawing, are called line blocks, while those using a dotted screen are called half-tone blocks.

All printing done from upraised surfaces, whether from engraved

wooden blocks, zinc plates or from type-matter is called letterpress printing, although it is sometimes called surface or typographical printing.

Lithographic printing is still used today, although it is rarely done from stone. A method of making lithographic plates from sheets of aluminium was invented at the beginning of the present century, and a later development still is offset photolithography, which is described later.

Another method of printing, rarely used for books, is called recess, or copperplate printing. This is mostly used for printing postage stamps or banknotes. The design is engraved into the surface of a copper plate, and an inked roller passed over it so that the ink is pressed into the engraved recesses. A knife blade is passed over the surface of the plate, wiping this clean and leaving ink only in the recesses.

When the plate is printed, the ink is taken up on the paper from the recesses only. Anything printed by this method can be recognised by the bold 'feel' of the lines in the engraved print.

Production and Bookbinding

Almost all books printed today are printed either by the letterpress method, or by offset photolithography. Letterpress machines are now very sophisticated and work at very high speeds, but the basic principle of printing from an upraised impression remains the same as it was in the time of Gutenberg. Almost all type is now set by machine, either by Linotype or Monotype.

The Monotype type-casting machine is in two parts: first there is a keyboard, something like that of a typewriter, but larger. The operator types on the keyboard, and the machine produces a roll of perforated paper. The roll is taken from the keyboard machine and placed upon a casting machine. Working by compressed air, the caster 'reads' the perforations on the paper roll, and tiny moulds produce metal castings for each letter required. The moulded letters slide into a tray, and are then taken to be inserted into the pages required. When all the type has been assembled into the page, it is 'locked' up and placed in the printing press.

Offset lithography came into use about the beginning of the present century, and today is probably the most widely used system of printing.

The picture below is a section of the illustration on page 187. It demonstrates the sequence of four-colour printing and shows the separate colours and the order in which they are printed.

The matter to be printed is first photographed and then lightly etched onto a lithographic aluminium plate. This plate is quite thin, and is bent round a cylinder on the printing machine. Next to it is another cylinder made of rubber, and the two revolve together rather like the two rollers on a laundry mangle. The printing cylinder is also in contact with a smaller inked roller.

When the machine runs, the printing cylinder receives ink from the roller. It is also damped with water, so that the ink is only taken up on the parts required to be printed. The printing cylinder is also in contact with the rubber roller, which receives the printed impression in reverse. Paper is brought in contact with the rubber roller, which prints the design the right way round. The book you are reading has been printed by this method, but by a much more advanced machine which has several sets of cylinders each printing in a different colour.

The Bindery

Books are printed in sheets, each containing a number of pages, usually 16 or 32. After the sheets leave the printing machine, they are folded to size, each sheet then becoming a section of the book. Usually, the printer has marked each section so that it can be recognised and placed in its correct order in the book. Arranging the sections in the correct order is called 'collating', and the collated sections are then taken to the book-binding factory.

At the bindery, the sections are placed in a sewing machine, which stitches the sections together. Folded sheets of paper —called endpapers— are glued to the front and back and the sewn sections are then put into a press, glue is applied to the back (or spine) of the sections, and a strip of cloth placed in position.

Then the cover itself is made. This consists of boards covered with book-binding cloth made to fit the printed pages. The title of the book is printed, embossed or blocked onto the spine, and the cover or 'case' is ready to receive its pages.

The glued sections of the pages are placed in a machine called a guillotine, which trims the top, bottom and front edges of the pages. Glue is applied to the inside of the cover, or case, the pages are placed inside and the book goes into a press to dry. All that remains is for the coloured dust jacket or wrapper to be placed around the book before it is sent away from the factory.

This method of bookbinding is used for modern books, but there are still many hand-bookbinders who use methods similar to those of the crafts-men of earlier times. The first books were put together by hand, the pages being sewn onto a leather thong which was attached to heavy boards bound in leather. The thongs made ridges

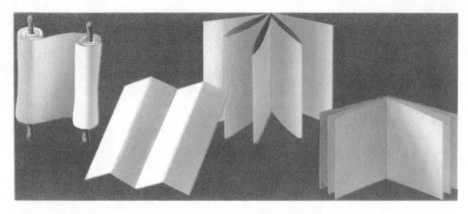

The present-day book, with pages secured together down one side, has evolved from the rolled-up scrolls of the ancient world.

across the spine of the book, and this is sometimes imitated in modern books with a so-called 'luxury' binding.

Papermaking

Paper has been known in China since the first century, and the secrets of its manufacture appear to have come to Europe by way of the Arabs, who had learned about it from Chinese prisoners. The craft of papermaking reached Morocco, and from there it was taken to Spain by the conquering Moorish tribes. From Spain, methods of making paper were learned by the

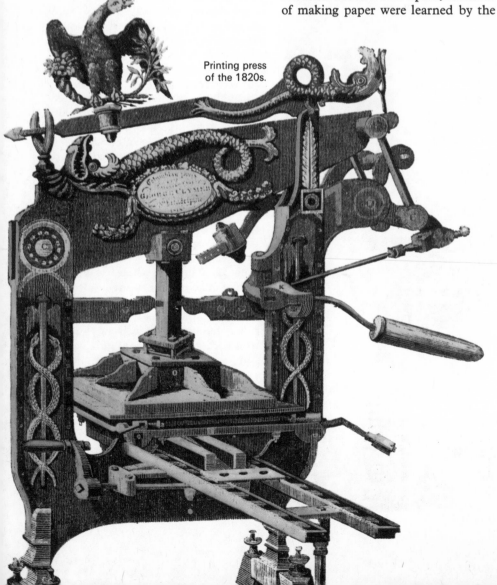

Printing press of the 1820s.

French and the Italians who carried their knowledge to the rest of Europe.

The invention of printing meant that a cheap, plentiful material for the presses was needed, and paper began to be made wherever the printing press was set up.

Briefly, paper is made by breaking down the fibres of a plant and then spreading them out in a fine web or flat sheet. In early times, paper was made by hand, suitable plant fibres being placed in a vat with water and thoroughly beaten until the whole mixture became a pulp which looked rather like thin porridge. A sheet of cloth stretched in a frame was then dipped into the vat and the pulp spread upon it evenly. The water was allowed to filter away, and the sheet of pulp left was placed between layers of felt to dry. The resulting sheets of paper were coated with size ready for printing.

Paper today is machine-made from wood, esparto grass or rag. The cheapest paper, such as newsprint, comes from wood pulp, while the finest is made from rag. Chemically treated wood pulp produces a better quality paper which can be used for books or magazines. A very good quality paper is made from esparto, which is a type of grass found in Spain and North Africa. Rag paper is very expensive and much less used nowadays.

Adding China clay to paper improves the surface for printing. A good example of paper made in this way can be seen in the glossy kind used for fashion magazines.

Access to Books

The first printers were also their own publishers and booksellers, and some-times they were authors too. Many printers had started out as booksellers, for this was a trade which dated back to ancient times. Early literature tells of the booksellers of Greece and Rome, when the stock-in-trade was not bound books, but handwritten scrolls.

In ancient times, the great book centre of the world was Alexandria, where there were many skilled scribes, and people came from Rome to have their books produced there. There were a number of well-known publishers in Rome, and later in Byzantium, when the capital of the Empire moved there.

The coming of Christianity brought an increased demand for books, and this was largely catered for by the monks. Bookselling actually took place in London within St Paul's Cathedral itself, and soon spread to the streets nearby. Many of these were religious books, some of which gave their names to the streets themselves: Paternoster Row, Creed Lane, and Ave Maria Lane.

It was not until the nineteenth century that publishers, as distinct from booksellers, really came into their own. Since then, bookselling has split into two component parts: the publishing houses who issue the books, and the retail booksellers who sell to the public.

Early libraries catered only for scholars and were few and far between. Some of the existing big libraries of

The national library in Paris (1861–9) designed by Henri Labrouste.

Europe date back to the fifteenth century, such as the Imperial Library of Vienna, the Bodleian Library at Oxford, and the Cambridge University Library. Many of the others were of later date, including the Vatican Library in Rome, which dates from the late sixteenth century. Among the great libraries of the world are the Bibliothèque Nationale in Paris, the British Museum in London, the Library of Congress in the United States and the University Library of Prague, founded as early as 1348.

Public Libraries

Public libraries now exist in almost every country in the world, although the first one is said to have been built in Rome in 39 B.C. The first public library in Britain was founded at Kirkwall in the Orkneys in 1683, but the public library system proper did not begin until about 1850. The world's largest public library is that of New York, which has about 5,000,000 books on the shelves of the central building and another 3,000,000 in branches.

In the present century, the Book Club idea has introduced many more people to the habit of book-buying. Members of the club undertake to buy either a book each month or a certain number each year as chosen by the club. This means that a special edition of the book can be supplied at a much cheaper rate than would be normal. The system began in the United States in 1926, when the Book of the Month Club was formed, and soon other clubs were formed in Europe. The first one in Britain was the Book Society, founded in 1929.

Another method of building a library came about when publishers started to issue a book in parts or sections. Because books were comparatively expensive, nineteenth-century publishers in Britain and elsewhere published them in 'penny numbers' or monthly parts. Most of Dickens's works originally appeared in this form. Once the buyer had collected all the parts he could take them to a book-binder and have them bound.

The system continued into the twentieth century, and was used to a great extent by Alfred Harmsworth, who published many works of popular education in this way, such as the *Children's Encyclopaedia*. The method is still being used by present-day publishers, and many part-works covering a wide variety of subjects are currently on sale.

179

Newspapers and Magazines

After the invention of printing 150 years passed before the first newspaper was published. This was not a newspaper in the modern sense, but really a kind of book. It was issued in 1594, and was called *Mercurius Gallobelgicus*, or the *Gallo Belgian Mercury*. Strangely, considering its title, it was published in Germany, first in Cologne, and later at Frankfurt-on-Main. Printed in Latin, it was edited by a Dutch priest named Jansen.

This 'newspaper' lasted for 40 years, and found its way into most countries of Europe, and very soon, other publishers had copied the idea. The first proper newspaper, published at regular intervals, was the German *Frankfurter Journal* which appeared weekly from 1615. The government of Venice in Italy had issued official bulletins from the sixteenth century, but these *gazetti*, as they were called (from the name of the coin needed to buy them), were not much more than leaflets.

The first newspaper in France was called simply the *Gazette* (the name taken from the Italian word), and was begun in 1631. Another was the *Mercure Galant*, which first appeared in 1672, and just over 100 years later, had reached the high circulation—for its time—of 13,000 copies.

In Germany, the *Frankfurter Journal* was soon followed by the *Frankfurter Oberpostamtszeitung* in 1616, and this paper lasted until 1866.

(Above left) London long song sheet seller. A long song was a single sheet containing several songs. (Left) A broadside sheet ballad. (Above) A 'trick' engraving sold in the streets which conceals within a landscape the heads of a man, a sheep and a cow. Turn the book on its side to see them more clearly. These are all examples of 19th-century street literature.

English Newspapers

The first English newspapers were simply letters containing news sent from one wealthy citizen to another, but soon, news-books like the *Mercurius Gallobelgicus* began to appear. These had no proper title, but the first one was published in 1619. The first with any sort of title was the *Mercurius Britannicus* appearing in 1625, although a sheet called *The weekly news from Italy, Germany and other foreign countries* had appeared as early as 1622.

Several other newspapers with the word *Mercurius* (Mercury) in their title appeared shortly afterwards. In 1665 came the first issue of the *Oxford Gazette,* which was to change its title some months later to the *London Gazette.* Under this name it is still published twice a week, although today it is not strictly a newspaper, but the official government circular.

The first successful London daily newspaper was the *Daily Courant,* founded in 1702, and this was soon followed by many imitators, like the *English Post, Postman, Flying Post* and others, named in allusion to their predecessors, which were simply letters containing news. Daniel Defoe had started a weekly called the *Review,* while Richard Steele had issued the

Tatler, and Joseph Addison the *Spectator.* There were soon so many newspapers that the government decided that taxing them would net a useful income. In 1712, a halfpenny tax was placed on half-sheet newspapers, and a penny on large ones. Despite this tax, there were 53 newspapers in London alone by 1776, selling over 12,000,000 copies a year. By the beginning of the nineteenth century, the newspaper tax was as high as fourpence a copy, but this was totally abolished by the middle of the century.

In the days before newspapers it was the custom for the Lord of the Manor to read out to his tenants the news sheet which he alone was privileged to receive from the nearest city.

The world's most famous newspaper began its life in 1785 under the title of *The London Daily Universal Register,* but this was changed in 1788 to *The Times.* By 1815, the newspaper was selling 5,000 copies a day, rising, 40 years later, to 50,000 copies a day.

The nineteenth century saw the birth of many famous British newspapers. The *Daily News* was founded in 1846 with Charles Dickens as its editor. In 1861 the *Daily Telegraph* appeared, and later reduced its price to the sum of only one penny. It was another 35 years before anyone was able to improve on this price.

In 1896, Alfred Harmsworth and his brother Harold introduced the *Daily Mail,* the first daily newspaper to sell at one halfpenny a copy, but this was soon followed by others all at this price. They were the *Daily Dispatch,* the *Daily Express,* and the *Daily Herald.* With the coming of the First World War prices of all newspapers rose, and none was ever sold for less than one penny.

The Boston News-letter

In the United States, the first newspaper to be published was the *Boston News-letter,* which appeared in 1704. There had been earlier attempts, but these were banned by the government of Massachusetts. In 1719, a rival called the *Boston Gazette* appeared, and in the years that followed there came the *New England Courant,* the *Massachusetts Spy,* and in 1831, the Boston *Liberator.*

The *New York Gazette* was born in 1725, but the first *daily* newspaper published in the State was the *New York Journal and Register* which began its life in 1788. The *New York Times* was started in 1851, while the famous *Chicago Tribune* began in 1847.

The development of the modern newspaper was only possible after the invention of the power printing press. The steam-driven machine press was invented in 1814 by a German named Friedrich König, working for *The Times* in London. By 1860, the powered newspaper press was able to print 25,000 impressions per hour. The invention of the Linotype in 1884 made it possible for newspaper type to be set by machine.

The Linotype, like the Monotype machine, casts type, not as individual letters, but in complete *lines* of type. The operator sits at a keyboard and types his copy, and the cast slugs, or metal type, slide into a tray by his side.

Newspapers today are printed on large rotary machines which produce thousands of copies per hour. Type, cast on the Linotype machine, is placed into a frame or forme the size of the newspaper page, and together with line and half-tone blocks for pictures, is locked up ready for casting. A thick sheet of papier-mâché, called the flong, is placed over the page of type and put under pressure.

This produces a mould from the flong, and a curved metal plate is cast from this. The plate is then placed on to the rotary printing machine. Several duplicates of this plate can be made, so that identical copies of the newspaper can be printed on more than one machine.

The Modern Newspaper

Modern newspapers are much more than simple *news*papers, since much of the issue is taken up with feature material, like articles on important subjects of the day, readers' letters, a 'diary' of gossip or politics, a cross-word puzzle, cartoons and picture-designers and writers. Almost as important as the news pages are the columns of classified advertisements, where readers and others can offer for sale, houses, cars and other goods, as well as find notices of jobs.

Today, the services of a newspaper are being rivalled by radio and

After a time, magazines on other subjects were published by different learned societies, but it was not until the nineteenth century that a magazine containing a mixture of subjects appeared. Some of the cheap magazines which began in the early part of the century were badly written or unpleasant in tone, but in 1813, John Limbird published *The Mirror*, an attractive, illustrated paper selling for twopence, intended for the working people of Britain. In the same year,

strips. In the United States, the picture-strip has become so important that special sections of the newspaper, known as the 'funnies', are entirely devoted to cartoon picture-strips in full colour.

The Sunday newspaper, in Europe and in the United States, has developed into a giant-size publication, containing a news section, a magazine section dealing with books, theatre, cinema and leisure, a business section, sometimes a sports section and often a special magazine in full colour, with editorial matter and advertisements.

Costs of newspaper production are very high, so that it is essential for a newspaper to carry advertisements to enable the price to be kept low enough to attract sufficient readers. Displayed advertisements are prepared by large advertising agencies using skilled

television, and the number of daily newspapers has fallen in recent years. A rise in price of newsprint, due to world shortages, has caused owners to increase the selling price of their papers. In spite of this, millions of daily newspapers continue to be sold in every part of the world.

Magazines and Periodicals

The first magazines were practically the same as newspapers. But it was not long before periodical publications appeared which dealt not with news, but with specialised subjects such as books and literature. A very early magazine in Britain was the *Mercurius librarius*, which appeared in 1680, and very soon there were dozens of such magazines, nearly all containing reviews of new books, both English and foreign.

another, similar paper, the *Mechanics' Magazine*, was published.

The mass of ordinary people were now learning to read, and as their numbers rose, more new magazines and periodicals appeared. They consisted of serial stories, popular science, natural history and similar subjects, usually with illustrations printed from wood engravings. Best of these were *Chambers's Journal*, the *Penny Magazine*, and the *Saturday Magazine*, all of which first appeared in 1832.

The *Penny Magazine* was published by Charles Knight, who decided he was going to give his reading public the best authors and artists possible, and all in a paper costing only a penny. Within a year, his magazine had reached a weekly sale of 200,000, a staggering total in those days. Many other such papers followed, including the *Family Herald, Household Words* and *All the Year Round* (the last two edited by Charles Dickens). Some, like the *Leisure Hour*, were sponsored by religious or temperance organisations.

It was also during the nineteenth century that the first true children's magazines appeared. The early ones were little more than illustrated schoolbooks, but later, papers intended solely for children's entertainment came on the market.

The very first boys' periodical to appear was *The Young Gentleman's Magazine*, which was published in Fleet Street for some months at the beginning of 1777. Later came the *Juvenile Magazine*, but neither was

Modern four-colour letterpress printing machine.

truly a magazine as we understand it. The first *weekly* juvenile paper did not appear until 1832, with the publication of the *Boys' and Girls' Penny Magazine*.

Following the success of this paper, imitations followed, but some of these were very cheaply produced and badly written, so that they soon became known as 'penny dreadfuls'.

Children's Papers

To combat these somewhat crude magazines, the first of the well-known children's papers was put on the market in 1879. This was the *Boy's Own Paper*, appearing weekly at the price of one penny. For the next 80 years, this magazine appeared continuously, weekly for most of its life, and monthly towards the end, which came as recently as 1967, having

served many generations of boys. Very soon after the *Boy's Own Paper* began, a similar paper for girls was launched, which lasted almost as long as its brother magazine.

By the end of the nineteenth century, there were dozens of popular magazines catering for all tastes and interests, ranging from beekeeping to bicycling —serious, diverting or even comic in tone. *Punch*, the world's most famous humorous weekly, began its life in 1842, and soon was selling 90,000 copies a week. An imitator called *Judy* was less successful.

Some of the most successful magazines, like the *Strand, Pearson's*, or the *Windsor*, were richly illustrated, and sold for only sixpence a month. Cheap weeklies like *Tit-bits* and *Answers* sold in very large numbers, owing to the genius of such publishers as George Newnes, Sir Arthur Pearson and the Harmsworth brothers.

The turn of the century was the golden era of periodical publishing, and great empires were set up, each publishing vast quantities and varieties of magazines ranging from serious political weeklies to women's papers and children's comics. It was now possible to print cheap, if crude, colour

on newsprint, and one result of this was the appearance of a host of brightly coloured children's weeklies.

The publishing empires which controlled both newspapers and magazines, continued to expand. The First World War was something of a setback, but after 1918, periodicals reappeared in an even more attractive guise. Photogravure presses were responsible for the success of the new women's weeklies which began to appear in the 1930s, and, because women are the main buyers of everyday products, manufacturers were prepared to spend enormous sums in placing advertisements in the weeklies.

Some of these are still being published with great success, but the competition from other entertainment sources, principally television, has been

Hand proofing press

When several pieces of type are placed together to form a word the serifs of certain letters will overlay the body surface of adjacent type.

The Monotype machine is in two parts. Seen here is the keyboard on which an operator taps out the words to be set in type. He produces a spool of paper perforated with small holes which is placed in another machine that casts individual pieces of type automatically.

These Egyptian hieroglyphics carefully arranged on a wooden panel (3000 B.C.) have all the abstract elegance of a page of print in a modern book.

responsible for the death of many. Despite this, more and more new magazines appear each year, although the tendency today is for periodicals to specialise in particular activities or interests, such as sports, hobbies or domestic matters.

American Magazines

In the United States, the early history of magazines was very similar to that of Britain. Probably the most famous of all American magazines was the *Saturday Evening Post*, which started its life in 1728, and which survived until only recently. Other American magazines which reached large circulations and achieved international fame were *Harper's Magazine*, launched in 1850, *Scribner's Magazine*, which began in 1870 and lasted until 1939, and the *Ladies' Home Journal*, which started in 1883.

Time, founded in 1923 and still published, was unique as a magazine which specialised in news, but it now has a serious competitor, *Newsweek*. Second only in fame to the *Saturday Evening Post* was *Life*, a lavish weekly that specialised in journalism in pictorial form. So successful was *Life* that imitators sprang up, not only in the United States, but in such countries as Britain, which produced *Picture Post* and *Illustrated*, and France, with its *Paris Match*.

Unlike Britain, the United States has few children's magazines. Some existed before the First World War, but the newspaper comic supplements or 'funnies' proved to be too severe a competition. The American comic, which has become an institution, is peculiar to the United States, although it has since been copied elsewhere. These comics, although read avidly by children wherever they appear, are not strictly speaking intended as juvenile fare.

European Magazines

As in Britain, the earliest magazines in France were concerned with literary matters, and the first to appear was the *Bureau d' adresse* in 1633. First to be published at regular intervals was the *Journal des Savants* in 1665, also literary in content. In France, the literary magazine became very important, much more so than elsewhere, and dealt, not only with French literature, but with that of other countries as well. There were even special periodicals on English literature, such as *Bibliothèque Anglaise* (1716), while *Bibliothèque Germanique* (1746) was devoted to German writing.

In the latter half of the eighteenth century, magazines on other subjects became very popular, covering the theatre, music, military matters, commerce and economics. By the nineteenth century, French magazines were appearing in great variety. There were fashion magazines such as *La Mode Illustreé*, sports journals, geographical reviews, children's papers, such as *L'Ami de la Jeunesse* and *Le Jeudi de la Jeunesse*, and even special magazines for motor-car enthusiasts and those interested in the new pursuits of ballooning and flying.

There were also popular general magazines, such as *A Travers le Monde*, *Les Lectures pour Tous*, and *La Revue Encyclopédique*, which was a monthly extension to the famous *Larousse* encyclopedia. *Le Magasin Pittoresque*, which began in 1832, was a particularly well-illustrated general magazine, which lasted into the twentieth century.

Among the best known of the modern French periodicals are the fashion magazines *Elle* and *Marie France*, the picture-paper *Paris Match*, and other illustrated papers such as *France Dimanche* and *Réalités*, as well as a large number of juvenile papers, among which are *Mademoiselle Caroline* (for girls), *Les Enfants S'Amusent*, *Pif* and *Tintin*.

In Germany, the earliest magazines were also literary, but these at first were annual editions. One of the best was *Acta Eruditorum*, which began in the middle seventeenth century, and remained with the same publisher until 1745. German literary magazines continued to flourish, and had greatly increased in number by the nineteenth century. Some of these papers began to deal with other subjects, such as fashion and science, and then came the specialist papers, such as *Natur* in 1852, devoted entirely to science, and *Bazar* in 1855, covering fashion.

Popular general magazines then followed, among them the *Hausblätter*, a bi-monthly, the *Salon*, and the very popular illustrated *Gartenlaube* of 1858, followed by *Daheim* in 1864. These contained fiction serials as well as general articles. The *Illustrierte Zeitung* (illustrated paper) appeared in Leipzig in 1843, and by the end of the century, there came the well-known *Berliner Illustrierte Zeitung* and *Die Woche*. The last-named soon reached a weekly circulation of 500,000 copies.

Probably the best known of the modern German magazines is *Der Spiegel*, a large-circulation weekly illustrated paper dealing with news, politics and similar subjects. Another is the equally popular *Stern*. Popular women's papers include the weekly *Frau*, *Brigitte*, published fortnightly, and the monthlies *Feminin*, *Monika* and *Lady International*. There are several papers devoted to films, radio and television, including the weekly *Bild und Funk Burda Fernsehen* and the monthly *Bravo*.

The Family Magazine

Modern Italian magazines include the very well-known weekly family magazine *La Domenica del Corriere*, well illustrated and popular in all Italian-speaking areas of the world. *Oggi* is another popular illustrated weekly paper, while the best known women's papers are *Amica* (monthly), *Gioia*, *Grazia*, *Alba* and *Eva*, all weekly. Italy has a number of very good children's periodicals, among them the well-produced *Corriere dei Piccoli*, a bumper weekly magazine. There are many sports magazines, some specialising in one particular sport, but many covering a whole range of sporting activities.

In Europe, a number of magazines have become international, especially in countries in which the same language is spoken. Belgian magazines are commonly sold in France and Switzerland, and French periodicals are found in Brussels and Berne. In some cases, special editions are produced in other languages. The best known of all international magazines is the Reader's Digest, originating in the United States, but appearing all over the world in a number of languages.

Millions of newspapers, magazines and comic papers are sold and read throughout the world, providing entertainment and information through words and pictures. Many of these publications have acquired international reputations and have taken their place as a regular part of their readers' lives.

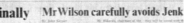

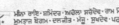

Index